The Positions of Adjectives in English

The Positions of Adjectives in English

P. H. MATTHEWS

OXFORD
UNIVERSITY PRESS

OXFORD
UNIVERSITY PRESS

Great Clarendon Street, Oxford, OX2 6DP,
United Kingdom

Oxford University Press is a department of the University of Oxford.
It furthers the University's objective of excellence in research, scholarship,
and education by publishing worldwide. Oxford is a registered trade mark of
Oxford University Press in the UK and in certain other countries.

First Edition published in 2014

Impression: 1

Published in the United States of America by Oxford University Press
198 Madison Avenue, New York, NY 10016, United States of America

British Library Cataloguing in Publication Data
Data available

Library of Congress Control Number: 2013956957

ISBN 978-0-19-968159-4

Printed and bound by
CPI Group (UK) Ltd, Croydon, CR0 4YY

In memory of
Stephen Matthews
1937–2009

Contents

Preface

This study is dedicated to the memory of my brother, who after a working career in what was then the Inland Revenue, began a new life, in retirement, as a historian. He was elected to the Royal Historical Society in 2008, and is described by a co-author, in an article which came out after he died, as 'an enthusiastic, inspiring, and multi-faceted scholar, who will be sorely missed' (*Medical History* 54 (2010): 29). His death came after a year's terminal illness, inseparable in my memory from the earliest botched attempt to get the subject matter of this book in order.

It will appear in the calendar year in which, if all goes well, I will turn eighty. I am therefore getting old; and superannuated scholars have a tendency to live, if not in the past, in an intellectual world of their own, centred on ideas and preoccupations that may not entirely coincide with those of their successors. I have therefore been helped enormously by comments from others, especially in conversation with Rosanna Sornicola and Sylvia Adamson, both of whom read earlier drafts of some chapters; and from the reports of three very well chosen referees. It has been a great pleasure to work with John Davey, who stepped down this March after truly distinguished work as the linguistics editor for the Press.

Cambridge
June 2013

Preface

[illegible]

1

Introduction

1.1 The latest and best-informed account of adjectives, as a part of speech defined across languages, is by Dixon (2010: 62–108). He does not assume that every language has a category that can be so named. But English is one of many languages throughout the world which have a class of words whose grammar is clearly different from that of others, which can be identified as adjectives by, in particular, the 'semantic tasks' they can perform.

One 'major' task, as Dixon puts it, is to 'make a statement that something has a certain property'. Thus, in English, *The chief is tall* could state, of someone referred to by *the chief*, that they have a property of being tall. Another task, which is also 'major', is 'as a specification that helps identify the referent of the head noun'. Thus, in English, a phrase *the tall chief* could refer to someone identified as a chief who is, more specifically, tall. There are languages in which the category as Dixon sees it has one of these tasks only: the first certainly; also, perhaps, the second (2010: 71). Nor do adjectives always have the same wide range of meanings: in an extreme case (2010: 74), only a handful of units are so distinguished. In English however, as in other familiar European languages, words like *tall* are members of a large and open class whose tasks, or functions, typically include both those that Dixon illustrates. In their syntax and morphology, they differ from, in particular, both verbs and nouns.

In grammars of English the distinction of functions has long been familiar. To 'make a statement about something' is to express what is traditionally a predication, and when adjectives are predicated they are in what is traditionally the 'predicative position'. As a verb has such a function in *The chief spoke* or *The chief talked nonsense*, so does either *tall* itself, or else a larger unit *is tall*, in *The chief is tall.* The second function is performed by adjectives in another 'position', which is traditionally 'attributive'. In *the tall chief*, the function of *tall* is as a unit attributive to, or as a modifier of, a noun. In both positions *tall* is the same part of speech. It can be characterized accordingly by two main functions, one predicative and one attributive: one in the structure of a clause or sentence, and the other within the structure of phrases.

We are talking, however, at a high level of abstraction. For it is well known that, while *tall* and many other adjectives can have both positions, there are others that traditionally at least have been assigned to the same part of speech, but whose uses are more limited. *Main*, for example, is attributive in *the main town in the Highlands* or *their main argument for resigning*: its task, as Dixon would put it, might be to help identify a town or argument in question. One would not say, however, *This town is main*, or *Their argument is main, not merely subsidiary*. The uses of words in *a-*, in particular, are the opposite. *The chief is afraid* or *She is awake* are normal; but not *the afraid chief* or, for example, *an awake baby*.

English is a language in which, in Dixon's words, 'just a few adjectives' (2010: 71) are confined to one of his two functions. Are these, however, no more than exceptions, or do they perhaps form part of a more general pattern?

How far have uses diverged?

1.2 The straightforward answer is that of current reference grammars. For Quirk and his colleagues, an adjective like *tall* is a 'central' member of the category. It 'can freely occur' in both an attributive and a predicative function; and in their analysis an adjective is central only if, among other things, it does so (1985: 404). If not, it is one that they class as 'peripheral'. *Afraid*, for example, is attributive only 'in exceptional cases' (1985: 403). It is called an adjective because, among other things, it is predicative in *People are afraid.* But *afraid people* is marked with '?*' as a phrase 'tending to unacceptability' (see their explanation of symbols, x). The opposite case is represented by *utter*. It is an adjective because one can say, for example, *That is utter nonsense*. But ?**That nonsense is utter*, though not marked as 'fully unacceptable', again tends to be so. *Afraid* and *utter*, though for opposite reasons, are both adjectives; but each is a peripheral member of the category, not one that is central.

The 'default' for an adjective, as Huddleston and Pullum put it, is 'to be able to function' in positions which include both the attributive and the predicative (2002: 553). *Utter* and *main* are instead one of a set that 'do not normally occur' except with the function *tall* has in *the tall chief.* They are therefore classed, as Quirk and his colleagues had classed them earlier, as 'attributive only'. 'The major distinction we need to make' is between adjectives restricted to that position and others, such as *afraid*, that are normally excluded from it. For Quirk and his colleagues, *afraid* and the like were 'predicative only' (1985: 432). For Huddleston and Pullum they are, more precisely, 'never attributive'. In the light, then, of the positions in which they are used, the part of speech as a whole can be divided into a default type, whose positions are subject to no restrictions, and two other types which are restricted in ways that are mutually exclusive. The default class is large, and includes words with an extensive range of meanings: *tall*, which is an adjective of size or dimension; *good*, which is one of value; *red*, which denotes a colour; and so on. Others have in common only that they are not of the default class. They are assigned to the same part of speech; but are subject to restrictions that are complementary and, at first sight at least, independent.

If that were all, it would be easy to say that *utter*, for example, is a lexical exception. By the attributive position we mean that of a premodifier: of *tall* in *the tall chief*, or of *good* in *a good dinner*. An adjective that is not a premodifier is predicative; and if restrictions are marked by features in the lexicon, *utter* can be assigned a feature [−Predicative]. A word such as *afraid* can again be entered as an adjective; but assigned a feature [−Attributive]. Adjectives of the default class will be assigned neither of these features, so that their uses are limited in neither way.

1.3 How many exceptions, however, must we recognize? It is tempting to say, with Dixon, 'just a few': few, that is, which have no use, or again no normal use, except in one of the traditional positions. But restrictions on the functions of adjectives are also associated, as both these grammars make clear, with specific meanings. In particular, there are 'numerous cases where an attributive adjective has a meaning that it cannot have in predicative position' or stands in a different 'semantic relation', in that position, to a head noun (Huddleston and Pullum 2002: 553).

Take, for example, *late*. It can be attested, as a form, in either position: attributively in a phrase such as *a late bus*; predicatively as in *The bus is late*. We can point at once, however, to a semantic complication. By *a late bus* one could refer in principle to a bus that happens, on a particular occasion, to be running behind schedule. But the phrase could also refer, and might perhaps more obviously refer, to one whose place in the timetable is late in the evening. In predicative position *late* could again mean 'behind schedule': thus one could say, for example, *The late bus* ('scheduled late') *was late* ('running late') *as usual*. But *The bus is late* would not be said of a bus whose place on the timetable is, as we might label it in inverted commas, 'late'. Such statements could be made, but with the adjective attributive, for example, to *one*: compare *The last bus I can catch is a very late one*. These senses of *late* are close, though a good dictionary will define them separately. But the same form has another, more distinctive sense, of 'having died in recent memory': compare *our late colleague* or *the late Queen*. With this meaning it is still more obviously not predicative. As Huddleston and Pullum point out, with the tacit exclusion of word play, *She is late* 'cannot mean "She recently died"' (2002: 554).

Another case they cite is that of *old* in, for example, *my old school.* The reference could be, in principle, to a school that has existed for a long time: this might be one, perhaps, of several schools, others all much newer, that the speaker owns or manages. With that sense *old* can also form a predicate, as in *The school is very old.* But a far more likely reference, in most uses, would be to a school at which the speaker was a pupil; and with that meaning *old* will not be used predicatively. As Huddleston and Pullum make clear, *This school is old* 'cannot mean "This is the school that I (or someone else) formerly attended"'. Another sense of *old* is as in *an old friend of mine.* As Quirk and his colleagues point out, this refers most naturally to someone that the speaker has known for a long time. With that sense, however, it too is 'attributive only' and 'cannot be related', as they put it, 'to *My friend is old*' (1985: 428).

The history of such uses cannot be known entirely. We have written evidence, which we may take as reliable, for what speakers could at one time have been able to say; but judgements of what they could not have said are at best problematic. It seems clear, however, that a use like that of *late* in, for example, *the late Queen* is in origin no different in kind from that of *utter* as in *utter nonsense. Late* developed a sense, attested in late Middle English, of 'not long ago'; thus, in an example from 1474:

John the monke late cardynal of Rome

(cited from the *O[xford] E[nglish] D[ictionary]* in the entry for *late* as an adverb). A sense of 'recently dead' developed alongside it. Compare, from 1490:

Her swete and late amyable husbonde

But other uses, as in *The bus is late,* may still be distinguished alongside it. *Utter* is related in form to *outer* and did once have similar senses. Compare, from Tyndale in 1526:

Ye make clene the utter side off the cuppe

These, however, became obsolete. In the fifteenth century *utter* is already attested in a sense of 'to an extreme degree', which is common from the sixteenth century onwards; thus, in a passage cited from 1511:

To the . . . vtter displeasure of the Kynge

Like that of *late,* this sense developed alongside others. The difference is merely that it is now the only normal sense the word has.

The classifications in grammars are in this light of both adjectives and senses of adjectives. For Huddleston and Pullum the default class, in the scheme displayed in Fig. 1.1, is opposed to others which together we may call 'restricted'. Of these one subclass is restricted to the attributive position, and will include both *utter* and the sense of *late* as in *the late Queen.* It will also include *old* in the senses that it can have, when it does not mean 'of some or of great age', in *an old friend* or *my old school.*

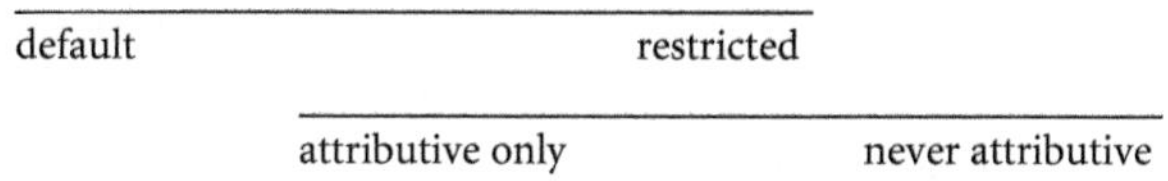

FIGURE 1.1

1.4 Other examples can easily be found, especially in specific collocations. In *white sauce*, with the meaning it has for cooks, a combination is formed by a noun, which in itself has a meaning no different from the one it has in general, and an adjective with a meaning it has in relation to this noun specifically. This is a meaning it would not have in *The sauce is white*. Nor, for example, can *an English summer* be matched by *The summer was English*; or *a tall story*, except conceivably in word play, by *Their story was tall*. Combinations and compounds, such as *white admiral*, of a species of butterfly, or *whitethroat*, of a species of bird, can be related as historically extensions. It is also natural that, as adjectives like *utter* are restricted to attribution, there should be others which in general can have both positions, but are used attributively only when their meanings are so restricted. *Sorry* is a premodifier in, for example, *It was a sorry mess*, or in *the sorry state of their finances*. These uses are not matched, however, by sentences such as *The mess was very sorry*. The same adjective is predicative, in what we may see as its basic sense, in *Everyone was sorry* or *They are terribly sorry for what happened*. But in that sense, as Huddleston and Pullum make clear, it is never attributive (2002: 560). If one could say *He was a sorry man* it would not be of someone referred to as apologetic.

Are we dealing still with mere sets of exceptions? If so, one way to describe them would again be in specific entries in a lexicon. In senses for which there is no restriction, adjectives have neither of the features [−Predicative] or [−Attributive]: thus *tall* in the sense it would have in *the tall chief* and *The chief is tall*. An adjective like *utter* would be marked as [−Predicative]; but so too, in an entry for *late*, could the sense it would have in *the late Queen*; so could another sense of 'scheduled late in the evening'. *Afraid* would again be marked as [−Attributive]. So could *sorry* in the sense of 'apologetic', just as in others it too would be [−Predicative]. This is not only technically feasible. It would also conform neatly to the way in which, in the philosophy or theory of linguistics, syntax and the lexicon have long been distinguished. Syntax, on the one hand, would be the domain of general statements, about how adjectives combine with head nouns, with forms of *be*, with modifying adverbs, and so on. These distinguish structures in terms of the parts of speech and other categories. The lexicon, on the other hand, will be the domain of individual statements about individual units, which enter individually into one range of structures or another.

How far, though, does this cast light on a language as experienced by its speakers, or the possibilities open to them? The question is one that cannot be answered wholly by appealing to the evidence, and for that reason it may be prudent to see this as an issue more in the 'philosophy of grammar', in the sense of Jespersen's famous study in the 1920s, than one of 'theory' in the sense that is now familiar in science. What does seem true, however, is that the attributive position is the one in which the uses of individual adjectives tend to be most systematically distinguished. *Hard* in *a hard worker* is another of Huddleston and Pullum's examples, whose sense they compare with that of the same adjective in *The work is hard* (2002: 554). Whatever one might mean by *The worker is hard*, its meaning would be different again. Technically, therefore, *hard* can be assigned a sense which we could mark in the lexicon as [–Predicative]. As a modifier, however, of the agentive *worker* it stands in the same relation to a verb and adverb, in (*She*) *works hard*, as do many others. Sometimes the same sense is possible when the adjective is predicative: compare *a fast runner* with, for example, *The next runner is very fast*. But with others, as with *hard*, it is excluded. *Light* in *a light sleeper* can be related to the adverb in *sleeps lightly*, but the meaning is not the one it would have in a sentence like *Some sleepers are very light*. *Good* can also modify *worker*, and again we can compare the adverb in *They work well*. But that sense of *good*, with a noun whose meaning is purely agentive, can be distinguished from the one it would have in *Some of these workers* (or *Some of these people*, or *Some of these children*) *are very good*. What kind of pattern we are faced with is a further, partly theoretical or partly philosophical issue. It would not be right, however, to describe a sense of *hard* in which it is [–Predicative], as a mere detail of an individual entry in the lexicon, in the same way as we might describe a meaning that is truly idiosyncratic, as of *late* in *the late Queen*.

1.5 The 'positions' of adjectives differ, if we may make the point as neutrally as possible, in the restrictions to which some members of the category are subject. But they also differ in their syntax: in the structures distinguished, in detail, in one position or the other. We cannot simply say that, on the one hand, adjectives can be premodifiers; and, on the other hand, they can combine with *be*. Not only do they have other uses, as we will remind ourselves in a moment. Their uses in the attributive position are syntactically more complex, in ways that again reflect the history of the language since the Middle Ages.

One well-known complication is that premodifying adjectives form sequences. A sequence of *late* and *amiable*, cited earlier from the end of the fifteenth century, may not or may no longer be normal. But combinations are in general common: of two adjectives in *an ugly black stain* or *some enormous wooden tables*, of three in *a nice large comfortable sofa*, and more. We will need to consider what exactly is the structure of such phrases. Crucially, however, this is a problem that arises only where adjectives are attributive. One would not normally say, for example, *The tables were enormous wooden*. One could say, for example, *The stain is dark black*; but *dark black* would be a unit that can itself form part of a sequence: thus, as we may write it with commas, *an enormous, ugly, dark black monstrosity*.

It is also well known that in sequences like these the order of the adjectives will reflect the types of meaning that they have. Those that denote a size or dimension tend, for example, to come before ones that denote a colour: *a large red sofa* rather than *a red large sofa*. Adjectives such as *nice* will tend to come before both: *a nice large sofa, a marvellous green wallpaper*. Types like these are therefore relevant in the attributive position and not relevant, or at least they are not distinguished similarly, beyond it. The difference between positions is in this light partly one of lexical divergence: the meaning of *sorry* as a predicative adjective does not match its sense or senses as a premodifier, and *late* or *old* have senses in which they are premodifiers only. But this is matched by a divergence in syntax. In both respects, moreover, the attributive position is the one in which divergence leads, or has led historically, to the most differentiation. The range of meanings that individual adjectives can have is greater; and, as attributive adjectives form sequences, their functions too are subdivided.

Are there other positions?

1.6 The divergence between positions is the theme that ties this book together. Can we take it for granted, however, that there are just two? In, for example, *They met someone tall* the 'position' of *tall*, in a literal sense, is different. Nevertheless it is a modifier; can we say then that, in a more abstract sense, it has the same 'position', or the same syntactic function, as in *the tall chief*? In *I forced the door open* an adjective follows *the door* and cannot be part of the same phrase: there is, for example, no corresponding passive *The door open was forced*. Does this illustrate another function in which adjectives are predicative? In *They turned blue*, the function of *blue* is like, at least, the one it has in *They were blue*. But do adjectives have the same syntactic relation to both *turn* and *be*?

The last question seems at first the easiest to answer. Both for Quirk and his colleagues (1985: 1171–2), and for Huddleston and Pullum (2002: 263–4), a sentence such as *They turned blue* has a structure in which a verb is followed by a complement. As a verb which is transitive takes an object, so *turn*, or *turn* in the sense it has here, takes a complement which can be an adjective. So too, among others, do *become* and *seem*. *Be* is described no differently. It is seen as a main verb, which like others is inflected for tense. In *They have been quiet* it combines, like others, with an auxiliary. Verbs take complements and, as represented in both grammars, an adjective in predicative position is one kind of complement that can be taken by *be*.

But there is another view. The verb 'to be', in European languages in general, is traditionally a 'copula'; and in one analysis, which can be traced back to antiquity, its role is literally that of a bond or link, in the sense of Latin *copula*, that can join an adjective, among other units, to a subject. If we say of certain things that they are blue we are predicating 'blueness' of whatever, in such a sentence, will be referred to by its subject. In *They are blue* the adjective is related, therefore, to *they*. If one cannot simply say, in English, *They blue* it is because, it will be argued, there must always be, in English, an expression of tense. Therefore there has to be a unit which is verb-like to the extent that *are*, for example, can be distinguished from *were*; and can combine with auxiliaries. *Be* is like a verb, however, in these ways only. It has no relation either to the subject or to a unit predicated of it, other than as a 'link' by which these are themselves related.

This is an old, old story. If it is right, however, it can be right for *be* alone. We can argue that this one verb has no lexical meaning: that, although it has the same inflections and can take the same auxiliaries as the others, and has the same apparent function in the structure of such sentences, it is not in direct contrast with them. But we cannot claim this for both *be* and *turn*, both *be* and *become*, both *be* and *seem*, or *be* and any of the other verbs that would be relevant. It is not surprising that in an analysis by Ferris, to which we will return in a much later chapter, 'ordinary predicative position', which is that of an adjective after *be*, is distinguished from another position which he calls 'postverbal'. This would instead be that of *blue* in *They turned blue* or, in the example with which he illustrates it, *angry* in *The crowd remained angry* (1993: 36).

Alternatively, *be* does have a lexical meaning, which contrasts with those of *become*, *seem*, and so on in a function that is the same for all. Its treatment as a copula was not originally proposed for English, and linguists who advocate it have appealed in part to languages which either have no such verb or have one which is not obligatory. In part too, arguments are philosophical rather than empirical. We will therefore need to ask if there is evidence in English, in particular, that might be taken to support one or the other analysis.

1.7 If *be* is no more than a copula, the *tall* of *The chief is tall* may be represented, in abstraction from it, as in a direct relation to *the chief*. The *tall* of *The chief became tall* is instead a complement, as current grammars describe both, of the verb. In either function, however, the adjective is predicative rather than attributive. This is confirmed by the range of adjectives that can combine with *turn*, *become*, and so on. They are variously restricted: one is more likely to say *They turned blue* than *They turned big*, or *He grew tall* than *He grew stupid*. The restrictions are to a subset, however, of the default type and of those described in Fig. 1.1 as 'never attributive'. Where adjectives or senses of adjectives are classed as 'attributive only', they are excluded in relation to any of these verbs, not only *be*.

The traditional predicative position may in that light be extended to include all functions in which adjectives combine directly with a verb. But take then the role of *open* in *I forced the door open*, or of *brilliant* in *I thought him brilliant*. As *blue* in *They turned blue* has in some sense a predicative relation to *they*, so, in these examples, *open* and *brilliant* stand in some way in a similar relation to *the door* and *him*. The result of the forcing was that the door was in the state of being open; what was thought of a certain person was that he was brilliant. The adjectives, moreover, that are so used are again those that in general can combine with *be*. Therefore, for many linguists, just as adjectives can be related to a subject, with verbs such as *become* or *grow*, so there is another class of verbs, which includes both *force* and *think*, with which they can be related, in what we can see as a further extension of the predicative position, to an object.

For other linguists, the predicative relation is again between, for example, *open* and *the door*. *The door* is not, however, an object, as it would be if no adjective followed. It is instead part of a larger unit, *the door open*, which the verb, in this use, will take as a whole. The extension, therefore, is that of an adjective in the basic predicative position, as in *The door is open*, to a role in which it stands in an immediate relation to a subject, with no *be* intervening.

One major problem, which will be central to the discussion of such sentences in Chapter 8, will be to try to clarify the pros and cons of this and the competing analysis. But we will also do well to remember that, in the predicative position generally, the role of adjectives is often shared with that of other classes of unit.

With *be*, in particular, the point is obvious. As one can say, for example, *They are dangerous* or *His sister was always very helpful*, so one can say, with the substitution of a noun phrase, *They are a menace* or *His sister was a woman you could always rely on*. As the adjectives denote properties ascribed to the individuals referred to, the second pair of sentences are similarly, in the term proposed by Lyons, 'ascriptive' (1977: 469–73). A predicative noun phrase, as we may describe it, is not possible with all verbs. One can say *He grew tall*; but not, for example, *He grew a tall man*. But there are plainly other cases where an adjective in an extended predicative position can be replaced similarly by a phrase whose function is not at least self-evidently different. Compare *He became tall* with *He became a tyrant*; or, in the type of sentence whose analysis is an issue, *I thought him brilliant* with *I thought him a genius*. The dispute itself can also be extended to structures involving other categories. In, for example, *I photographed them going into the house*, there is a predicative relation, again in some sense, between *going into the house* and *them*. Compare the simple *They went into the house*. Is *them*, however, the object of *photographed*, and the participial phrase a unit separate from it? Or does it form part of a single unit, *them* plus *going into the house*, which *photographed*, in turn, relates to as a whole? It seems clear that though the syntax of predicative adjectives can be explored in isolation, the issues they give rise to will be part in the end of a much wider pattern.

1.8 The 'predicative position', as extended beyond combination with *be*, is that of adjectives whose functions are within the structure of clauses. The 'attributive position', as current grammars define it, is that of an adjective in a noun phrase that both modifies and comes before a head noun. In *I met someone tall* the adjective has again a position, literally, in the structure of a phrase. But it is a modifier that comes after *someone*. There are also larger units, headed by adjectives, that regularly follow nouns: thus the 'adjective phrase', headed by a comparative, in *a chief taller than the others*. Is a postmodifier, as a unit with such a function is called, not in turn 'attributive'?

In current grammars this is presented simply as a third function. We may therefore speak, as Quirk and his colleagues do speak, of 'three positions of adjectives': the attributive, the predicative, and the 'postpositive' (1985: 418). For Huddleston and Pullum, the postpositive is likewise one of three 'main functions' (2002: 528), separate from both the others. An adjective with this function 'commonly occurs' after units such as *something* or *anyone*, and 'under restricted conditions they occur' in phrases headed by nouns. It is tempting, however, to ask if 'function' and 'position' have precisely the same meaning. By a 'position' we might mean, literally, a place in a sequence. A postmodifier has in that sense a position different from that of a premodifier. By a 'function', however, we would mean a role within what is traditionally a 'construction'. The nature of constructions is an issue in the philosophy of syntax on which various views are possible. Traditionally, however, units are construed one with another independently of which comes first or whether, indeed, they are adjacent. It is therefore possible, at least, to argue that all modifiers have the same construction. The adjective in *someone tall* would in this light have a function it would also have in *a tall chief*. One would not say *a chief tall*, any more than one would say, for example, *I met tall someone*; but that would be a matter of 'position' only, which is determined in such examples by the type of unit, which can be a noun or a pronoun, that is modifed. This would also be the function of a phrase beginning with an adjective, in *a chief taller than the others*. One would not say, in turn, *a taller than the others chief*. But it is tempting to argue that this too is a difference in the positions in which functions are realized, which is determined in this example by the internal structure of the modifier.

An analysis that is tempting may not always, however, be right. Let us accept that functions and constructions can be established independently of order: in many languages, if we do not accept this, we will be pathetically at sea. Let us also accept that the order of modifiers is in part determined by rule. *The chief tall spoke to me* is one sentence, for example, that we could exclude as ungrammatical. But order is not entirely determined. Phrases with a structure like that of *the chief tall* cannot be excluded entirely, and it has been claimed that, where both orders are possible, it is with a potential difference in meaning.

One famous example is originally from an article by Bolinger, now more than fifty years old. 'If we say', as Bolinger himself put it, '*The only navigable river is to the north* we normally mean "regularly navigable"'. The river, in a term which other linguists have since taken from him, 'is so CHARACTERIZED'. But 'if we say *The only river navigable is to the north* we mean "navigable at present"'. 'Out of several navigable rivers', as Bolinger explained it, 'there may be only one river navigable' (1952 [1965: 297]). If this is right, the reference of *the rivers navigable*, where the adjective is not 'characterizing', will be included in that of *the navigable rivers*: compare *For the moment, the only rivers navigable are the Rhine and the Danube*. It is only 'normally', as Bolinger put it, that the premodifier will be taken to be characterizing. The difference is therefore no more than potential and we may expect that, when it is there, it may be hard to pin down. But it should be true at least that adjectives are more easily postmodifiers if they are more easily 'non-characterizing'. If *the chief tall* is excluded, the reason could perhaps be that the property the adjective denotes is not one that can vary, like the navigability of rivers, from one state to another.

Is the function *navigable* has as a postmodifier different, in this light, from the one it has as a premodifier? The question is as much about the nature of constructions, and the criteria by which they can be distinguished, as about the evidence itself. Functions might be said, however, to form a hierarchy. In Huddleston and Pullum's system, which follows one that I adopted in the early 1980s, a modifier is in general one form of dependent (Huddleston and Pullum 2002: 24; Matthews 1981: 146–59). Complements, such as *tall*, as they describe it, in *The chief is tall*, are another. At a more specific level, the functions of adjectives or of adjective phrases are divided from those of other modifiers; and, at a level still more specific, the function or functions adjectives can have before a noun can be distinguished, as they are distinguished by both Huddleston and Pullum and Quirk and his colleagues, from the one they have when nouns precede them. But they have in common that they are dependents of the same kind.

1.9 If that were all, we could talk of a major division, as shown in Fig. 1.2, between the predicative position and the 'position' of a modifier, which is in turn divided into the attributive position and the postpositive. There is also, however, an important link between the postpositive position and the predicative. For the adjectives that form postmodifiers are in general those of the 'default' type and those that are 'never attributive'. Others are restricted, as we have seen, or restricted in some senses, to the attributive position. These are in general not postmodifiers.

modifying   predicative

attributive   postpositive

FIGURE 1.2

Take, for example, *former*. It is another adjective that Huddleston and Pullum class as only attributive (2002: 553): one could say *It is a former warehouse*, but not, for example, *Its use as a warehouse was former*. It does not usually head a phrase: therefore no rule applies by which it would come after a noun. Neither, however, does it come after pronouns such as *something*. One would not say, for example, *I had a vision of something former*, in the sense of 'something that no longer exists'. The same restriction applies to *utter* or *main*. One can say, for example, *Nothing dreadful happened*, but *nothing utter* would be at best not normal. *Main* is attributive in, for example, *The main speakers have still to arrive*, with the same function as *important* in *the important speakers*. In *someone important* the adjective is again postpositive; but one is unlikely to say, for example, *We are still waiting for someone main to get here*. The restriction also applies, for example, to the sense of *late* as 'recently deceased'. People who believe in ghosts would not say, straightforwardly, *I saw someone late in my bedroom last night*.

When Huddleston and Pullum talk, then, of an adjective as 'attributive only' they mean that it is excluded from both their other functions: as it is not predicative, neither is it postpositive. Those that can 'occur', in their term, in the postpositive function include not only those of their 'default' class (2002: 553), but others, such as *afraid*, that they class as predicative only. It is therefore possible to say, with Quirk and his colleagues, that 'a postpositive adjective . . . can usually be regarded as a reduced relative clause' (1985: 418). In *a chief who is taller than the others*, an adjective phrase is in predicative position within a modifying clause; in *a chief taller than the others*, the modifier is reduced to it alone. In *people afraid of the dark*, where the adjective is one classed as 'never attributive', it is reduced from *who are afraid of the dark*; and so on. As the postpositive position is more, however, than a mere variant of the attributive, it is also more than yet another extension of the predicative. For there is also a small class of adjectives, or of words traditionally classed as adjectives, that are either restricted to this position or are restricted, again, in certain senses.

Take, for example, the sense of *proper* in *the city proper*. The reference will be to a city 'strictly speaking', as distinguished maybe from its suburbs or as defined by an administrative or other boundary. *New York proper* might be used, for example, in reference to Manhattan only. But this is a meaning *proper* does not have, as Quirk and his colleagues point out, in any other position (1985: 418). Compare its uses as a premodifier in, for example, *Oxford is a proper city* (meaning 'a genuine city', 'a real city'), or *That was the proper* (meaning 'the correct') *reaction*. Compare too *That reaction was perfectly proper* or, in another conceivable use in predicative position,

Some people do tend to be rather proper. Other examples include the use of *elect* as in *the president elect* or *designate* as in *the chairman designate*; and, for Huddleston and Pullum (2002: 560), *galore* as in *flowers galore*. *Galore* is in origin a loan-word, from a form in Scottish Gaelic that is not an adjective. Its only use, however, is in phrases like this. Phrases in which it would be attributive, such as *the galore flowers*, can be safely described as ungrammatical. Nor is it normally predicative. Suppose, for example, that two people have been guests at a wedding reception, of which one says afterwards: *There was wine and food galore*. The other, who had sat alas at a less favoured table, might conceivably reply: *But I'm afraid the wine was less galore where I was*. The example, if it is possible, reminds us that we cannot always ignore word play and the verbal contexts that provoke it. But a predicative use of *galore*, or of *elect* or *designate*, does have to be forced.

1.10 An adjective of the 'default' class is one which, more precisely, can have all of Huddleston and Pullum's three main functions (2002: 553). In their classification, those whose distribution is restricted are again divided, as in Fig. 1.1, into those which are 'attributive only' and those which are 'never attributive'. The 'default', then, for the latter is that they can be both predicative and postpositive. This is the default, however, for what is already one class of exceptions. Within that class there is, however, a subclass, with members such as *elect* or *proper* in *the city proper*, which are 'postpositive only'. The scheme of classification is accordingly as set out, as a whole, in Fig. 1.3. The exceptions at a higher level, of adjectives such as *utter* or *afraid*, are again implicitly equal. This is one point, therefore, which might be disputed. At a lower level, adjectives which can only be postmodifiers are exceptions in any analysis.

default — restricted

attributive only — never attributive

predicative and postpositive — postpositive only

FIGURE 1.3

To what, however? The authority of standard grammars is never to be sniffed at. The assumption, however, which underlies this scheme is that postmodifiers are, in the first instance, not attributive. There are adjectives restricted to this position, and by that criterion, if no other, it is separate from the predicative. But they are adjectives distinguished, in the first instance, by their exclusion as premodifiers.

In another view, however, the main division among adjectives might be between those that have both the traditional positions and those, like *utter* and many others in specific senses, that are restricted to phrases. The first type we may describe as 'bipositional': these are again those that have both the 'major syntactic tasks' with which we began. The others, whether or not we see them as exceptions, we can call 'modifying only'. But postmodifiers, if we may return to the hierarchy in Fig. 1.2, also modify. An alternative scheme may therefore be set out in Fig. 1.4. The terms at the lower level are again those used by Huddleston and Pullum. But words like *afraid*, since they can form postmodifiers, are in this analysis an exception among the adjectives classed as bipositional. Words like *elect* are instead, in the first instance, modifiers. They are exceptions, however, within the class of adjectives that are modifying only, in that the default, for that class, is to be attributive and not postpositive.

modifying only		bipositional	
attributive only	postpositive only	default	never attributive

FIGURE 1.4

From this alternative scheme the term 'bipositional', at least, can usefully be added to the others already current.

Prospectus

1.11 No introduction can do more than hint at what is to follow. It may be helpful, however, at this stage to say briefly how the remainder of the book is organized.

The next two chapters, in particular, deal with the category of adjective in general. Chapter 2 addresses the basic question of which words belong to it. Criteria are less straightforward than they seem at first sight, and raise problems regarding parts of speech in general. Chapter 3 asks whether either of the traditional positions, or the 'semantic tasks' that Dixon distinguishes, can or should be seen as primary. A better conclusion, for English, is again that they have diverged. At this point, as an introduction to the problems arising in specific positions, it will be helpful to look back, in Chapter 4, at the earlier history of the language, through which they have arisen. The three chapters that follow will concentrate on the attributive position. Chapter 5 will be concerned with the division drawn by many linguists between premodifying adjectives and determiners; Chapter 6, in particular, with relations among successive premodifiers; Chapter 7, in the light of these, with the relations, more generally, of units within noun phrases. Chapters 8 and 9 will turn to the predicative position: to the status of *be*, as broached in 1.6, and problems associated both with its role and the extensions distinguished in 1.7. Chapter 10 will finally return to adjectives as postmodifiers.

Only brief conclusions are needed, but Chapter 11 will also attempt to draw some morals from the whole.

2

Which words are adjectives?

2.1 *Adjectives as a part of speech.* 2.2 *Parts of speech in general.*

Adjectives as added to nouns 2.3 *As modifiers.* 2.4 *Adjectives in ancient and mediaeval grammar.* 2.5 *Adverbs as modifiers of nouns.* 2.6 *Adjectives as attributive and predicative.* 2.7 *'Adjectives' and 'adverbs' in a-.*

Conversion 2.8 *The problem in general.* 2.9 *Conversions of adjectives to nouns vs. nouns to adjectives.* 2.10 *Is there a solution?* 2.11 *Adjectives, adverbs, and prepositions.* 2.12 *Some instances in detail.* 2.13 *Microsyntax and macrosyntax.*

2.1 There is no dispute that *tall*, for example, is an adjective. So are *old*, *blue*, *happy*, *fat*, and many others. As adjectives they form a part of speech distinct from others such as, in particular, nouns and verbs. In keeping with this they have similar syntactic functions, in what are traditionally the same positions. Other parts of speech have other functions. More precisely, adjectives have one range of functions, in relation to other parts of speech in one range of syntactic structures. Nouns, for example, have another range of functions, in relation to adjectives among others.

But things are plainly not that simple. One complication, to which we will return in the second part of this chapter, is that words that are in some sense the same unit are assigned to different parts of speech in different functions. *Fast*, for example, has the same form in *a fast train* and *She drives too fast*. Its meaning in one is also like its meaning in the other. Yet in phrases like *a fast train* it is traditionally said to be an adjective: this is a part of speech whose members have, to repeat, one range of functions. In *She drives too fast* it is instead classed as an adverb. This is a different part of speech whose members have, implicitly, another range of functions. A second complication, which we have struck already, is that not all words assigned to the same part of speech have precisely the same range of functions. *Main*, for example, is also classed as an adjective. It has only one, however, of the positions that *tall*, *old*, and so on can have. *Afraid* is another adjective, or another word traditionally said to be an adjective, whose range of functions, if this is right, is also restricted. Not only that, but the functions of *main* and *afraid* are mutually exclusive. In either system of subclassification (1.10), one would be only attributive and the other never attributive. Where words, however, enter separately into different relations in quite different syntactic structures, on what grounds should they be classed as if they were alike?

The question is obviously as much about the justification for the parts of speech in general, as it is about this part of speech specifically. They are classes that traditionally are both few and exhaustive. Adjectives are one of only nine in the scheme, for example, proposed by Huddleston and Pullum (2002: 22), and no word, implicitly, does not belong to one or another of them. Since they are few, however, they are largely heterogeneous. A more radical question will be why the lexicon of a language should be divided into classes of this sort.

We may accept at once that, if the scheme is justified, some parts of speech have members that we may call 'peripheral'. This is made clear, for adjectives in English, in the analysis, already cited, by Quirk and his colleagues (1.2; 1985: 403–4). Some words may be marginally members of one class, yet share functions with words that may be assigned to another. There may in that way be gradations between categories. Such insights have been familiar since the 1960s, and in part earlier. In proposing a system of five classes, Jespersen acknowledged that 'we are unable to define such categories so rigidly as to be left with no doubtful or borderline cases' (1924: 92). This does not, however, make our problem any easier. For if there are gradations within categories, and fuzziness, as it has since been called, at the boundaries between them, it is less obvious that boundaries fall at these points, between classes that are few, rather than in different places and more places, between classes that are smaller and more homogeneous.

2.2 What, if we may put it bluntly, are the parts of speech for? Quirk and his colleagues are among the few who indicate that such a question may need to be answered.

In the first of their grammars (1972: 44–5), they illustrate a scheme in which adjectives, for example, are distinguished from separate classes of both articles and demonstratives. This departs already from the one inherited from antiquity, in which demonstratives had themselves been adjectives. In their second and definitive grammar, articles and demonstratives are included in a new class of 'determiners'; and verbs, which had been earlier a single part of speech, are instead divided into three (1985: 67). There is, however, an 'important caveat', as they make clear a few pages later. 'Although', as they explain, word classes have 'deceptively simple labels', they 'tend in fact to be rather heterogeneous, if not problematic categories'. The 'adjustments' they have made to the traditional scheme are 'well-motivated', in their view, 'for modern English'. 'They do, however, raise questions about the justification for this or that classification' (1985: 73).

Many of the conventional arguments about the parts of speech 'have more to do', as they remark at the end of the next paragraph, 'with the labelling of categories than with the question of how we can best explain the grammatical behaviour of items on the basis of their varying degrees of similarity and contrast'. This is a wise observation. To explain how units 'behave grammatically', we must obviously make general statements about classes of units. A class of any kind, however large or however small, can be established if, as part of such an explanation, there is something to be said about its members. There is a class, for example, of determiners only if there are statements that apply to all the words included. This is a category whose status is reserved for a later chapter (see especially **5.12** and **5.13**); but, if it is not justified in that way, we may question whether its motivation, for modern English, is as good as Quirk and his colleagues claim. If they are right about verbs, it may be because there is no statement to be made about such words in general, over and above what are traditionally subclasses.

In practice, in English, that does seem to be true. Both *must*, for example, and *sing* are traditionally of the same part of speech. But the second has inflections that the first does not have, and its functions in sentences are different. Grammars need accordingly say little about verbs in general, but make separate statements about each of the classes that Quirk and his colleagues distinguish: about 'full verbs', as an open class of lexical units; about modal verbs, like *must*; about 'primary verbs', as they describe them, such as *be*. Another traditional part of speech is that of adverbs. Among the words, however, that are seen as included in it, *too* or *very* has one range of functions within larger units. The range of *not*, for example, is different; and in detail there is little overlap between one and the other. *Badly*, for example, has a function in *I did it badly* which is like that of *well* in *I did it well*. Therefore they may be classed together, not as adverbs but as members of a smaller class traditionally called 'of manner'. It does not follow that they must be further lumped with *not* or with, for example, *tomorrow*.

The heterogeneity of adverbs has long been familiar. According to one ancient source, the Stoics had already called this part of speech *pandéktēs* 'all-receiving' (Charisius, ed. Barwick 1964: 247). Adjectives in English are at least less diverse. Clear statements hold of most of the words so classified. It is not clear, however, that there is any statement we may make, or any rule that we may formulate, which will hold for all the words of all the subclasses that we distinguished earlier. Is there any reason for grouping them together other than that parts of speech have been assumed, traditionally, to be both exhaustive and as few as possible?

We may anticipate, perhaps, two answers. One is that the parts of speech are universal. They are justified at a level of abstraction above that of any individual language, and the scheme in any individual grammar is no more than a projection onto a particular language, or an instantiation in it, of categories that any language may have. If not all are universal, all are at least potentially so. Notional categories in particular were restored to favour, some fifty years ago, by Lyons (1966, 1968) and others. In Dixon's account of adjectives (2010; see 1.1), the semantic tasks by which they can be identified, though illustrated with examples from English and other languages, are explained independently. So too are the types of meanings by which, as Dixon adds, a class of adjectives can also be recognized (2010: 73). If parts of speech are distinguished, however, at this level of abstraction, it does not follow that their projection or instantiation, in any individual language, has to be exhaustive. Words assigned to any category, in any language, must first fall together in their morphology and syntax. But other notionally similar words may fall together separately.

Another answer might be more in the traditional spirit. A part of speech may well be heterogeneous. Not all members may have the same range of functions; many may be peripheral, and in ways that are mutually exclusive. But each part of speech has a definition, in a given language or a given type of language, that distinguishes its members from all other lexical units. The parts of speech in general are the smallest set for which such definitions can be formulated.

Adjectives as added to nouns

2.3 We might again ask what such schemes are for. But adjectives have often been defined in this way, by their role as modifiers of nouns. *Old*, for example, is a modifier in *an old man* and forms the head of a modifier in, for example, *a man older than me*. That it can also be predicative is not essential. *Main*, for example, is a modifier in *the main argument*; *designate*, which is classed as postpositive only, is a modifier in *the leader designate*. That neither of these is normally predicative is not an obstacle. *Afraid*, for example, is classed as never attributive. Nevertheless it heads a modifier in phrases such as *people afraid of flying*. All words classed as adjectives are modifiers in either one position or the other.

For current formulations we may look no further than ordinary dictionaries. The entry for 'adjective' in, for example, *The New Shorter Oxford English Dictionary* modifies in part the wording of the original *Oxford English Dictionary* (henceforth *OED*). It is 'a word', however, 'designating an attribute and added to a noun, to describe the thing, etc. more fully' (Brown, ed. 1993). This is not, in passing, an entry on which I (Preface, ix) was asked for advice. In a simpler formula, which may be cited at random from a smaller dictionary, an adjective 'describes or modifies a noun or pronoun' (O'Neill, ed. 2006). Some linguists may be tempted to ignore or disparage works of this kind. But this form of definition rests on a scholarly tradition that goes back to antiquity; and although it is clear, from the work of Dixon and others, that it may not be appropriate for all languages, we are concerned now with the parts of speech in a particular language, or in a type of language that it represents. For those of Europe generally, this characterization of adjectives has long seemed attractive.

One of the neatest formulations, in a specialist dictionary, is still that of Marouzeau (1951 [1933]). The French term *adjectif*, as he reminds us, is from Latin *adiectivum*; and, in Latin, it was morphologically transparent. These were words of a type that could be 'added to' (*ad-iec-t-*) other words, which are those we now call nouns. In Greek they were similarly *epítheta* 'put next to'. They could be related to nouns, however, in one of two ways. In one case they were added 'directly', as part of what would now be called a noun phrase. This is the relation illustrated, in French, by the role of *bel* in:

(1) un bel arbre
a-MASC.SG beautiful-MASC.SG tree
'a fine tree'

where in the written form its gender and its number both agree with those of *arbre*. In the other case an adjective is added to a noun 'by way of predication'. This is the relation of *grande* in:

(2) la maison est grande
the house is big-FEM.SG
'The house is big'

which is by implication indirect and mediated by *est*. Here too, written *grande* agrees in number as in gender with *maison*.

In my own *Dictionary of Linguistics* (2007a), 'the most characteristic role' of adjectives is the one that Marouzeau distinguishes as 'direct'. The authors of such dictionaries are liable to be biased by the types and families of languages that they know best, and both entries may perhaps reflect too much the structure of the older forms of Indo-European. But English too is Indo-European. A class of words called 'adjectives' was first identified, in the Western tradition, in the grammars of Ancient Greek and Latin. If they could be defined in antiquity as words 'added to' others, has their status in English, as ones which can all stand in a direct relation to nouns, changed fundamentally?

2.4 It may be helpful, at this point, to look back at the history of the category. For the syntax of adjectives in Ancient Greek and Latin, we may refer to a masterly summary by Wackernagel (1926, 2: 51–8). Two general points, however, are worth noting.

The first is that syntactic relations were for the most part between words that might or might not be adjacent. In a sentence in Latin which we may gloss as follows:

(3) domus est parva
house-NOM.SG is small-NOM.SG.FEM

parva agrees with *domus* in number, gender, and case. But while the adjective in (2), in French, is clearly predicative, it may be pointless to ask if (3) has a structure like that of, in English:

(4) [[the house] [is small]]

where *the house* is a subject noun phrase and *small* a unit separate from it, or like that of, in what might be a likelier translation:

(5) [it [is [a small house]]]

in which the adjective in Latin would be a modifier divided, by *est*, from its head. One important development, in the Germanic and the Romance languages, is that the positions called attributive and predicative are now fully differentiated.

A second feature is that adjectives and nouns had similar inflectional endings. *Parva* in (3) has the same inflection as, for example, the noun form *puella* (girl-NOM.SG). The ending of *domus* 'house' is also that of, for example, the adjective form *bonus* (good-NOM.SG.MASC) in *vir bonus* 'a good man'. The genitive plural *bonarum* (good-GEN.PL.FEM) has the same ending as the noun form *puellarum* (girl-GEN.PL), and so on. These were languages in which it is very easy to distinguish verbs, in general and in detail, from all words of other classes. A distinction between adjectives and nouns was far less obvious. It is hardly surprising, therefore, that while words called 'adjectives' were distinguished in ancient grammars, they were not seen as a major class distinct from nouns. In the ancient system the term '*pars orationis*', which is traditionally rendered 'part of speech', referred literally to the parts into which a sentence or utterance (Latin *oratio*) was divided. The classification was therefore of words not as lexical units, as the term is usually applied in modern grammars, but of specific word forms with specific inflections. The first 'part' of (3), for example, was the word form *domus* 'house', which was classified as a *nomen* or 'name'. The second part was *est* 'is'. The third part was *parva* 'small', also nominative and also singular, and inflected as *puella* 'girl', which is a 'name', is also inflected. In this light it too was a 'name'.

The 'names' called *adiectiva* were distinguished in school grammars, such as that of Donatus, as a subclass on a par with, for example, patronymics or diminutives (*Ars maior*, ed. Holtz 1981: 616). Even, however, in a grammar as summary as his, they were different from other subtypes in that, among names in general, they could form a comparative and a superlative (ed. Holtz 1981: 617). In the tradition followed by Priscian, adjectives were again a subclass. They were singled out, however, as names not only added to other names, but as denoting properties independent of the 'substance', in the Aristotelian sense, that these others denoted (ed. Keil 1855: 58). Such properties were of, in Latin, *qualitas* (literally 'what-sort-ness') and *quantitas* ('what-size-ness'), and could vary without diminishing the essential nature (*sine substantiae consumptione*) of whatever entity was referred to. In retrospect, at least, this passage is significant. It was only, however, in the Middle Ages, in the work of scholars in whose native language a distinction between adjectives and nouns was much clearer, that the insight was developed further. For Thomas of Erfurt, seven centuries after Priscian, the category of *nomina* or 'names' was first divided, as it had been in antiquity, into names 'proper' and those that 'signified', in the terminology of the Modistic school to which he belonged, through the mode 'of commonness' (*communis*). But 'common names' were in turn divided into two main categories. A 'substantive name', or *nomen substantivum*, signified through the mode 'of standing by itself' (*per se stantis*). A *nomen adiectivum*, or 'name added', signified differently, through the mode 'of lying next to' (*adiacentis*) (ed. Bursill-Hall 1972: 156, 158).

2.5 English 'noun' derives from Latin *nomen*; and common nouns were divided into 'nouns adjective' and 'nouns substantive' until the early twentieth century. For Jespersen, for example, the separation of adjectives from substantives, as two different parts of speech, had to be justified (1924: 72–81). Since his time, it has come to be taken for granted. A division between them is also clearer in English than in older forms of Indo-European, in that, in the wake of changes in the transition from Old to Middle English, adjectives lost an inflection for number which nouns retained. We will return to this transition in a later chapter (4.2). Another consequence, however, was that words which had been inflected as adjectives became hard to separate from those traditionally labelled adverbs. A further complication, in Modern English, is that adverbs too can modify, or be 'added to', nouns. Compare *tomorrow*, traditionally an adverb of time, in *the meeting tomorrow*; or *inside*, traditionally an adverb of place, in *the people inside*; or *there* in *everybody there*. All three are postmodifiers: one would not normally say, for example, *I must go to the tomorrow meeting*. But not all adjectives, so-called, are premodifiers either. Other words described as adverbs can have either position: *a window downstairs*, but also, as part of a tendency to which we will return, *a downstairs window*. Each of these can fulfil the 'semantic task', if we may refer again to Dixon's criteria, of helping to identify a referent. *The meeting tomorrow* refers to one meeting where *the meeting on Thursday* would refer to another; a downstairs window is specifically not an upstairs window. If adjectives, therefore, are a part of speech defined, in the traditional style, as words that can at least have the syntactic function of a modifier, on what grounds do words like these not also belong to it?

One natural response is to appeal to lexical meanings. In a dictionary definition cited earlier an adjective is not only 'added to a noun'. It is also a word 'designating an attribute'; and no 'attribute', it might be argued, is denoted by, for example, *tomorrow*. Is being downstairs not, however, an attribute or property of a window? Or, if it is not, does *main* in *the main argument* denote a property of an argument? If *absent* in *the people absent* is an adjective by this criterion, how is *abroad* in *the people abroad* to be excluded? Such niggling is notorious, and was the basis on which definitions of the parts of speech were rubbished in the first half of the twentieth century. Most linguists have accordingly retreated from the attempt to give both necessary and sufficient criteria. A 'cluster of syntactic properties' (Huddleston and Pullum 2002: 528) can be said to characterize the 'central' members of a part of speech. In their analysis, a central adjective has positions which include the 'postpositive'; is gradable and takes 'degree modifiers' such as *very*; and 'characteristically' takes other adverbs. It is in the light of this that other adjectives, which are not central, are delimited.

This brings us back, however, to the question implied at the beginning of this chapter, as to whether we have good reason to include them in this category, other than to ensure that somehow, somewhere, they will fit into the traditional scheme.

2.6 English has been studied for so long, and studied against the background of Latin and other European languages, that it is hard to imagine how a field linguist would work out its structure if confronted with it for the first time. It may be instructive, however, to recall a distributional analysis by Fries (1952), which relied ostensibly on that evidence alone.

Of the classes that Fries established, 'Class 3' was defined by 'frames' shared by, among others, *good* and *large*. *Good*, for example, can be inserted in either slot in:

(6) The — coffee was —

where *coffee* was, more generally, a word of 'Class 1' and *was* a word of 'Class 2'. All words insertable in either slot, in frames of this form, belonged 'in a single part-of-speech class' (1952: 83). Like the others, however, this did not coincide 'in either what is included or what is excluded' (1952: 87) with the parts traditionally distinguished. Thus *main* or *utter* would not be insertable in the second slot, nor *afraid* in the first. This form of distributional analysis has since been lambasted, by Croft (2001) among others. But there is perhaps no need, for present purposes, to spring to its defence. Let us assume, with Dixon (2010), that adjectives in any language may be identified as words with certain semantic tasks. A prior condition, however, is that they are grammatically both similar and distinct from others. It would then be reasonable to ask if English, as a language which we are pretending to see as unfamiliar, has such a category and what category it is. If its grammar had to be discovered directly with the help of speakers, it is Fries's Class 3, or at least one very like it, that seems likely to be identified.

But Fries did not classify all words at once. In his account, 'four parts of speech... make up the bulk of the "words" in our utterances' (1952: 87). This implies, however, that some words are, initially at least, left over. *Main* or *utter* would not belong in Class 3; nor in Class 4, which is closest to the traditional category of adverbs; nor in either of the others. We can imagine a field linguist whose analysis has reached a similar point. It might be reasoned, however, that the second slot in (6), in which the adjective has one of Dixon's functions, can be filled by many other units. These include words he assigns or would assign to Class 4: compare *The coffee was there* or, with a different member of Class 1, *The meeting was yesterday*. They also include units larger than words: *The coffee was in the kitchen*, *The coffee was where you left it*, or *The coffee was a disaster*. This is not a function characteristic of adjectives especially. But the first slot in such a frame is typically filled by words of Fries's Class 3. If this then is the slot that distinguishes adjectives most clearly, it might seem reasonable to extend the term to other words that fill it, and have one of Dixon's major semantic functions, even though they do not have the other. This would be confirmed by evidence that adjectives which are distributionally bipositional (1.10) often have senses (1.3) in which they are so restricted.

An adjective might again, in this light, be a word that is 'added to' nouns. It would be added in the relation that Marouzeau distinguished as 'direct' (2.3), even if in no other. But the crucial function would be that of a premodifier, or a modifier in the attributive position; not, in the way in which it is possible to read a traditional definition, of a modifier which is either attributive or postpositive. This would exclude words that are traditionally adjectives, but classed as never attributive.

Those restricted to postposition need not detain us. In one way or another, they are a class on their own. Words like *afraid* are not so simple, and call into question a boundary that for many linguists might in any case be 'fuzzy'.

2.7 These are words that can be predicative and can form postmodifiers. They are thus distinguished by a pair of functions that they share with words traditionally classed as adverbs: compare *The meeting was yesterday* and *the meeting tomorrow*, or *The people are inside* and *the people abroad*. They are exceptions, in the received view, in that while they are adjectives, and have meanings characteristic of that class, they do not have the attributive function, by which adjectives are most clearly distinguished. This insight could, however, be turned round the opposite way. They are words, that is, whose functions are included in those of adverbs. But they are exceptions in that they have meanings more like those of adjectives.

Most are 'formed', as Huddleston and Pullum describe them, 'with the *a-* prefix' (2002: 559). It might be disputed whether *afraid* is strictly transparent; but *asleep* is plainly *a* + *sleep*, *alive* is *a* + *live*, and so on. Huddleston and Pullum also distinguish a small set of words that 'have to do with medical health or condition' (2002: 560); this includes, for example, *unwell*. But those in *a-* have come together, from varied sources, in the history of the language; and if they are adjectives, they are restricted in comparison with others morphologically related to them. Compare, for example, *the children asleep* with *the sleepy children* or *a live fish* with *a fish still alive*. Boyd and Goldberg (2011) ask how it can be that a speaker who will learn to use most adjectives as premodifiers nevertheless learns not to say *the asleep children*, *an alive fish*, or *the afraid people*.

Theories of learning are not our concern. One observation, however, that may be relevant is that as words such as *asleep* tend not to be attributive so they tend not to be 'characterizing'. The term is borrowed from Bolinger (1952), and used as he used it in a passage cited earlier (1.8). *Sleepy* has a transferred sense, as in *a sleepy town*, in which it is as characterizing as *large* in *a large town*. *Live* in *a live interview* characterizes an interview as one not recorded earlier, and in *They sell live fish* it characterizes what is sold. But *asleep* denotes a state that a child, for example, will be in at one time and not at another, and *alive* a state in time opposed to that denoted by *dead.* If their syntax is exceptional, it is exceptional in a way that accords, if Bolinger was right, with a more general tendency. Another observation is that these are not the only words formed with this prefix. *Ahead,* for example, is transparently *a* + *head.* Traditionally it is an adverb; but it too comes after a noun, as in *the road ahead. Abroad,* as in *the people abroad,* is another. It is hard to see how learning not to say *an asleep child* or *the afraid people* is separate from learning not to say *the ahead people* or *the abroad roads.*

Ahead and *abroad* are among ten words in *a-* that Huddleston and Pullum (2002: 614) class as prepositions: their reasons for not treating them as adverbs need not, for the moment, distract us. As prepositions, they are separate from twenty-four described as adjectives (2002: 559). The boundary, however, is a fine one. *Ashore,* for example, is another word that they describe as a preposition. *Afloat* is instead described as an adjective. But it is worth noting that in, for example, *The New Shorter Oxford English Dictionary* (Brown, ed. 1993) both have entries headed '*adv*[erb] *&* *pred*[icative] *a*[djective]'. On what grounds might one authority be right and the other mistaken?

The 'most decisive criterion', according to Huddleston and Pullum, is that 'prepositions...can occur as head of a non-predicative adjunct in clause-structure' (2002: 606). *Alone,* for example, is an 'adjunct' or the head of an adjunct in *Alone, they are nothing. Alone,* however, is classed as an adjective, and must be linked to a 'predicand' (2002: 530); the predicand, in this example, is whatever would be referred to by *they. Ashore* is an adjunct in, for example, *Ashore, there was much drunkenness.* But here there is no predicand, and *ashore* is a preposition. Replace *ashore,* in the same context, with *alone* and the example is marked, with an asterisk, as unacceptable (2002: 531). While this criterion, however, may seem natural enough, the evidence may be less than decisive. *Afloat* is described, once more, as an adjective: compare then *Afloat, they are in their element.* If its classification is right, one should not be able to say *Afloat, there will be no drunkenness. Aground* is classed with *ashore,* as a preposition. This implies that one could say, for example, *Aground, there will be a problem.* Such judgements are at the limit, however, of those that can be made reliably.

One conclusion might be that the boundary may be 'fuzzy'. But on what evidence is there a boundary at all? The alternative is that words in *a-* belong together. The main distinction is instead between words that, as modifiers, are basically postpositive, and others that are adjectives and basically attributive. Among the former is a subclass that includes, for example, both *afraid* and *abroad*; both *alive* and, for example, *away.* If this were the real division for speakers of the language, it is not clear why they might be expected to say *an asleep child* any more than *a child sleepy.*

Conversion

2.8 It is time now to return to the other complication mentioned at the beginning of this chapter. In *She drives fast* the function of *fast* is like that of, for example, *slowly* in *She drives slowly*. Compare, however, *slowly* with *slow*. Their meanings are related; but where one is traditionally an adverb, the other is an adjective. Other words are related similarly: *badly* and *bad*, *carefully* and *careful*, and so on. We may therefore speak of a process:

(7) $_{\mathrm{A}}[\mathrm{X}] \rightarrow {}_{\mathrm{Adv}}[\mathrm{X} + \mathrm{ly}]$

by which a suffix, *-ly*, is added to an adjective (A) to form an adverb (Adv) corresponding to it. 'X' in (7) is a variable of which *slow*, in this case, is one value. But *fast* can have a function similar to that of words formed in this way. It is therefore natural to posit another process:

(8) $_{\mathrm{A}}[\mathrm{X}] \rightarrow {}_{\mathrm{Adv}}[\mathrm{X}]$

by which nothing changes other than the part of speech to which X is assigned. The values of X, in this case, include *fast*. The process in (8) could be described as one of 'zero-derivation', by which one lexical unit, as in (7), is derived from another. Alternatively, it is a process of 'conversion', by which a lexical unit is reassigned from one class to another. If this is right, we need to ask if words can also become adjectives, by conversion from other categories.

Let us assume, as is usual, that parts of speech are few and exhaustive. Another assumption, which is crucial to one line of argument, is that syntactic functions, such as that of a head and a modifier, are established independently of the classes of units that can have them. This is made explicit by, among others, Huddleston and Pullum (2002: 20–26); and implies that a construction, if we may use this term in something like its traditional sense, can be identified on two levels. That of *fast*, for example, in *fast cars* is at one level of a modifier to a head, and at another level that of an adjective, which can have the function of a modifier, to a noun. This has the attraction, for them and for other linguists who have reasoned similarly, that the same function may in principle be that of units which belong to different classes; and the same unit may have different functions, in different constructions.

Take then a phrase such as *the library carpet*. *Library*, we will argue, is a modifier: in that respect at least it has the construction of *big* in *a big carpet*. In *a big library* it has the function of a head; and in that role, we will argue, it is a noun. Where it is a modifier there will then be logically two options. The function could be of both adjectives and nouns. In *the library carpet*, the construction of *library* can thus remain that of a noun. Alternatively, *library* is a noun in one construction but an adjective in the other. It might accordingly be subject to a process of conversion:

(9) $_{N}$[library] → $_{A}$[library]

by which, though basically a noun (N), it is reassigned to the same part of speech as *big*. Adjectives have the property of modifying nouns, and it is by virtue of its conversion that *library*, as an adjective, can do so.

There is also, it is perhaps worth noting, a third possibility. In an appendix to Huddleston and Pullum's grammar (2002), with the title 'Lexical word-formation', Laurie Bauer and Huddleston speak only in passing, in their section on conversion (1640–44), of a process such as that in (8), converting an adjective to an adverb. But it is made clear elsewhere that some words are syntactically members of both parts of speech (chapter signed by Huddleston and Pullum, 530). Conversion may be implied. In principle, however, we could avoid assuming that in every case one part of speech is basic. A word such as *library* could be classed equally as a noun, with one function or range of functions, and as an adjective, with another.

A treatment possible in principle may also in principle be wrong. If conversion, however, can be justified in some cases, in which is it and in which not?

2.9 Take for comparison a process by which adjectives would be reclassified as nouns. According to Huddleston and Pullum, 'a considerable number of nouns', such as *brown* in *a dark shade of brown*, 'are formed by conversion' in that way (2002: appendix by Bauer and Huddleston, 1642). This implies a process we could represent as follows:

(10) $_{A}$[X] → $_{N}$[X]

where X is a variable one of whose values would be *brown*. One argument in particular that might be made in favour of (10) is that words denoting colours, for example, have a function in which they can be plural: compare, for example, *The browns are starting to fade*. To be inflected for number is a property that nouns have and adjectives, or words that are for certain adjectives, do not have.

Conversions in the opposite direction are, as Bauer and Huddleston see it, 'very rare'. The process, for them, is one of word-formation and, to justify it, we are required to show that the derived word 'has acquired distinctively adjectival properties' (2002: 1643). The problem, therefore, is what such properties are. It seems that they must be positive: it is not sufficient, for example, that as adjectives are not inflected for number, neither would one say *the libraries carpet*. One property of 'central adjectives', for Huddleston and Pullum, is that they can take 'degree modifiers' (2002: 528; **2.5**). These include, in particular, the intensifier *very*: a conversion, therefore, that Bauer and Huddleston do allow is that of *Oxbridge* in, for example, *He has a very Oxbridge accent*. But central adjectives are not distinguished, in this account, by any single function or position. Above all, it would not be sufficient that in *an Oxbridge accent* the function of *Oxbridge*, like that of the adjective in *a nice accent*, is attributive.

Others have seen the modifying, and in particular the attributive role, as central. It is not surprising, therefore, that they argue differently. *Glass*, we will take it, is a noun when used as in *The glass is too thick*. But in a phrase such as *a glass door* its function is like that of, for example, *wooden* in *a wooden door*. *Wooden* can be classed as an adjective, derived by a process of word-formation from a noun *wood*:

(11) $_{\text{N}}$[wood] → $_{\text{A}}$[wood + en]

Glass in *a glass door* does not have, for Bauer and Huddleston, the cluster of syntactic properties said to distinguish central adjectives. For them therefore there is no conversion, which they describe (in Huddleston and Pullum 2002: 1640) as another process of word-formation. If not all properties, however, were relevant a noun *glass* could be converted in parallel:

(12) $_{\text{N}}$[glass] → $_{\text{A}}$[glass]

The process would be regular for words denoting materials of which something can be made. Compare *wood*, without a suffix, in *a wood floor*; *steel* in *a steel frame*, *silk* in *a silk shirt*, and so on. As a class of adjectives, these would acquire a syntactic property characteristic of the part of speech in general, of being attributive.

This logic underlies, in particular, the practice of dictionaries. In, for example, *The New Shorter Oxford English Dictionary* both uses of *glass* are covered in a single entry (Brown, ed. 1993). This implies that it is a single lexical unit. It is classed grammatically, however, as both '*n*[oun] *&* *a*[djective]', and its meanings are divided accordingly. The one it has in, for example, *Bring some glasses* is explained and illustrated in a section headed '*n.*' (A II, 'a glass vessel or receptacle'). The one it would have in *a glass door* follows in another section (B 1 'made of glass', or B 2 'glazed, having pieces or panes of glass set in a frame'). This second section has the heading '*attrib*[utive] or as *adj*[ective]'. *Steel* is similarly '*attrib.* or as *adj.*' when it is used as in *a steel frame*; *gold* is labelled '*adj.*', abbreviating 'adjective' or 'adjectival' (xxiii), as in *a gold ring*; and so on. The sense of 'attributive' is either taken for granted, or as 'designating', in the wording of its own entry, 'adjectives (or their equivalents) that premodify or occas. immediately follow nouns'. Crucially, that is, they premodify.

Library, for comparison, has an entry headed '*n.*'. This implies that when attributive, in the definition cited, it is an 'equivalent' of an adjective, not an adjective itself. There may, accordingly, be an additional criterion: that for derivations like (12) to be justified the adjective must have what we can call an adjectival meaning. In the same dictionary, *chief* is a word that has two entries: one as a noun; the other as an adjective, in phrases such as *the chief cook*; and, though this need not concern us, as an adverb. Compare *top* in *the top woman* or *head* in *a head gardener*. If these are basically nouns, this would imply conversions such as:

(13) $_{\text{N}}$[chief] → $_{\text{A}}$[chief]

where the meaning of the adjective can be seen as similar to that of *main* in *the main cook* or *leading*, as a participial adjective, in *the leading woman*.

2.10 For Huddleston and his colleagues, whose criteria are different, words like *glass* and *chief* remain nouns. As modifiers, that is, they are not '*attrib.* or *adj.*', but simply members of another part of speech whose function, as '*attrib.*', is one they and an '*adj.*' will share. The treatment, therefore, that prevails in dictionaries is excoriated in a later paper by Pullum (2009). *Head*, for example, is a modifier in *a head librarian*. As such it has a function like that of the adjective in *a tall librarian* or *a nice librarian*. But it is a word that has 'no adjectival properties other than... the possibility of occurring', as it does here, 'as an attributive modifier in the structure of a noun phrase'. Hence it is not itself an adjective. Words of this kind may have 'special meanings', as Pullum acknowledges, 'when used as attributive modifiers'. *Top*, for example, would have a meaning in *the top cook* that could not simply be predicted from its uses as a head noun, in *the top of the hill* or *This is the top*. A dictionary must explain this, but not as that of another lexical unit. It is merely a meaning the noun has in an attributive function.

Pullum's paper is a useful polemic. But conversions cannot in general be ruled out: *brown* might again be converted in *The browns are fading*, and while *head* might not be converted to an adjective, it is in most accounts a verb in, for example, *She headed the list*. 'A notable property of English', as Bauer and Huddleston put it in their section on conversion, is the extent of 'homonymy' between verbs and nouns (Huddleston and Pullum 2002: 1640). The issue is one of criteria: of whether *head*, for example, has or has not, if we may repeat their wording, 'acquired distinctively adjectival properties'. There is, however, a new problem: that words may acquire properties in part, but not wholly.

One property of 'central adjectives', still according to Huddleston and Pullum, is that they are gradable (2002: 528). It might thus be seen as relevant that when *glass* is attributive it does not normally form a comparative. But neither does *wooden*, so long as it means literally 'made of wood'. *Wooden* would still be an adjective: it is merely, in that sense and to that extent, not central. It is not clear, however, why adjectives derived by conversion need be central either. Another property ascribed to central adjectives is that they 'characteristically take adverbs as modifiers'. For Pullum it is relevant, for example, that the modifier in *a cotton shirt* cannot in turn be modified by adverbs such as *flimsily* (2009: 259). The explanation, he would argue, is that it remains a noun. It is only 'characteristically', however, that adjectives take modifiers of that kind, and the property is again of central adjectives only. If we exclude *a flimsily cotton shirt*, we may also exclude, with an adjective that might again be peripheral, *a flimsily wooden door*. There are also problems when we turn to 'degree modifiers'. Words like *cotton* or *glass* cannot be modified by the intensifier *very*. But they can take other words that indicate the degree to which a thing is made of one material or another. Compare, for example, *a partly cotton shirt* or *It has lots of largely glass walls.* There are no phrases, in comparison, such as *a partly cotton* or *these largely glasses.* The explanation, we might argue in a spirit similar to Pullum's, is that *cotton* and *glass* are nouns in one construction but are adjectives in the other. As adjectives, with the type of meaning they have, they take some degree modifiers, or more generally some kinds of adverb; they just do not take all.

It may seem tempting, in this light, to follow linguists such as Aarts, and argue that one part of speech shades into another (2007: 129–36). It is at least worth raising, however, the more fundamental question, as to why a classification into parts of speech is relevant. We have assumed implicitly that if there is a process of conversion it is one we can represent as follows:

(14) $_{\text{N}}[\text{X}] \rightarrow {}_{\text{A}}[\text{X}]$

at a level of abstraction as high as possible. 'X' is again a variable whose values must be made clear; and, if we are guided by dictionaries like the one referred to, the words involved will not be nouns in general, but specific units which form smaller classes. *Glass*, again, is one of a class whose members denote materials of which things can consist or be made. This is a good candidate for a category that might be real for speakers, and one statement can be about such words in general. A statement about words such as *chief* may be harder to formulate: there are semantic complications, certainly. But they too can be said to belong together. A statement that they can be modifiers need say nothing about their part of speech. It is merely about their function, under another assumption made at the outset, in relation to a head. Have we any reason to say more?

The traditional answer is that we must address the question which has echoed down the millennia, *Quae pars?* 'which part', of what were originally defined as the successive parts of every utterance or sentence, is it? It is not unreasonable to ask why must we.

2.11 A conversion affecting *glass*, if that is how it is seen, affects several such words similarly. It may be helpful, however, to look at another case where dictionaries, for reasons that make good sense from the viewpoint of a lexicographer, describe words as adjectives when they are attributive. In this case, there is little regularity.

Let us return, for a first example, to the *downstairs* of *a downstairs window.* The word in general has two entries in the dictionary cited (Brown, ed. 1993), which assign it to three parts of speech. It is a noun, with stress on either syllable, when used as in *They would be given the downstairs to live in. It is an* '*adv*[erb]', stressed on *-stairs*, in, for example, *They walked downstairs.* But it is an adjective, with a variant *downstair*, in phrases like *the downstairs window.* For another view we may turn again to Huddleston and Pullum. In *I walked downstairs* it is in their analysis a preposition. There are prepositions, that is, whose complements are obligatory; others with which a complement is optional; and still others, such as *downstairs*, which exclude one. In, for example, *I walked through the door* a preposition (P), for example, would form a prepositional phrase (PP):

(15) $_{PP}$[$_{P}$[through] the door]

So, as a unit in the same construction, does *downstairs*:

(16) $_{PP}$[$_{P}$[downstairs]]

Such a unit can also be predicative, as in *Everyone is downstairs*, or a postmodifier, as in *the windows downstairs*. The word itself is then of the same category, at least, when it is attributive. As Huddleston and Pullum put it, 'a few prepositions . . . are found', in phrases like *a downstairs window*, as attributive modifiers (2002: 444). This implies that they do not form prepositional phrases, as in (16). To that extent the change of function is linked to a change of syntactic category. But in this account there is no lexical conversion.

The same type of preposition, that excludes a complement, is taken to include, among others, *here* and *there*; other compounds such as *overseas* or *downhill*; also, as we have seen, one set of words in *a-* (Huddleston and Pullum 2002: 614). Of these *overseas*, for example, is attributive in phrases such as *the overseas members*. So is *indoor*, which can be described as a variant of *indoors*, in *an indoor swimming pool*. Other prepositions, which may or may not take a complement, include *through* or *opposite*. In this analysis, they are prepositions both when they do, as in *the house opposite ours* and when, as in *the people inside*, they do not. Such words are premodifiers in, for example, *a through road* or *the opposite wall*. In this use they too could be represented as bare prepositions: as words whose part of speech does not change, but which no longer form a phrase as in (16).

In *The New Shorter Oxford Dictionary*, the entry for *overseas* is headed '*adv., a., & n.*'. An entry for *indoors*, headed '*adv.*', is separate from one for *indoor*, headed '*a.*'. The entry for *opposite*, for example, is headed '*a., n., adv., & prep.*'. This again implies that such words are adjectives when they are attributive, whatever part of speech they may belong to when their functions are different.

2.12 It is tempting to assume that one or other treatment must be right. The more closely, however, we look at the evidence, the more we open up a hornet's nest of details, and it is ultimately these, at a far lower level of abstraction, that we have to deal with.

Both *downstairs*, for example, and *opposite* form what may be characterized, more neutrally, as locative expressions. *Opposite ours* is such an expression in *Their house is opposite ours*, as is *downstairs* in *The party is downstairs*, whether or not it has the structure Huddleston and Pullum assign to it. In construction with *be*, locative expressions are used freely and regularly. They are also regularly postmodifiers. We may now speak more clearly of a class of units that, as modifiers, will be basically postpositive. Words in *a-* were tentative examples mooted earlier (2.7). Locative expressions, which include some words in *a-*, are others for which this is, in one sense of a term traditional in linguistics, an unmarked function or an unmarked realization.

None are used so regularly as premodifiers. *A downstairs window* may in practice have a meaning like that of *a window downstairs*; or *an indoor swimming pool* like that of *a swimming pool indoors*. What holds for these holds also for their antonyms *upstairs* and *outdoor(s)*. But the attributive use of all four is restricted. *An upstairs window* would again be normal; as would, for example, *a downstairs bedroom.* Windows and rooms can be characterized, as Bolinger would have explained it, by their location (compare Bolinger 1952, cited in 1.8). But for people, in particular, that is far less usual. Imagine a speaker living in a house with children in a flat below. They could be referred to, in whatever context, by *the children downstairs*. It is harder, however, to think of one in which *the downstairs children* might be as or more appropriate.

Many locative expressions are not normally premodifiers. Among them are both *here* and *there*, which again, for Huddleston and Pullum, form prepositional phrases without complements. They also include, very obviously, most expressions that are undisputed prepositional phrases, such as *opposite ours* or *in the garden. An on the spot decision* can, in comparison, have a meaning like that of *a decision on the spot*, and *an out of court settlement* one like that of *a settlement out of court.* A premodifying use is possible, however, only for specific phrases. One would not say, for example, *an away from court settlement.* It can also involve a restriction of meaning. *On the spot* has a structure like that of, for example, *at the scene* and, as a postmodifier, can be locative in the most literal sense. *The children on the spot* would refer to children in a particular place, as would *the children upstairs.* With this noun as the head, *the on the spot children* is at best less likely. In *an on the spot decision*, the meaning of the modifier could instead be seen as transferred, to that of an expression of time. The decision was taken there and then, the location where it was taken being irrelevant or unknown.

Other restrictions are specific to varying degrees. *Uphill*, for comparison, is a straightforward locative in *the buildings uphill*, and *the uphill buildings* is similarly less likely. It is a premodifier in *an uphill journey*, which could be said of what would also be referred to by *a journey uphill.* It is as a premodifier, however, that its use is most likely to be metaphorical. Compare, for example, *Writing such a long book is an uphill struggle. Opposite* is a locative, whether a preposition or an adverb does not matter, in *the wall opposite.* But it has another, figurative use in, for example, *an opposite view* or *the opposite argument.* So has *outside*, in *an outside chance* or *another outside possibility.* Neither would have these meanings, though others might at a pinch be possible, as postmodifiers in *a chance outside* or in *the argument opposite.* Other contrasts are still more specific. *Outside* is also attributive in, for example, *an outside door.* In *the door outside* its meaning is again as a straightforward locative, as it would be if a complement were added. The reference could be to a door, say, that has been delivered by builders' merchants and has not yet been brought in. But *an outside door* refers instead to one by which a person can leave, for example, a house. *Overseas*, if we may add yet one more detail, is a locative in *the roads overseas*. Compare *the roads in France* or *the motorways abroad*. It too can be a premodifier, as in *the overseas members*. The reference would not, however, be to people who at some time merely happen to be out of the country. For that one could say *the members overseas*. It might instead be to the members of a club who, in its books, are domiciled abroad. They could be characterized, for example, as members who pay less.

2.13 The question raised by the practices in dictionaries is whether it helps to say that *overseas* or *outside* can be adjectives. But this raises a complementary question, as to whether it is of any greater help to insist that they are always adverbs, or are always prepositions.

Any word has a range of uses which can be studied, in detail, individually. We would be naïve to kid ourselves that we are describing 'the phenomena' or 'the data': to talk of a word is to talk already of an abstraction. But at the lowest level of abstraction that concerns us, *downstairs* has what we may call a 'microsyntax', in which it combines with other individual words and sequences of words, such as *walked* in *I walked downstairs* or *window* in *a downstairs window*, which is different in part from that of *indoors*, which as a form does not combine in the same way with *window*, and still more that of, for example, *opposite*. *Brown*, to return to an earlier example, has a microsyntax different from that of *large*. *Large* does not combine with *the* as *brown* does in *the browns*, and they combine as in *a large brown animal*, rather than as in *a brown large animal*.

All this is banal, and only the term 'microsyntax', which I hope I can be forgiven for introducing, may be original. It is obvious too that at successively higher levels of abstraction, many words are easily classed together. *Brown* belongs with *red*, *blue*, and the like as words denoting colours, which all, for example, combine in the same order with words such as, in a parallel abstraction, *large* or *small*. At a still higher level, of what we might distinguish as 'macrosyntax', *brown* and *large* in turn fall together. We have no reason to contest that a category which includes both is in some sense real for people who have learned to speak the language. This leads us back, however, to the central issue, as to whether we have any reason to see macrosyntax as exhaustive. Have we any motive, that is, other than precisely to achieve exhaustiveness?

Let us accept, for the sake of argument, that we can abstract away from the traditional distinction between adverbs and prepositions. We can say that many such words are used regularly both in what is for adjectives the predicative position, and as postmodifiers. We can add, in general, that some have uses as premodifiers. But these we have to describe for each word individually, or for pairs of antonyms at best. What would be the point of saying more?

3

Can one position be primary?

3.1 At the level of macrosyntax (**2.13**), there is a class of adjectives that includes at least *large*, *happy*, *brown*, and many others. In a wider extension, it has other members that are only attributive (compare **2.6**). In the conventional account, in which its extension is the widest, it includes words that are not attributive or may be no more than postmodifiers. The members, however, described as central to it have two main functions, or traditionally 'positions': the predicative and the attributive. Are these, in English at least, simply independent? Or are adjectives a part of speech for which one role is primary, and others are in some sense secondary?

In what sense a position might be secondary is part of the problem. One possibility, however, is that when an adjective is in the attributive position its category is specifically that of an 'attributive adjective'. When it is in the predicative position, its category is instead that of a 'predicative adjective'. It is the same word: but its category is different and might be seen as changing, therefore, by a process of conversion. The *brown*, for comparison, of *The browns are fading* can be classed as a noun derived by conversion, as in **2.9**, from the adjective in, for example, *a brown carpet*. The attributive adjective in *a brown carpet* could also be converted, in principle, into the predicative adjective in *The carpet is brown*.

We will begin by looking briefly at two analyses, of adjectives in general, that have developed this insight. Though formulated decades apart and in quite different terms, they agree in taking the modifying role of words like *brown* as primary. In this they follow the traditional definition of an adjective (**2.3**). In another view, however, what is primary is precisely the opposite. The relation in which one unit is predicated of another is central to the formation of a sentence, and the unit predicated can be an adjective, in combination in the case of English with *be*, as well as, in particular, a verb. Verbs also enter into the formation of phrases: thus, in English, as one type of participle in phrases like *the vehicles arriving*, or as another in, for example, *the houses destroyed*. So do adjectives, in a position that in English is especially attributive. But the formation of phrases is subsidiary to that of sentences, of which they are parts. The functions of participles and of attributive adjectives are both, in that light, secondary.

Analyses in which adjectives are parallel to verbs can be traced at least to the tradition of 'philosophical grammar'. For James Harris, in particular, both were 'attributives', or attributives of a 'first order', that 'denoted attributes' (1751: 87, 184–91). In living memory, however, an analysis in which the predicative use of adjectives is primary was developed above all in the tradition of transformational grammar from the 1950s onwards.

Adjectives as basically attributive

3.2 For an alternative to it, we may look first at a scheme of categories proposed by Croft (2003). It forms part of a book on 'typology and universals', in the tradition of Joseph H. Greenberg, and it might perhaps be questioned whether the way it deals with adjectives is appropriate for all languages. We are concerned, however, with a language of one type in particular.

The guiding principle is that categories can be distinguished from one another on two dimensions. On the one hand, they may differ in their 'semantic class': in what their members characteristically denote. The distinction is threefold, between 'objects', 'properties', and 'actions'. On the other hand, they may differ in what in Croft's term is a 'propositional act'. The distinction of acts is also threefold, between 'reference', 'predication', and 'modification'. He therefore posits a system of nine categories, each defined by a different pairing of a type of meaning with, if we may use another term, a function. Take again, for example, the *tall* of *the tall chief*. Its semantic class is that of words denoting properties, and its function is as a modifier. Its category is thus defined by a pairing we may represent as follows:

(1) <property, modification>

Compare then the *tall* of *The chief is tall.* Its semantic class remains that of words denoting properties. But its function, or propositional act, is of predication. Therefore its category is different, and is defined by the pairing:

(2) <property, predication>

A finite verb, such as *arrived* in *The vehicles arrived,* is in turn defined by the pairing:

(3) <action, predication>

while a participle, as in *the vehicles arriving,* is distinguished from it by the function of a modifier:

(4) <action, modification>

which (4) shares with (1).

So far (2) is to (1), on the dimension of 'propositional acts', as (3) is to (4). In more traditional language, a predicative adjective is to an attributive adjective as a verb is to a participle. Three, however, of Croft's nine pairings are described as 'typological prototypes of parts of speech' (2003: 88). One defines what in his terms is an 'unmarked noun':

(5) <object, reference>

The function of a noun, that is, is 'prototypically' neither as a modifier nor as a predicate. (3) similarly defines an 'unmarked verb': a verb is unmarked, therefore, when it is predicative. (4), in comparison, is not prototypical. An adjective, still in accordance with the traditional definition, is unmarked when, in the pairing in (1), it is a modifier. While the participle, therefore, in *the vehicles arriving* is marked by a function other than predication, the predicative adjective in *The chief is tall* is marked, in the opposite way, in that its function is not one of modification.

3.3 Croft's analysis dates from 1990, and his treatment of adjectives has been criticized by Baker (2003). Its roots lie deep, however, in an ancient tradition; and in spirit, though not in terminology, it recalls a bolder proposal by Tesnière, over thirty years earlier. In Tesnière's analysis (1959), a sentence like *The chief is tall* did not merely include a unit whose category was secondary to that of the adjective in *the tall chief.* It was not itself an adjective. It was a verb; but a verb derived from an adjective.

Tesnière's categories are distinguished in a system that was his alone: the traditional 'verb' and 'adjective' will suffice, however, for our purposes. To say then that a verb can be derived from an adjective is to say that it undergoes a process of (in French) *translation*, by which it is 'transferred', as we will put it, from one category to another. The transfer may involve no further change, and in that case it is similar to conversion, in the sense of **2.8**. It may instead, however, be effected with what Tesnière called a *marquant de la translation* (1959: ch. 160), or 'marker of transfer'.

This may be, for example, a suffix. It may alternatively be a larger unit. Thus, for illustration, the participle in *the vehicles arriving* is again a modifier. It has a function, as others might put it, like that of an adjective. But for Tesnière it actually was an adjective. It was therefore derived by a transfer which might be represented, in a later system of notation, as follows:

(6) $_{\text{V}}$[arrive] → $_{\text{A}}$[arrive + ing]

The marker of transfer is, in this case, *-ing*. In *the centre of London*, a noun is modified by a phrase, as it is conventionally called, *of London*. *London*, however, is in itself a noun, and for Tesnière it too would be transferred to the category of an adjective:

(7) $_{\text{N}}$[London] → $_{\text{A}}$[of + London]

the marker of transfer being, in this case, what is conventionally the word *of*.

A unit transferred from category A to category B may in turn be transferred to another category C, or back to A, and so on. Such elaborations are explored in detail in Part 3 of Tesnière's treatise. The point, however, that concerns us is that while, for Croft, an adjective is 'unmarked' as a modifier, it is an adjective, in this analysis, only when it is so. Its transfer to a verb is effected, in English, by the addition of what is traditionally the copula. As *arrive*, or *arrive* with its inflection, is the verb in *The vehicles arrived*, so *be tall*, or *be tall* with the inflection of *be*, will be the verb in *The chief is tall*. A transfer, therefore, may be represented as follows:

(8) $_{\text{A}}$[tall] → $_{\text{V}}$[be + tall]

where *be* is a marker just as *of* is a marker in (7) or *-ing* in (6).

It is an unfortunate accident of history that when Tesnière's work was published posthumously, at the end of the 1950s, English-speaking linguists in particular had to grapple with Chomsky's theory of transformational grammar, which had burst on them two years earlier. Even where other ideas of Tesnière's have been influential, that of a transfer of category has not been. A transformation was, moreover, a competing process, and it was not until the end of the 1970s, in the work of Bresnan and her followers, that operations on lexical units, which changed their classification or syntactic properties, came to be exploited in the generative tradition (Bresnan 1978; ed. 1982).

The sole strategy, before then, had been to relate syntactic structures, such as that of a phrase in which an adjective is attributive to that of a clause in which it is predicative, as wholes. In this treatment the predicative structure was ineluctably primary.

Adjectives in early generative grammar

3.4 The starting-point, for transformations generally, was that units with different structures are subject to the same 'selectional restrictions'. *Numerous*, for example, 'selects' a plural subject in *The children are numerous*, which has the structure of a clause or sentence. It correspondingly selects a head noun which is plural, in a phrase *the numerous children*. As *sour*, for example, selects nouns such as *milk* in phrases such as *sour milk*, so it selects the same nouns as a subject, in clauses such as *The milk is sour*. Restrictions like these had to be described; and unless the structures were linked, they had to be described twice over, once in clauses and once more, separately, in phrases. Therefore Chomsky proposed a 'nominalizing transformation', by which, as he originally explained it, 'any string' whose form is as follows:

(9) T – N – is – Adj

(where *T* stands for 'article') can be converted to 'the corresponding noun phrase of the form *T+Adj+N*'. Selectional restrictions can be stated over (9): there is no clause, for example, *The child is numerous*. They would then carry over automatically to any structure derived from that of (9). It was 'not difficult to show', in Chomsky's words, that such a transformation 'simplifies the grammar considerably, and that it must go in this, not the opposite direction' (1957: 72).

The argument was spelled out further in a book whose published version is two decades later (Chomsky 1975: 539–40). It is from this that I have taken the example of *numerous*. But the proposal as it stood did not cover postmodifying adjectives. What Chomsky had said was also strictly untrue. If *afraid* is an adjective, as was assumed then as it is assumed now, it can form part of a 'string' whose form is as in (9): *the – child – is – afraid*. But this is not converted to a corresponding noun phrase *the+afraid+child*. Let us therefore turn to a more nuanced and detailed study by Lees (1960), whose subject was 'nominalization' generally.

A first transformation, as Lees argued, would convert the structure of an independent sentence, such as *The children are afraid*, into that of a relative clause. Clauses were classed as sentences, and a sentence (S) such as *who are afraid* can form part of a noun phrase (NP) whose structure, insofar as it is relevant, we may represent as follows:

(10) $_{\mathrm{NP}}$[the $_{\mathrm{N}}$[children] $_{\mathrm{S}}$[who are $_{\mathrm{A}}$[afraid]]]

This process will apply to sentences generally. From *The party is tomorrow* we can accordingly derive (*the party*) *which is tomorrow*; from *The book is on my desk* we can derive (*the book*) *which is on my desk*; from *The vehicles are arriving* we can derive (*the vehicles*) *which are arriving*; and so on. By a second transformation, sequences or 'substrings' such as *who are* or *which is* can be deleted. The structure in (10) can therefore be the source for one in which an adjective alone is the postmodifier of a noun:

(11) $_{\mathrm{NP}}$[the $_{\mathrm{N}}$[children] $_{\mathrm{A}}$[afraid]]

The same process can again apply more generally: to *the party which is tomorrow* to derive *the party tomorrow*; to *the book which is on my desk* to derive *the book on my desk*; or to *the vehicles which are arriving*, though *are* in this example is an auxiliary, to derive *the vehicles arriving*.

By this second transformation, the structure of a phrase such as *the chief who is tall* would be reduced to one where *tall* is likewise a postmodifier:

(12) $_{\mathrm{NP}}$[the $_{\mathrm{N}}$[chief] $_{\mathrm{A}}$[tall]]

It was from structures like (12), therefore, that a third transformation derived phrases in which adjectives of this type are premodifers:

(13) $_{\mathrm{NP}}$[the $_{\mathrm{A}}$[tall] $_{\mathrm{N}}$[chief]]

by a process of inversion. This was subject, as Lees acknowledged, to 'many as yet unanalyzed restrictions' (1960: 98). But it could be stipulated that it would not apply to postmodifiers such as *afraid*; nor, for example, to prepositional phrases such as *on my desk*. For some adjectives it might be optional; for others, like *tall*, it could be obligatory.

3.5 In reviewing early work on generative grammar it is important to remember, first, that grammars were quite literally 'generative'. The 'fundamental aim', as Chomsky had put it, was to generate the sentences of a language and 'none of the ungrammatical ones' (1957: 13). Each sentence would be assigned a structure, determined by how it was derived. But the evidence taken to be relevant was simply that of distributions. Meanings were to be the subject of a separate investigation, of the ways in which 'syntactic structure is put to use in the actual functioning of language' (Chomsky 1957: 102). For the background to these ideas I may refer, I hope, to my own commentary (Matthews 1993: 128–41 especially). The first objective, however, of a grammar was to achieve the simplest overall account of how words were distributed in sentences.

The case for Lees's solution was in these terms overwhelming. The restrictions called 'selectional' restricted the distribution of words, and wherever they held across two different structures, the simplest treatment would again relate one structure to the other. The classic illustration had been Chomsky's argument for a passive transformation (1957: 42–3). Evidence of that sort did not in itself determine the direction in which structures should be related. But the argument for nominalization fitted beautifully, when Chomsky first proposed it, with the theory of what he called 'kernel sentences'.

Their technical definition was as sentences whose derivation did not include 'optional' transformations (Chomsky 1957: 45). It was by such transformations that, for example, passives were derived from actives, or relative clauses, as an initial step in Lees's proposal, from sentences that could stand on their own. In practice, therefore, kernel sentences were those whose structure was not reduced to that of others. Take then *The tall chief arrived*. It could, in principle, be a kernel sentence. But obviously, if modifiers are derived from predicates, its structure can be reduced to those of, on the one hand, *The chief arrived* and, on the other hand, *The chief is tall*.

An underlying motive, both for transformations generally and for the direction taken for specific transformations, was to establish kernel sentences that would be as simple and as few as possible.

Finally, it was simpler to derive premodifiers in successive stages, not directly by the transformation Chomsky had originally proposed. *Tall*, in *the tall chief*, was a part of a noun phrase seen as deriving from an independent sentence. So was the relative clause in *the chief who is tall*, and a grammar would be simpler if *the tall chief* was derived in part by the same process that applied to that; not independently, in a single operation, from *The chief is tall*. The premodifier in *the tall chief* and the postmodifier in *the party tomorrow* could in principle be derived by separate processes, each from a relative clause in which a sequence *who is* or *which is* would be independently deleted. But the grammar is simpler if the deletions are all part of the same process, to be followed by an inversion, in the order of what is left, for units such as *tall*. Compare then the derivation of a modifying adjective and, in particular, a participle. In a treatment like that of Tesnière (**3.3**), their relations to predicates are the opposite. In Lees's account, *the chief who is tall* was instead derived by precisely the same operation as *the vehicles which are arriving* or, with a passive participle, *the towns which are destroyed*. All three were reduced by the same operation of deletion, and the order of modifier and noun is the only difference remaining.

3.6 In the past half century a great deal has changed. Transformational grammar is water under the bridge, and arguments such as these, which at the time were partly implicit, may seem of no more than historical interest. An argument from simplicity can often however be reformulated as a claim that, if a treatment is adopted, generalizations can be made that would not be made otherwise.

One relation that remains attractive is that of clauses and postmodifiers. We have noted already that postpositive adjectives or adjective phrases 'can usually be regarded', in the words of Quirk and his colleagues, as reduced relative clauses (1985: 418; **1.9**). In Lees's analysis this holds true of postmodifiers generally. The adjective phrase in *the people angry with us* or the adjective in *the rivers navigable* was in this respect no different from the adverb in *the party tomorrow*, the prepositional phrase in *the books on my desk*, or the participle, once more, in *the vehicles arriving*.

This insight is elaborated later by McCawley, in a major survey of English syntax that appeared first in the 1980s. But the case for what he described as 'Relative Clause Reduction' (1998: 393) was by then not merely, as had been argued in the 1950s, that it simplifies an account of distributions. The appeal was also to the meanings of noun phrases. For when phrases are postmodifiers they 'can always', in McCawley's words, 'be paraphrased by restrictive relative clauses'. In *a lecture extremely rich in insights*, to take one of his own examples, the postmodifier has a semantic role like that of the relative clause in *a lecture which was extremely rich in insights. The little house on the prairie* was paraphrased, in the same sense, by *the little house that is on the prairie*, and *a vehicle moving in this direction* by *a vehicle which is moving in this direction*. This notion of 'paraphrase' might now be questioned. But the way the term was used reflected a 'heuristic principle', proposed by Katz and Postal in the 1960s, by which 'paraphrases' were seen as important clues to possible syntactic derivations (Katz and Postal 1964: 157).

McCawley's 'always' is not strictly justified. *Proper*, as used in *the city proper*, has no 'paraphrase' since, with that meaning, it is postpositive only (see again 1.9). Nor, to take a fresh example, can *the 1960s redux* (from a recent magazine) be paraphrased by *the 1960s which are redux*. The 'usually' of Quirk and his colleagues, as underlined by Ferris, is more accurate (Ferris 1993: 49). But evidence of paraphrase was not all. For some postmodifiers, as McCawley saw it, actually demanded this analysis. Take, for example, the reflexive pronoun in *a person proud of himself* (McCawley's (10b)). Pronouns of this type are commonly understood as anaphoric: thus, with *he* as subject, in *He is proud of himself*. It had therefore been assumed that where a reflexive was used, a syntactic analysis 'must provide' an antecedent for it. This requirement was 'immediately met' if *proud of himself*, as a postmodifier, is reduced from a relative clause, *who is proud of himself*, in which *himself* has its antecedent in *who*. If some postmodifiers 'must', in this light, be derived from clauses, so could all of them, 'at no extra cost', even when they did not 'absolutely have to be' so treated (McCawley 1998: 393–5).

This style of reasoning had been much in vogue in the late 1960s and the early 1970s, when transformational grammar was at its zenith. The basic point, however, was that 'Relative Clause Reduction' makes explicit an important generalization, about the way in which postmodifiers of all categories are understood. If participles, for example, were derived from finite clauses, while postmodifying adjectives and adjective phrases were not, no statement as general would be possible.

Adjectives such as *tall*, which are lexically of the 'default' class in 1.10, are instead attributive. For these a 'fairly obvious proposal', as McCawley saw it, was that of 'Modifier preposing' (1998: 397). It was 'considerably harder', he acknowledged, to find compelling arguments for such a transformation. But let us accept that premodifiers too derive from relative clauses. It might be indirectly, via a structure in which they are postmodifiers, or it might not. Then compare the participle in, for example, *the crying children*. As *the children arriving* is to *the children who are arriving*, so this phrase would be to *the children who are crying*. The proposal thus has 'the advantage', as Lyons had put it in his study of semantics in the 1970s, 'that it enables us to account for the semantic relationship between all kinds of attributive and predicative expressions in the same way' (1977: 448).

Adjectives in underlying structures

3.7 By the time when Lyons was writing, let alone McCawley, the case for transformations in general had been rethought. A generative grammar, as conceived in the mid-1960s, was no longer restricted to an account of distributions, but paired 'semantic interpretations', as they were called, of sentences with representations of their syntax that at first, by definition, were 'deep structures' (Chomsky 1965; commentary in Matthews 1993: 172–4). Transformations were needed where these underlying structures differed from 'surface structures'. There is no sign that problems with adjectives influenced this or any subsequent development. But the derivations that Lees had proposed in 1960 were immediately in doubt.

One complication, which by then was sufficiently well known to any linguist who had searched for evidence, was that some of the words called adjectives do not form predicates. This had not at first been recognized. But a 'string' such as *an+utter+disaster*, if we may return to Chomsky's way of talking in the 1950s, could not be derived from one of the form *a – disaster – is – utter*, unless a sentence that this source would represent can be excluded. In an article written before Chomsky had published his theory of semantic interpretations, Winter (1965) cited several other instances where adjectives would form, as he described them, 'transforms without kernels'. But by the time this had appeared the problem had become more serious. For if the aim of a grammar was simply to generate a set of sentences, there could always be some mechanism that would deal with adjectives like *utter* as exceptions. Compare, for the record, a solution of my own (1967: 143). But if a grammar dealt with meanings, it would also have to deal with adjectives such as *late* or *old* (1.3), which had meanings varying between positions. A sentence that included *the late Queen* would have a semantic interpretation in which one meaning was assigned to *late*; in the semantic interpretation of *The Queen is late* it would have another. If their interpretations were determined as Chomsky had proposed, their deep structures would in turn be different. Alternatively, semantic interpretations could be determined by surface structures; this is the conclusion Chomsky was to reach, for other reasons, in the early 1970s. But then their structures may be independent. *The Queen is late* would have what is traditionally one construction, which is also that of *The chief is tall*, in which an adjective is in one position. *The late Queen* could simply have another, which is also that of *the tall chief*.

There were also differences between premodifiers and postmodifiers. The argument did not surface fully from the critique of Winter and others. But only attributive adjectives could be, as Bolinger had put it, 'characterizing' (1952; see again 1.8). Bolinger's contribution at this stage (1967) was also important, and is underlined by McCawley in the 1980s. 'Postnominal modifiers', in his words, 'can only express "ephemeral" properties', while 'prenominal modifiers can express not only ephemeral but also "permanent" properties' (McCawley 1998: 392). Both, we may add, can also be expressed by adjectives in the predicative position. Thus *The Danube is navigable* could confirm that the river is navigable at the time of speaking: nothing, at the moment, blocks it. Alternatively it could characterize the Danube as distinct from rivers such as the lower Congo, that can never be navigated. In *the rivers which are navigable*, the relative clause would similarly express what is either 'ephemeral' or 'permanent'. But when *navigable* is a postmodifier the property it denoted would in this account be strictly temporary. What Lees had proposed, whatever its attractions in the early days of transformational grammar, was that clauses with a wider range of meanings should first be reduced to postmodifiers whose meanings would be restricted; then these would be moved to a position in which a wider range of meanings would be restored.

3.8 Two insights, however, were left unscathed. One is that units in different constructions could be subject to similar 'selectional restrictions'. The point may now seem obvious, but it was Chomsky and Zellig Harris (1957 and earlier) who first pointed to its significance. A second insight, also shared with Harris, was that the structure of more complex sentences, including ones in which nouns took a modifier, could be related to structures that were simpler. The simplest were those of what Chomsky in the 1950s had called 'kernel sentences'.

For Chomsky in the 1960s, these played 'no distinctive role in generation or interpretation of sentences' (1965: 18). They could certainly not be defined in the technical way he had originally proposed. Nevertheless the notion had, he thought, 'an important intuitive significance'. Exactly where this lay he did not explain. But it is perhaps revealed by his understanding, still in the mid-1960s, of the grammar of Port-Royal. What Arnauld and Lancelot had said was that in the 'proposition':

Dieu invisible a créé le monde visible

three 'judgements' are included: that God (*Dieu*) is invisible, that He created the world (*a créé le monde*), and that the world is visible. 'In other words', as Chomsky interpreted their analysis, 'the deep structure underlying' the whole 'consists of three abstract propositions', of which 'its surface form expresses' only one (1966b [2009: 80]). An abstract proposition, or 'judgement', can be distinguished from a sentence. But at this underlying level the essential aim appears still more explicit, of reducing complex propositions to a set of elementary propositions that will be as simple as possible.

'Les messieurs de Port-Royal' did not, in the seventeenth century, have the benefit of modern predicate logic. But in one of Chomsky's propositions French *créer*, or in English *create*, can be represented as a two-place predicate whose arguments are *God* and *the world*:

(14) create (God, the world)

In the others, *visible* and *invisible* can be represented as one-place predicates, whose arguments are *the world*:

(15) visible (the world)

and *God*:

(16) invisible (God)

It is not surprising, therefore, that by the end of the 1960s many who believed that they were following Chomsky came to question at what level adjectives were separate from verbs. At the level of 'surface form' the difference in English remained obvious: no underlying proposition could be realized by *The chief talled*, with an adjective inflected for tense, or *The chief was arrive*, with a verb linked to a copula. But at an underlying level surface differences could be discounted. It could instead be argued that, in other respects, these categories belonged together. 'Recent research into the nature of underlying syntactic structure' had indicated, as Ross put it, that verbs and adjectives 'should really be looked upon as two subcategories of one major lexical category, *predicate*' (1969: 352, referring in particular to Lakoff 1970).

Ross's view did not prevail. In a doctrine, however, which has been widely taught for many years, syntactic structures form one level of representation, and representations of 'meanings' form another. A distinction between deep and surface syntax was in time perceived to be redundant, and as parts of speech adjectives and verbs remained separate. The ghost, however, of the kernel sentences of the 1950s can be seen to live on in the view that in, for example, *The tall chief arrived* the verb and adjective both realize one-place predicates whose argument would be realized by *the chief*.

3.9 It is not clear how far this idea is thought to be open to empirical argument. But it is at least worth asking why, if adjectives realize semantic predicates, they cannot all, in English, be syntactically predicative.

An underlying predicate is implicitly a unit 'of meaning', as distinct from its realization, which 'has meaning'. If we may return, however, to a more conventional way of talking, an adjective such as *old* has a sense in, for example, *an old friend* (1.3), not matched in *My friend is old*. The question, therefore, as it might have been presented in the 1960s, was whether the phrase could be a 'transform' of a clause in which the meaning of *old* was different. The sense of *new* in *the new president*, said of a president who has taken up or is about to take up office, is not matched precisely by the predicate that would be realized in *The president is new*. Compare *a new car* and *The car is new*. There is still less correspondence between *the old president* and *The president is old*. *Current* in *the current leaders* is temptingly related not to a predicative adjective, but to an adverb as in *They lead currently*. The use of *current* is no different, however, in *the current champion* or *the current president*, where the nouns have meanings not related regularly to those of *champion* as a verb or of *preside*. *The last chairman* could refer either to the chairman who has most recently retired, or to the one who is last of all before, for example, a company goes bust. In either case, *last* has an attributive meaning that would not be realized predicatively in *The chairman was last*.

It was through the critique of Chomsky's or Lees's transformations that many details like these were first made familiar. They are, if we may again cite Huddleston and Pullum, 'numerous' (2002: 553). The divergence, however, that they illustrate is one we may expect if adjectives are primarily attributive: in a secondary function, it is natural that some units and some meanings, which will be possible in the primary construction, should be excluded. It is also consistent with the view that neither function is primary. Let us remind ourselves (again from 1.4) that *sorry* is an adjective with a sense in the predicative position which is not matched, conversely, when it is attributive. The uses, however, of *old, new, current*, and so on offer no support for a proposal that adjectives realize underlying predicates.

Technically, without doubt, it is feasible. Any sentence can be represented, at a sufficient level of abstraction, by a structure of predicates and arguments: see for example, from the period when analyses like that of Ross were all the rage, a study in Italian by Parisi and Antinucci (1973). While 'cry', for example, and an argument 'children':

(17) cry (children)

might be realized in any of *The children cried, the children crying*, or *the crying children*, it could be stipulated somehow that a predication:

(18) current (president)

could be realized only in a phrase such as *the current president*, a predication:

(19) late (queen)

only as in *the late Queen*, and so on. We should surely explain, however, why the realizations of one type of semantic predicate, which are verbs, all have a syntactic function in relation to a subject, while those of another type, which are adjectives, can tend not to.

Is there a conclusion?

3.10 Transformational grammar had the enormous virtue, if no other, of putting a cat among the pigeons. The conventional view of adjectives had been, since antiquity, that they were units added to nouns. Their function in phrases could be related to their function in clauses; but in the opposite way, as Tesnière's notion of *translation* underlines, to that of verbs to participles (3.3). In Croft's analysis of categories, the modifying function is similarly that of an 'unmarked adjective', while an 'unmarked verb' is predicative. Both are described as 'typological prototypes', and are distinguished as such from others, variously not prototypical (3.2), in a system whose symmetry, as displayed in a table (Croft 2003: 88) is perfect. Lees's analysis was in this respect the opposite. But it had the considerable attraction that any structure in which a noun is modified, whether by an adjective or by, for example, a participle, is derived by similar processes of 'nominalization'.

It is hard to say that either view is straightforwardly right or that either is straightforwardly wrong. In part at least they are based on different assumptions, as to whether what might be primary is basically a syntactic structure, from which a secondary structure can be derived by a syntactic process, or is basically a category associated with such a structure, to which a second category is related by a process affecting lexical entries. The distinction had been drawn earlier: a paper by Kuryłowicz (1936) is still worth recalling. It was only, however, through the critique of transformational analyses that linguists came to appreciate that either kind of relation was possible, that a choice between them can be difficult, and that the function which is primary, assuming that one should be, may accordingly be disputed.

Take, for example, the adjective in *a hard worker*. In such a use, as we have noted, it is only attributive. So, among others, is *light* in *a light sleeper* (1.4), or *current* (**3.9**) in *the current leaders*. It can be related, however, to the adverb in a clause such as *She works hard*; and in the years when transformational grammar was carrying all before it, it was tempting to propose a syntactic process by which *hard worker* and *work(s) hard* would be related as wholes. As *a young worker* or *a tall girl* could be derived by a nominalizing transformation, so in this case too the clause or predicate would be seen as primary. One obvious problem, however, is raised by adjectives such as *fast*, in *a fast worker*, or *lazy*, in *a lazy worker*. They have senses in which they are restricted neither to attribution nor to nouns with an agentive meaning. As *a fast car*, for example, could be related by a transformation to *The car is fast*, so *a fast worker* could be related to *The worker is fast* as readily as it could be, on the model of *a hard worker*, to a clause such as *She works fast*. We have no reason, however, to posit two alternative derivations. In, for example, *a lazy worker* there is no ambiguity, in practice, between a meaning 'worker who has the property of being lazy' and a contrasting meaning 'worker who has the property of working lazily'.

The alternative is that structures like these are related not syntactically, but through the mediation of processes within a lexicon. There is a relation, first, between a set of adjectives and a set of corresponding adverbs. For *lazy*, it implies a process of suffixation:

(20) $_{\text{A}}$[lazy] → $_{\text{Adv}}$[lazy + ly]

as for *light* and *lightly* and for many others. For *fast* it implies conversion (**2.8**):

(21) $_{\text{A}}$[fast] → $_{\text{Adv}}$[fast]

as too for *hard*. Secondly, and separately, there is a process by which an agentive noun like *worker* will be derived from a verb:

(22) $_{\text{V}}$[work] → $_{\text{N}}$[work + er]

To assign a word to a category is to say that it can, in general, have a certain range of syntactic functions. An adverb as derived in (20) can modify a verb, as *lazily* modifies *work* in *They work lazily*. An adjective can instead be both attributive and predicative: thus the roles of *lazy* both in, for example, *a lazy child* and in *The child is lazy*. What holds, however, in general may be subject to specific qualifications, which apply to some words in particular. Thus *hard*, as an adjective, has one sense in which it is only attributive; and in *a hard worker* it combines in this sense with an agentive. The agentive is related, as a lexical unit, to the verb in *They work hard*, as the adjective too is related to a corresponding adverb. If we can talk, however, of a relation between syntactic units, it is simply by virtue of the lexical relations, of conversion and suffixation, that link words separately.

This spells out briefly what many linguists will now see as obvious. It is obvious too that when Croft saw an attributive adjective as 'prototypical', or Tesnière proposed a process by which adjectives would be 'translated' to verbs, what is primary is a lexical unit, not a syntactic combination of which it forms part. It would be perverse to maintain, however, that in languages in general there are no syntactic processes. The structure, for example, of an interrogative is related systematically to that of a corresponding declarative: *They are coming* → *Are they coming?*; *They arrived* → *Did they arrive?*, and so on. Such relations were another subject of Chomsky's earliest transformations (1957). It would be possible, of course, to argue that in the first example, the auxiliary undergoes conversion from one category to the other. In one case, that is, it is lexically declarative, and as such can form part of a declarative sentence. In the other case it is lexically interrogative and can therefore form part of a sentence that is syntactically interrogative. *Do*, we could say, is in this use also lexically interrogative. But these are technical fiddles whose only justification would be that in this way a direct syntactic relation can be eliminated.

Have we any better grounds for saying that an adjective in the predicative position is lexically 'predicative'? The argument hinges, in particular, on the way we choose to deal with partial regularities. A process of nominalization, as represented by Lees and others, is straightforward in many cases: the adjectives involved are bipositional (1.10) and the meanings they have when they are predicative are ones that they can also have when they are attributive. Some have further meanings, like that of *hard* in *a hard worker*, which are restricted to the attributive function only. These must be made clear in the lexicon, but in individual entries that are strictly irrelevant to the general process. If *hard worker* cannot be derived from *The worker is hard*, that is no reason why *hard work*, where the sense of *hard* is bipositional, should not be related syntactically to *The work is hard*, or *a tall chief* to *the chief is tall*, and so on.

Alternatively, adjectives have meanings that will individually determine the positions they can have. *Late*, for example, has among its senses one in particular that will restrict it to attribution. In many other senses, adjectives will instead be bipositional. This does not imply, however, either a syntactic process or a lexicon in which the same point has to be made individually for each. The uses of adjectives when they are predicative can be derived in general, in a regular lexical relation, from uses of the same words when they are attributive. The duplications claimed originally to be removed by transformations (3.4) can be removed in that way also. Statements about words individually will instead be needed only for the attributive position, and in cases where the regular relation does not hold.

3.11 The character of a language may often be revealed more clearly by the problems its analysis gives rise to than by any specific solution imposed on it. The insight is Bazell's (1958) and is one I have tried to develop in other contexts (Matthews 2000; 2007c). It would be easy to imagine, for example, what the language would be like if a process of nominalization were to be uncontroversial. Adjectives would be more like verbs, and the senses they would have as modifiers would either correspond to those they have in clauses or would be restricted relative to them. But this is precisely not how English has evolved. If we try with whatever motive to reduce it to this model, we are faced with the reality that attributive and predicative uses have diverged, through the development of patterns that it is hard to dismiss as mere exceptions. Yet at the highest level of abstraction, each of the main positions remains connected, in whatever way connections are to be represented, to the other. It is only at lower levels of abstraction that we are forced to focus on each function, or on specific constructions, in isolation.

The closer we approach the level of microsyntax, however, in the sense in which this term was introduced in 2.13, the more it is clear that an analysis has, in practice, to be polysystemic. The term is Firth's and was applied, in his own work, mainly in phonology (papers in Firth 1957). A system of, for example, vowels in unstressed syllables was treated as independent of the system in stressed syllables; the contrasts between consonants at the end of the word as independent of those medially or at the beginning; and so on. In a strictly Firthian mode the role of *current*, for example, in *the current president* can be contrasted with that of *last* in *the last president*, of *serving* in *the serving president* or *retiring* in *the retiring president*, of *then* in *the then president* or *post-war* in *the post-war president*, regardless of the range of functions any of these words may have in other constructions.

The alternative in phonology was the monosystemic theory, as Firth called it, of the phoneme. In syntax it might have been, above all, that of the traditional parts of speech. *Then*, for example, is in a monosystemic analysis the same word in *They left then and not earlier*, *Then they told me*, and so on; it is classed in grammars as a type of adverb; and its use in phrases such as *the then president*, like that of *downstairs* (2.12) in *a downstairs window*, calls for comment in a way that *current* in *the current president*, since it is classed as an adjective, will not. This is precisely, however, in a monosystemic perspective. In a polysystemic analysis, the way a word is used in one construction can fit better with the use of others in the same construction than with its own uses elsewhere.

Take, for example, *ready*. In the predicative position it is used with a wide range of subjects: *The house was ready, Your mother won't be ready, Dinner is ready*, and so on. The sense is variously that of being or having been prepared. It denotes a state, however, that is not characterizing: being ready, for whatever passing purpose it may be, is in McCawley's term (3.7) 'ephemeral'. Uses like these can accordingly be linked with those of adjectives, as they are called traditionally, such as *afraid* and *asleep*, and other units that are not regularly attributive. In *Your mother is asleep* the state denoted is again not 'permanent'; nor, for example, the location denoted by *outside* in *Everyone is outside*. By the same token the predicative use of *ready* may be distinguished, in a polysystemic analysis, from a characterizing use of *kind*, for example, in *Your mother is kind* or of *clever* in *The children were clever*. These could precisely denote a property in the nature of the people referred to. They are also adjectives with which the form of the copula can be progressive: compare *Your mother is being kind*, of an act of kindness on a specific occasion, or *The children were being clever*. We will return to the progressive of *be* in a later chapter. But *They are being ready* is not normal, any more than *They are being asleep*.

None of this is relevant when *ready* is used attributively. One does not normally say, for example, *a ready house* or *your ready mother*, and it is easy to find records of earlier uses that are at best no longer current. Compare, for example, *upon a light and readie horse*, cited in the *Oxford English Dictionary* from 1603, or, from Mayhew in 1851:

He knew that he was a ready man

(glossed by Mayhew 'a quick workman'). Where uses survive the meaning varies with nouns individually. One, for example, is with *wit*; but the adjective is 'polarized', as Bolinger remarks at one point, 'to the extent that *a ready wit* is not easily interconvertible with *?His wit is ready*' (1967: 9–10). In a polysystemic analysis it is irrelevant whether it is convertible or not. One can say, for example, *I paid ready money* or *They had a ready answer*. But what is meant is not explained by a comparison with the use of *ready* where these nouns are subjects, as in *Money is always ready* or *My answer will be ready next week*.

In another mode, though Firth himself might have demurred, a description of syntax is monosystemic. The more that mode can be maintained, the more attractive it is either to oppose or to assimilate the relation of predicative and modifying adjective to that of verbs and secondary participles. The more a polysystemic account takes over, the stronger is the case for seeing neither position as primary. This causes problems, but it is the problems that reveal most clearly the nature of the category.

4

How the syntax of adjectives has changed

4.1 Enough has been said, for our purposes, about the part of speech in general; enough too about problems that may impinge on wider typologies. Those that remain concern specific positions, and where they have wider implications they are for the theory or philosophy (1.4) of grammar, more than they are empirical.

The problems are in part those of a *Sprachbund*, of what Whorf perceptively called 'Standard Average European' (Carroll, ed. 1956: 138). They are a reflex, that is, of a history partly shared with other Germanic and with neighbouring Romance languages. One development, important in English as elsewhere in western Europe, is of a system of articles, which distinguished indefinite from definite noun phrases. But English has its own history, and in the past five hundred years its structure has evolved in ways that distance it not just from its origins in West Germanic, which are immediately obvious in Old English, but from French and other European languages with which direct bilingual contact has been closest. One familiar idiosyncrasy is the progressive. It is the outcome of this history, on the relations of adjectives within noun phrases (Chapters 5–7), and with *be* and in other predicative positions (Chapters 8–9), that we are now faced with.

It has been, and is still, a history of divergence. Before we turn then to the details, it may be helpful to look back in general at the changes by which the functions of adjectives have diversified, since the Norman occupation and over the Modern period especially. For it is in these changes that the origins of our problems lie.

Adjectives in Middle English

4.2 'Much work needs to be done on the status of adjectives in OE and ME, which has been meagrely investigated so far': thus Fischer and van der Wurff (2006: 122). With this warning in mind, the transition between these periods has to be interpreted with caution. Two developments, however, have long been familiar and have a direct bearing on what was to follow.

One is the loss of case and other inflections. Old English was in this respect like Latin (2.4) and other older Indo-European languages, in that adjectives agreed with nouns in number, case, and gender. The only features that survived in Middle English were the distinction in nouns between a singular and plural, and the genitive ending that was to become the phrasal clitic *-'s*. The corresponding properties of adjectives were lost, and the relation of agreement between adjectives and nouns was lost with them.

A second change, which may or may not have been separate, affected the distinction in Old English between weak and strong forms of an adjective. These are the terms conventional in Germanic philology, and for non-Germanists, especially, are scarcely the most helpful. But in Old English, as it is described by Quirk and Wrenn, the forms of adjectives 'in general use' were those traditionally called 'strong'. They were the forms 'found when the adjective is predicative' (1957: 68); hence more generally, as Fischer and van der Wurff make clear, in constructions where it followed the noun to which it was related (2006: 123). In the position that Fischer and van der Wurff call 'prenominal', an adjective could instead be either strong or weak. In (1), for example,

(1) se blinda man
that blind-WEAK man
'the blind man'

(glossing restricted to what is relevant), *blinda* is weak, or is in the form that Quirk and Wrenn describe as 'definite', in association with a demonstrative. This was, more generally, 'the specifying and particularising form, usually signifying that the item modified is the one expected in the context or the one referred to just previously' (Quirk and Wrenn 1957: 68). In (2), however,

(2) blind man
blind-STRONG man
'a blind man',

the adjective is strong, or in their term is 'indefinite', in a phrase whose meaning is not specifying or particularizing. In a brief historical account by Traugott, from whom these examples are taken, strong forms such as *blind* had come to be 'associated', in Old English, 'with the indefinite only' (1992: 173).

The forms that Germanists call 'weak' can thus be said to represent the marked term in an opposition. But in Middle English, as the relevant changes are summarized by Fischer and van der Wurff, the 'remnants' of this opposition, in the shape of forms reflecting those in (1) and (2), ceased to be 'functional' (2006: 111, Table 3.1). For qualifications see the relevant chapters in *The Cambridge History of the English Language*, by Lass (1992: 115–16) and Fischer (1992: 217). But phrases with definite and indefinite reference came to be distinguished by articles. The distinction in adjectives became redundant, and in the end the remnants vanished.

All this, in outline, is well known and well understood. One major consequence, however, was that adjectives no longer had inflections that distinguished them from adverbs. A distinction has since been supplied, in many cases, by the formation of an adverb in *-ly*. But this affects some types of adverb only, and in at least one other case in Modern English, of words in *a-* such as *asleep* and *ashore*, the conventional division can, as we have seen, be problematic (**2.7**). Another consequence, it might be argued, is that the order of adjectives and nouns has tended to become fixed. In Middle English 'postmodification was not infrequent' (Fischer 1992: 215). In summary, however, modifying adjectives were 'mainly prenominal' (see again Table 3.1 in Fischer and van der Wurff 2006: 111). In the longer run, this order was to become increasingly dominant.

4.3 For the moment, however, either order became possible. The phrase in (1) was distinguished, as a definite referring expression, by a demonstrative and a 'weak' form of premodifier. Such expressions are the clearest instances of phrases, and it is no surprise that when the role of *se* became that of a definite article, the construction of (1) was the model for a corresponding pattern:

(3) Article + Adjective + Noun

where the article could also be indefinite. In the system, however, implied for Middle English, the order of adjective and noun could be the opposite:

(4) Article + Noun + Adjective

This too became an option for definite expressions, where the adjective in Old English had been a premodifier, as well as indefinite.

Exactly why need not concern us: noun phrases were evolving in a period when many speakers of English also commonly spoke Norman French. To the extent, however, that (4) has an origin in Old English, it is in constructions where the adjective had been in the predicative, or conventionally the strong, form. Thus, in an example discussed by Fischer and van der Wurff:

(5) nym betonican swa grene
take betony green-STRONG
'Take betony still green'

the noun for 'betony' (the plant *Stachys officinalis*) is related, in a structure that does not include a definite expression, to the strong form *grene*. In a position such as this the adjective, as they explain it, 'always conveyed "new" or extra information'. The instruction in (5) is therefore to take betony which, in addition, is green or in a fresh state. In the object phrase:

(6) grene betonican
green-STRONG betony

whose construction would be as in (2), the adjective might instead be taken, with the noun, to distinguish betony of 'a different species' (Fischer and van der Wurff 2006: 123). Their discussion refers to Bolinger's paper on 'linear modification' (1952), for the relationships imposed, in such ways, by the 'linear geometry' of units.

One pertinent question might be how far, in examples such as (5), the structure of a noun phrase was distinct within that of the clause as a whole. Compare, in Modern English, the construction of *Pick apples ripe*, where *ripe* does not form a noun phrase with *apples*, with that of *Pick ripe apples*. It is also worth reflecting, even at this early stage, on the positions to which adjectives and senses of adjectives have since come to be restricted. *Utter* was to become, in a later period, attributive only (examples in 1.3): it was restricted, that is, to the position in which adjectives in Old English could be either weak, as *blinda* (blind-WEAK) in (1), or else strong, as *grene* (green-STRONG) in (6) or *blind* (blind-STRONG) in (2). In the construction in (5) an adjective could only be strong, as when it was straightforwardly predicative. These were positions in which it was more generally, in Fischer and van der Wurff's analysis, postnominal.

A restriction whose roots, at least, lie in the Middle Ages concerns the attributive use of *sorry*. Its earliest sense is as in Modern English *They were sorry*, where it can now be classed as 'never attributive' (1.4; Huddleston and Pullum 2002: 560). But it has again another sense, in which it is now attributive only, in *It was a sorry mess* or *Everything has got into a very sorry state*. This use in general seems to have its origin in Middle English, in a sense defined in the *OED* as 'causing distress or sorrow; painful, grievous, dismal'. One citation, from before 1300, is in:

þat sari sight was on to se

Its use as so defined is marked as obsolete. But this is not that easy to distinguish from the modern sense of 'wretched, pitiful, deplorable', and so on. That too dates from the Middle Ages: of a person, for example, in 'that sory Judas' (around 1325). We can never be sure when uses are or become syntactically restricted. But a division available in syntax seems already to have been open to lexical exploitation.

For another possible example we may return to *ready* (3.11). Its form is an extension, in early Middle English, of Old English *ræde*, with a basic sense, in the predicative construction, like the one it has now. Compare one of the earliest citations in the *OED*:

if hie redie ben to golliche deden

(from around 1200). But its use in collocations such as *ready money* seems to have followed very quickly. Compare, from before 1300:

Al redi penijs for to tell

In this and later uses *ready* can be distinguished as 'characterizing'; as, with no change in its sense, can the premodifying *grene* 'green', in (6). But characterization 'sometimes makes', if we may cite Bolinger in another context, 'for partial or complete transfer of meaning' (1952 [1965: 297]). When it is not attributive, the uses of *ready* have remained non-characterizing, as was that of *grene* as a postmodifier in (5).

The attributive position in Modern English

4.4 In Modern English, if we may return to the summary by Fischer and van der Wurff, the position of modifying adjectives has become 'prenominal with lexical exceptions'. One form of exception, at least from a historian's viewpoint, is that of words like *asleep*, as in *the people asleep*. Another, we may add, is where the meanings of adjectives are divided, on the model of *sorry* or *ready*, between positions.

Both the general point and the exceptions can be illustrated with the fate of two adjectives 'borrowed', in the conventional term, from French, which Fischer and van der Wurff refer to. Take first *apparent*. It is attested in the fourteenth century, initially as in *heir apparent*, and when part of such 'idiomatic "French" expressions' (Fischer and van der Wurff 2006: 124) words like it have remained postpositive. But if the expression as a whole is idiomatic, it is only because the collocation is restricted. As a modifier generally, in *the apparent owner* or *an apparent successor*, the adjective has, like others, become attributive. As used by Shakespeare, for example, it was already mainly so: compare, for example, *these apparent prodigies* (from *Julius Caesar* 2.1.198).

Present dates from the same period, and in present-day usage, as interpreted by Fischer and van der Wurff, it illustrates a 'rare' case in which 'salience or new information in adjectives' can still be conveyed, as it had been in the case of (5), by postnominal position. They compare, for example, the postmodifier in *the present people* with the premodifier in *the present class structure* (2006: 122). But there is a more specific difference, between *present* in the sense of 'being there' and *present* in the sense of 'as it is now'. The word could be used indifferently in late Middle English: compare, from the *OED*, *this present parlement* (1466) with *alle present and absent* (1382). *A very present help in trouble*, in the Authorized and earlier versions of Psalm 46, may attest a use in which a distinction was as yet uncertain. But this translation is replaced in the *New English Bible* (1970) by *a timely help in trouble*; and when used in the attributive position *present* is now generally temporal. *The present parliamentarians*, for example, would refer to people who are the current members of a parliament, and is distinguished by this meaning from *the parliamentarians present*. Its sense in the latter is in turn as in *The parliamentarians were present*. Nor can *the Queen present* have the meaning of *the present Queen*, or *in circumstances present*, if it would be said at all, that of *in present circumstances*. This too is an adjective that in one sense can be listed, as by Huddleston and Pullum (2002: 556) as 'attributive only'; in another as 'never attributive' (Huddleston and Pullum, 560).

A distinction of 'salience', as Fischer and van der Wurff describe it, can instead be realized, as they point out, by a difference in stress. The equivalent, therefore, of the order in (5), in which the word for 'green' came after the word for 'betony', might be the intonation, in English as it is now spoken, of:

(7) Take a FRESH lettuce

where the adjective in small capitals in prominent. The history of intonation is a blank that we have little hope of filling. Note, however, that a distinction of 'salience', in the sense that seems to be envisaged, has come to be independent of the order of modifiers, both where it is fixed and where it can still vary. The place of the adjective is fixed by rule in, for example, *something green*, where the head it relates to is an indefinite pronoun. But in its intonation either unit can be prominent: *Just bring me something* GREEN (not any other colour); *Just bring me* SOME*thing green* (anything, so long as it is green, will do). The order is not fixed in, for example, *the possible movements*. But while one can also say *the movements possible*, the difference in the place of the adjective is overshadowed by a far more general and more regular opposition, in which *the* MOVE*ments possible*, on the one hand, contrasts with *the movements* POS*sible* as, on the other hand, *the* POS*sible movements* contrasts with *the possible* MOVE*ments*.

4.5 Of the other developments that have shaped the structure of noun phrases, the most far-reaching is the 'stacking', as Fischer and van der Wurff describe it, of attributive adjectives in sequence. In, for example, *a large black animal*, two successive adjectives are stacked, in this sense, in relation to *animal*.

The emergence of such sequences has been studied in part. They had not formed a pattern in Old English: it was 'virtually impossible', as Fischer and van der Wurff express it, 'to put one adjective after another in a row' (2006: 125). Where nouns took two adjectives as modifiers they could instead be joined by *and*; or 'very often one adjective would precede and one follow the noun'. A similar construction is familiar in Middle English, in phrases like *grete lobies and longe* 'big lanky yobs', in the prologue (52) of *Piers Plowman*. So too are examples without *and*. Compare, from Chaucer:

Ful of smale fishes lighte
(*The Parliament of Fowls*, 188)

as also another line in the same poem (442):

Ryght as the freshe, rede rose newe

where one adjective follows the noun, but two come before it. By the early Modern period the pattern which is now familiar had been clearly established. *A still small voice*, in the Authorized version of 1 Kings 19.12, had been preceded by Coverdale's *a styll softe hyssinge* from 1535. *Silent* follows *sweet* in a familiar line from Shakespeare:

When to the sessions of sweet silent thought
(Sonnet 30)

and other examples are easily found. Details may need to be investigated further, since a structure formally similar to the phrase from Langland survives. But it is increasingly restricted, in more recent periods, to a coordination where the adjectives apply to different referents. Compare *rich people and poor*, meaning 'rich people and poor people'.

Sequences of adjectives are peculiar, as we have noted (1.4), to the attributive position. It is therefore natural to see stacking as a new construction, and to ask exactly how it should be represented. Are *big* and *lanky*, for example, independently subordinate to *yobs*? Or do they form a unit that as a whole will modify it?

(8) [[big lanky] yobs]

Or do *lanky* and *yobs* form a unit that is modified, as a whole, by *big*?

(9) [big [lanky yobs]]

These are questions we will return to (6.1 and onwards). But from a historian's viewpoint it is obvious how this development fits with others. Not only had the order Adjective + Noun become dominant; but the syntax of premodifiers was now complex in a way not matched in the predicative position. Further complexities seem inevitably to have followed.

4.6 One well-known complication is the order in which adjectives form sequences. In another line from Shakespeare:

A good soft pillow for that good white head
(*Henry V* 4.1.14)

both pairs of modifiers have the order that would now, at least, be usual. As an adjective of 'value', in the typology proposed by Dixon, *good* comes before both *soft*, which denotes a 'physical property', and *white*, which denotes a colour (Dixon 1991: 78; repeated 2010: 73). In

An old black ram is tupping your white ewe
(*Othello* 1.1.89)

an adjective of colour in turn follows one of age. The pattern as it is now has recently been explored by Feist (2012) and considered, in a different spirit, by Cinque (2010). The principle, however, that examples like these seem to illustrate is one made clear, for present-day English, by Quirk and his colleagues (1985: 1341). In sequences in general, those placed nearer to the head noun tend to denote a property '(relatively) inherent in' the entity referred to, 'visually observable, and only subjectively assessible'. How size, for example, is perceived depends on the context in a way in which the perception of colour does not. In accordance, therefore, with this principle, the adjectives in *a large black animal* are in that order rather than the order *black large*.

Tendencies are not rules. In another line, for example:

The white cold virgin snow upon my heart
(*The Tempest* 4.1.55)

an adjective of colour comes before another which, in Dixon's typology, denotes a 'physical property'. Perhaps Shakespeare too could just as easily have written *cold white*. Could either *white* or *cold*, however, have come after *virgin*? It would be foolish to speculate too much about what may or may not have been possible in the early seventeenth century. But some types of sequence have since, at least, become fixed. It is reasonable, therefore, to suggest that in some cases different constructions may have evolved, in which an adjective closer to a noun has one kind of relation to it and one more distant has another. This is especially so where words develop uses in which they are only attributive.

One case is that of *criminal* in, for example, *a young criminal lawyer*. One could also say *a criminal young lawyer*, but its sense would then be as in, for example, *criminal behaviour*. The lawyer would be one whose actions, that is, are illegal or deplorable. In that sense it, like *young*, can be predicative. Compare, for example, *The law was criminal*, said of a law which a legislature was wrong to pass. But when *young* comes first, the reference will instead be to a lawyer who specializes in criminal cases. As described by Halliday, in an analysis of the noun phrase to which we will return in **7.8**, the modifier nearer to the noun would be a 'classifier', indicating 'a particular subclass' (1985: 164) of lawyers in general. *Young* is instead an 'epithet' (163), and as such comes first. Only *young*, moreover, has a meaning with which it can also be predicative. *My lawyer was criminal* would again be a statement about the lawyer's character or behaviour, not the class of lawyer he or she is.

Both senses of *criminal*, or uses from which they have developed, are attested, with the word itself, from the fourteenth century onwards. But many other adjectives have more recently been used and ordered similarly. The collocation of *marine* with, for example, *painter* dates from the late nineteenth century; with *biology* or *biologist* from the mid-twentieth. Compare *nuclear* in *a nuclear physicist*, *popular* in one sense (from the nineteenth century) of *a popular novel*, and so on. In, for example, *a tall marine biologist* the modifiers can be said to form more than a sequence. They have functions by which they are differentiated, as an epithet plus a classifier, in a pattern increasingly attested over the late Modern period.

4.7 Further complications, in the system as it now confronts us, lie in the intonation of noun phrases. Historians are once more at a loss for evidence. But where adjectives form sequences, three different patterns can now be distinguished.

Take first a phrase with one modifier. In, for example, *They bought a large* TABle, *a large table* forms part of a clause, whose rhythm is that of a single intonational unit. The pitch might fall, for example, on the stressed syllable of *table*, which, as the last, is prominent. Alternatively *large*, for example, might be emphasized: *a* LARGE *table* (not a small one). Add a second adjective, and either might be prominent: *a* LARGE *red table* (a red table which was not small); *a large* RED *table* (one which was large but not some other colour). Otherwise, however, the pitch might once more fall on the stressed syllable of *table*, and the adjectives would have the same weight in relation to it. The pattern is therefore one that may be represented, for our purposes, as follows:

(10) a lárge réd TABle

Table, that is, remains maximally prominent, as indicated by small capitals, and the modifiers have a rhythm in which they are equally subordinate to it. This pattern can be seen as an extension, to a sequence, of the rhythm that there would be with one adjective alone. Add other modifiers, and we can see it as extended further: *a lóvely lárge réd* TAB*le*; *a níce smáll whíte chína* TEA*pot.*

It is tempting to assume that this has long been normal. If that were right then in a line, for example, from Browning:

Played off the young frank personable priest
(*The Ring and the Book* 1.1022),

the rhythm could already have been one in which *young*, *frank*, and *personable* formed part of a single intonational phrase: *yóung fránk pérsonable* PRIEST. But the pattern of (10) can be distinguished immediately from one in which successive modifiers are divided among intonational units. Take for comparison *They bought an* ENOR*mous*, DREAD*fully expensive* TA*ble*. The rhythm of the last three words can vary, in ways we need not explore. What is crucial, however, is the boundary marked in writing by a comma, between an intonational unit in which the pitch might fall, for example, on ENOR*mous* and another unit that begins with *dreadfully*. The syntactic structure is again one where a noun takes two successive modifiers, but the rhythm of the phrase is broken between them, where in (10) it is not. It would be foolish to pretend that this distinction is always quite so easy to draw. It is plausible, however, to suppose that in the history of English over the Modern period, what we may call a broken and a continuous rhythm have progressively become distinct.

A clear differentiation may, of course, be quite late. In the following line from Shakespeare, some editors supply commas:

I spy a black, suspicious, threatening cloud
(*3 Henry VI* 5.3.4)

where the most recent, in the *Oxford Shakespeare* (Wells and Taylor, ed. 2005) prudently refrains. Contemporary punctuation is, as always, of no help (see, for example, Salmon 1999), and it may be that a variation real enough for modern readers or for modern actors was in Shakespeare's day not yet sufficiently established. Where the pattern, however, is now broken, it is natural to see the modifiers as syntactically parallel. Compare it with the coordination in, from Shakespeare:

you secret, black, and midnight hags
(*Macbeth* 4.1.64)

or, with repetition of the article, in *an enormous and a dreadfully expensive table*. The question then is how far, where there is no conjunction and the rhythm is continuous, the syntactic relation of a modifier to a head may have become different.

4.8 There is, moreover, a third pattern. In the line from Browning the adjectives, as read now, have the same weight as compared with *priest*. Compare, however, a line from Betjeman:

And my silly old collarbone's bust
('Hunter Trials', 1972: 248)

In a natural reading, the noun is once more prominent, but where the adjectives in (10) are perceived as having the same stress in relation to *table*, *silly* and *old* are linked in a rhythm which is more like that of a compound. Compare *an age-old collarbone* or, with an equal number of syllables, *some lily-white earthenware*.

One obvious comment is that *silly* + *old* is, as a whole, affective. Compare, for example, *little* + *old* in *a little old lady*, or *nasty* + *little* in *a nasty little insect*. It is especially, perhaps, when adjectives have this kind of meaning that there has developed what we may call a 'legato' rhythm, in which the second of two adjectives is intonationally subordinate to the first. This may be represented, for the last example, as follows:

(11) a násty little INsect

with an accent on the first adjective only. Compare with (10) a rhythm similar to that of (10) in, for example, *a húge púrple insect* or *a násty bítter taste*. The legato pattern may, for all we know, be fairly recent. But the problem again is how or whether it reflects the syntax of the sequences that have it.

Predication and attribution

4.9 Other changes since the Middle Ages have contributed further to a pattern of differentiation between the attributive and predicative positions. This warrants an analysis which will again be polysystemic (3.11).

It may be helpful to imagine, in contrast, what we might see as an 'ideal' system, for which a monosystemic account would be straightforward. 'Ideal' is and will remain in inverted commas: this is not a state of grace from which, in the course of history, the language as we know it now has fallen. But such a system might be more like that of English in the early Middle Ages than of English in any later period. First it would consistently distinguish adjectives and adverbs. This is true in general of the older Indo-European languages, Old English included. There would also be a clear division among verbs, between a copula as a link between predicative units and a subject (1.6), and others which themselves are predicates. At no stage in the earlier history of English has a copula been so clearly separate. But one major complication, in the Modern period, is that several more verbs have developed a construction in which adjectives, in particular, function similarly.

Take, for example, *sound*. Its source in Middle English is the verb in French whose reflex is the modern *sonner*; as originally used, it could be transitive or intransitive, and in either case it could and can be modified by adverbs. An extension, however, of its sense is illustrated neatly by examples from Shakespeare. In a speech from one play:

Is there no voice more worthy than my own
To sound more sweetly in great Caesar's ear
For the repealing of my banished brother?
(*Julius Caesar* 3.1.49–51)

its subject is *voice* and the sound made by a voice may literally be sweet. But what is crucial is the pleading that the voice would convey: it is not by its sound as such that Caesar might be persuaded. In *The Comedy of Errors* (4.4.7):

I tell you 'twill sound harshly in her ears

the verb is modified by *harshly*, as it could be still as a straightforward intransitive, in *The trumpets will sound harshly*. But its subject now refers not to a source of sound, which might not in itself be harsh at all, but to the news the speaker's wife, as it happens, is going to receive. In a third example, from *The Tempest* (5.1.200-1):

But O, how oddly will it sound, that I
Must ask my child forgiveness

the subject is explicitly a clause identifying what men might be told.

In these examples *sweetly*, *harshly*, and *oddly* are all adverbs in *-ly*. So is *oddly* in a citation in the *OED* from the mid-nineteenth century, *This sounds oddly to unmitred ears*, where what 'sounds' is in writing. But in similar uses a construction with an adjective is now normal. Compare *This decision may sound harsh*, or *Ideas of that kind always sound odd*. It is easy too to find examples where an adjective is obligatory, and a corresponding adverb cannot replace it. Take, for example, *What you say sounds obvious. What you say sounds* might be said at best if the verb means 'make a noise'. Nor would one say *What you say sounds obviously.*

Look is another verb with which, in uses like these, adverbs in *-ly* have been supplanted by adjectives. Either was still possible for Jane Austen (examples in Denison 1998: 232). Among others that have developed similar uses, *appear* takes an adjective in a citation in the *OED* from 1559: *to have appered most right*. This can be seen as modelled on a use of *seem* established earlier. *To taste very sour* is cited from 1681; *if it feels heavy* from 1694; *if old sawes prove true* from Spenser's *Faerie Queene* a century earlier. The resultative sense of *become*, as in *He became ill*, had been normal since the early Middle Ages, as a development of uses in Old English that were like that of the simple *come*. That of *get*, however, is another that can be illustrated from the seventeenth century, by a citation from 1662: *They were both gotten sufficiently drunk*. Other verbs appear to have developed uses like these even later, especially when extended by a preposition. That of *turn out*, for example, is attested in the *OED* from the mid-nineteenth century: *not... seeming to be true and turning out false.*

4.10 One important question, mentioned briefly in **1.6**, will be whether these verbs have the same construction as *be* in, for example, *What you say is obvious.* Whatever the structure may be, it can be distinguished from that of, for example, *It sounds repeatedly*, where *sound* remains a simple intransitive. But the process has historically been one of differentiation, in which verbs have developed a new use while retaining, in most cases, those they had before. Compare, for example, *grow* and *look* with adjectives, in *She grew tall* or *You look tired*, with their continued use as intransitives that can be modified by adverbs, in *She grew quickly* or *I looked carefully.* The changes, moreover, have been in the uses of verbs individually, over periods that vary. *Appear*, for example, regularly takes an adjective as used by Shakespeare; but *sound*, as we have seen, does not. It can therefore be hard to say how far, at a particular stage, a change may be complete.

We may take for illustration *smell.* In a line from Shakespeare:

Lilies that fester smell far worse than weeds
(Sonnet 94.14)

it is natural for a modern reader to construe *worse* as an adjective, with the same construction as *rotten* in *They smell rotten*. But *worse* could equally be an adverb, and in *The feast | smells well* (in *Coriolanus* 4.5.5–6) the simple form is *well* and not, as it would now be, *good.* Shakespeare also uses *smell* with *sweet*, in:

To see him shine so brisk, and smell so sweet
(*1 Henry IV* 1.3.54)

or famously of the rose in *Romeo and Juliet* (2.1.85–6). As with *sound*, however, a form in *-ly* was also possible: thus...*gift after gift, smelling so sweetly*, in a prose passage in *The Merry Wives of Windsor* (2.2.69). In *a rose would smell as sweet*, does the form without *-ly* also have the function of an adverb?

For *smell*, as for *sound*, a change in syntax may at this stage have been no more than incipient. Go back two centuries and it is clear that in an example from Chaucer:

But first he cheweth grein and likoris,
To smelen swete
(*Miller's Tale* 3690–1 in one system of numbering)

to smell is modified by an adverb, whose form was only starting at this stage to be distinguished by *-ly*. If we look ahead, however, to the present century it is the use of *smell* with adverbs that is problematic. One might not perhaps be likely to say *It smells well* or, for example, *It smells rancidly.* One could say *It smells sweetly.* But when *sweetly* is deleted, as when an adjective is deleted in *It smells sweet*, the verb has a sense it has had since the later Middle Ages, not simply of 'to have a smell', but 'to stink' or 'to have a smell that is offensive'.

In other cases a distinction between adjectives and adverbs can again be difficult. *Quick*, for example, tends to be classed both ways in dictionaries: as an adverb when used in, for example, *Come quick!*. This implies conversion (as for *fast* in 2.8). Alternatively, it remains an adjective but has a function shared with *quickly*. In *It sounded loud and clear*, two forms without *-ly* are in one view either a single adverb or two adverbs coordinated. Or are they coordinated adjectives? An answer would be obvious only if an older construction in *It sounded loudly* could now be distinguished neatly from the newer construction of *It sounded loud*.

4.11 In an 'ideal' or unproblematic system, adjectives and adverbs might be different at all points, and just one verb would have the role that *be* has in, for example, *He is happy*. With that verb, and with it alone, an adjective would be used to 'make a statement', in Dixon's words, 'that something has a certain property' (2010: 70; see also 1.1). There could therefore be a neat distinction, where a subject has an animate referent, between sentences which have such a meaning and others that describe an action or a form of behaviour. The verb in these would be intransitive, as in *He smokes*; or, among others, a simple transitive. In the system, however, that has actually evolved, sentences like *He looks tall* or *It smelled nice* have in this respect a function similar to that of *He is tall* or *It was nice*. *Look* and *smell* are accordingly among a set of verbs called 'copular' by, for example, Quirk and his colleagues (1985: 1171–2). But *be* itself has other uses where its combination with an adjective or other unit is instead more like that of verbs generally.

In a strict sense it has always been so, whenever *be* is used as an imperative. One can say, for example, *Be quiet!* or *Be careful!*, where the adjective denotes a state that someone can control; and, for comparison, one is far less likely to say *Be tall!* or *Be red!*, where it does not. If we fancy, as philosophers are prone to, that the raison d'être of language lies in making statements, it is tempting to represent imperatives as a modulation of the corresponding declaratives. A person or persons addressed would thus be enjoined to be in such a state that being quiet, for example, can truthfully be predicated of them. But this is precisely to say that they should act, or should not act, in a certain way. It is not surprising that as an imperative *be* can combine with the auxiliary *do*. One cannot say *They do be quiet* or *I did be careful*. But one can say *Do be careful!* or *Do please be quiet!*, as easily as, with other verbs, *Do come along!* or *Do please help me!*.

This use of *do* with *be* appears to have become established in a period before and after 1800. When Elizabeth Bennet is urged by Jane,

My dearest sister, now *be* serious
(*Pride and Prejudice* 3, ch. 17)

the emphasis that Jane Austen represents is in a different form, though one still possible two centuries later. But *don't be*, in a negative imperative, was already normal, and in an example from Fielding, often cited in the handbooks, a positive *do be* combines with a noun phrase:

Come, do be a good girl, Sophy...
(*Tom Jones* 16, ch. 2).

Denison has an example with an adjective from 1796 (1998: 252):

pray do likewise be content

and in these uses we may see the beginnings of what soon became normal. The pattern can be linked, moreover, to another yet more telling, in which *be* is used in the progressive. Thus in English as it is spoken now, one can say not only *He was careful* or *The children were quiet*; but also *He was being careful* or *The children were being quiet.*

The development of the progressive can be followed across three volumes of *The Cambridge History of the English Language* (Fischer 1992: 250–6; Risannen 1999: 216–18; Denison 1998: 143–60). Its use with *be* is on the evidence no earlier, however, than the first half of the nineteenth century. There are no examples from Jane Austen; and in comparison, where Mrs Gardiner says to Elizabeth:

Elizabeth, you are not serious now
(*Pride and Prejudice* 2, ch. 3)

the progressive *You are not being serious* would now be more likely. But Denison cites, from Jespersen, an example in a letter of Keats:

...how diligent I have been, and am being

and by the beginning of the twentieth century, as Jespersen had remarked, they are 'more and more frequent' (Denison 1998: 146–7; Jespersen 1909–49, 4: 225–6). Now the progressive also tends to be excluded with such adjectives as *tall* or *red*, that denote a property not normally under the control of an individual who has it. If it is normal, instead, with adjectives like *careful* or *quiet*, it is because their combination with *be* has a meaning more like that of an intransitive verb. Compare, for example, *The children are being naughty* with *The children are misbehaving* or, with a verb and an adverb, *are behaving badly*. What is described is less a property that the children have, than something they are doing or the way they are acting.

The progressive of *be* can be distinguished in turn from that of *look*, *appear*, and other verbs that have been classed as copular. In *The children look tired*, tiredness is a property, as the term 'copular' implies, that may be ascribed to children. The meaning of *look tired* is then no different in *The children are looking tired*; that of the progressive, in turn, both separate and no different from the one it has with verbs of other types, as in *The children are waiting* or *The children are having dinner*. A subject could, moreover, have inanimate reference: compare *The carpets are looking frayed* or, with another verb, *The garden is getting untidy.* But one would not say *The garden is being untidy* or, except as a passive, *The carpets are being frayed.*

4.12 To say that adjectives can be used to ascribe a property to individuals is to propose no more than a criterion, as in Dixon's account (2010) and others, for the category in general. It is only in an imaginary 'ideal' system that this might be their only role when they are predicative. In such a system they might also have just one role when they modify nouns. This might be to supply 'a specification', if we may again cite Dixon's formula, 'that helps identify the referent of the head noun in an NP'. This too, however, is intended as no more than a criterion. As predicative adjectives do not always fit an 'ideal' model, neither do all in the attributive position, especially when senses have become restricted to it.

Uses peculiar to attribution include some, like that of *ready* in *ready money*, whose origin dates from the Middle Ages (4.3); others, like that of *present* in *the present parliament*, are later (4.4). In these instances, as in many others, adjectives continue to denote what is traditionally a 'quality' (compare 2.4) by which a referent may be identified. Money may be on the nail or may be on account; a parliament may be as it is now, or as it once was, or as it will be in the future. In other instances, an attributive adjective does not denote a property or quality of a referent, but may still help to identify it. This is the role that *main*, for example, has had since the sixteenth century, in phrases such as *my main motive*, and to which it has progressively been limited. But in still other instances, an adjective in this position has a sense like that of an intensifier. In, for example, *It was a real* CATA*strophe*, the function of *real* is not to distinguish one sort or quality of catastrophe from others. An event would not be identified as real rather than illusory, or as happening in the real world rather than one which was virtual. It would simply be one that was genuinely catastrophic.

We may recall the development of *utter* early in the Modern period (1.3). Towards the end of it, however, several adjectives have tended to develop similar uses.

Take, for example, *decided.* It seems not to have been established as an adjective, as distinct from a participle, until the late eighteenth century; and in a citation in the *OED* from 1790, *it is difficult to form a decided opinion*, its sense is still linked to that of *decide.* But an intensifying use is illustrated, in the middle of the next century, by an example from Dickens's letters:

It was a most decided and complete success

In this sense it may not, when Dickens used it, have been limited to attribution. He could also perhaps have written *Their success was most decided.* But in later usage, *decided* can intensify a noun with which it has no corresponding use in the predicative position. Compare *They were a decided nuisance* with, if they have any meaning at all, *The nuisance was decided* or *As nuisances go, they were quite decided.*

The other adjective in this example has been investigated, though from another point of view, by Davidse (2009). The sense with which Dickens used it would again be hard to separate from the one it has predicatively, in *Their success was complete.* But in at least one other use its syntax may already have been restricted: compare, in the mid-seventeenth century, the title of Izaak Walton's *The Compleat Angler.* Davidse also cites an example from the eighteenth century, where a superlative is, as she describes it, 'unambiguously intensifying':

He is the completest tyrant God ever made for the scourge of an offending people

Current examples are common, as in *This is complete nonsense* or *I was a complete fool.* For Quirk and his colleagues, *complete* is one of a set of adjectives to be classed as 'noninherent', and as such is attributive only (1985: 429). As they mark, as unacceptable, *The fool was complete,* so Huddleston and Pullum would implicitly mark, as ungrammatical, *The nonsense is complete* (2002: 554). A restricted sense is made clear too in, for example, *It was a complete accident.* The meaning is not as in, for comparison, *There was complete devastation.* It is simply that what happened was entirely accidental; no human or other agent was responsible.

4.13 The microsyntax (2.13) of a word such as *complete* may seem a matter of mere detail, even though it is in part like that of other intensifiers. In a monosystemic analysis, which focuses on adjectives of a central or default type, it is tempting to see its use in these examples as, with that of *utter*, an 'exception'. The inverted commas are there, however, to remind us that exceptions are identified and discounted in relation to a specific generalization in a specific mode of description. From another viewpoint, uses in which this and other words are classed in grammars as 'attributive only' are a natural part of a much wider tendency, throughout the history of Modern English, for the functions of adjectives in noun phrases to evolve independently of their functions in clauses. If they are 'exceptions' they are ones that in particular reflect innovations, not the persistence of what had once been regular. The syntax of adjectives in clauses has also evolved, in general, independently. There too differences in detail may be seen as part of a historical pattern.

5

Modifiers and determiners

5.1 One crucial change in Middle English, as in several other European languages, was the development of a contrast between articles. In Old English, a definite expression could be distinguished by a demonstrative, from an indefinite expression that could consist of a noun alone. As in the examples given earlier ((1) and (2) in 4.2), an adjective had been in a corresponding weak or strong form. But the system then became one with both articles and demonstratives. Thus, in Modern English, *the* contrasts with *a* and, at the same place in the structure of phrases, *this* with *that*. In analyses by linguists over the past fifty years, both have come to be classed together as 'determiners': as a part of speech which is separate from that of adjectives, and whose members have a function, in the structure of expressions like *a tall man* or *these happy children*, which is separate from that of the adjectives as modifiers.

What exactly distinguishes this function? We have tacitly assumed that such expressions have nouns as their head. They are thus 'noun phrases', within which other units are subordinate or are dependents. They are dependents, however, that are often seen as forming two layers of constituency. In *these happy children*, as its structure would be represented by, for example, Huddleston and Pullum, an inner layer is formed by *happy* as a modifier of the noun:

(1) [these [$_{A}$[happy] $_{N}$[children]]]

For Huddleston and Pullum, this layer is that of a 'nominal' (Nom) within a larger noun phrase (2002: chapter signed by John Payne and Huddleston, 329):

(2) $_{\mathrm{NP}}$[these $_{\mathrm{Nom}}$[$_{\mathrm{A}}$[happy] $_{\mathrm{N}}$[children]]]

Where a noun has two or more modifiers, each is seen as forming its own layer. Thus in *a large black animal*, the first adjective depends, within a nominal, on a smaller nominal:

(3) $_{\mathrm{NP}}$[a $_{\mathrm{Nom}}$[$_{\mathrm{A}}$[large] $_{\mathrm{Nom}}$[$_{\mathrm{A}}$[black] $_{\mathrm{N}}$[animal]]]]

formed by *animal* and an immediate dependent *black*. The role of *a*, however, as a determiner, as of *these* in (2), is to combine with a nominal to form what is, instead, a noun phrase.

One aim of this chapter and of the two which follow will be to question how far an analysis on these lines can be justified. We will also need to bear in mind a partly different treatment, promoted widely by the end of the last century, in which expressions like these are no longer represented as noun phrases. *These happy children* is in this view headed not by *children* but by *these*. It is therefore a 'determiner phrase' (DP), whose head is a determiner (D), and the only unit *children* heads will be a noun phrase *happy children*:

(4) $_{\mathrm{DP}}$[$_{\mathrm{D}}$[these] $_{\mathrm{NP}}$[$_{\mathrm{A}}$[happy] $_{\mathrm{N}}$[children]]]

The 'DP hypothesis', as it has been grandly called, has been widely discussed, by me among many others (Matthews 2007b: 61–75). It too, however, proposes a layered analysis, in which the smaller units that would make up *a large black animal*:

(5) [a [large [black animal]]]

are no different, in abstraction from a difference in headship, from those in (3). Whether (5) itself is right is therefore a question we may address in the context of either proposal.

5.2 The function of a modifying adjective, if we may focus on an account like that of Payne and Huddleston, is to combine with the head it modifies to form a nominal. That of determiners, such as *these* or *a*, is to combine with a nominal to form a noun phrase. Either kind of unit can, however, have the semantic role of making clear a referent. In *the happy children* we might see this as primarily the role of *happy*: the reference could be to a set of individuals identified as happy rather than sad. In *these happy children* it could be primarily that of *these*: the reference would be to a set identified by the demonstrative. It is therefore natural to ask how clear a line it will be possible to draw between one syntactic function, characteristic of adjectives, and the other, characteristic of a part of speech seen as separate from them.

It is easy to imagine an 'ideal' system (in the sense in which this term was used in 4.9), within which a line could be drawn very confidently. Adjectives would be words denoting properties; and, in keeping with that, all adjectives could also be predicative. Thus, in *The children are happy*, a property of happiness could be ascribed correspondingly to the referent of the simpler phrase *the children*. But a determiner would not denote a property, and could therefore not be used, in a predicative construction, to ascribe one. The system, however, that has evolved in Modern English is in this light only partly 'ideal'. On the one hand one cannot say, for example, *The children are the*; and in *The children are these*, where a demonstrative has a place which is at first sight like that of the adjective, it forms on its own an expression referring to a set of individuals, not one which ascribes a property of 'thisness'. On the other hand, the words we are calling adjectives include ones such as *main* or *utter* that do not have the role that others have when they are predicative.

Do all, moreover, so clearly denote properties? *Same*, for example, follows *the* in *the same children*. Traditionally it is an adjective and in Payne and Huddleston's analysis might form a nominal with *children*:

(6) $_{\mathrm{NP}}$[the $_{\mathrm{Nom}}$[same children]]

But one cannot say *The children are same*, and in *The children are the same* a unit in which *same* combines with *the* has the structure, at least, of a referring expression. Indeed it could be one: a set of children would be identified as the same set of individuals that have been mentioned, for example, earlier. With another meaning, the sentence could ascribe to the set of children the same property, of being happy, exhausted, or whatever, that has been ascribed to other individuals mentioned already. But this use of *the same* makes clear that *same* does not itself denote a property. An alternative, obviously, to the analysis in (6) is that *same* might form a larger unit with the article:

(7) $_{\mathrm{NP}}$[[the same] $_{\mathrm{N}}$[children]]

and it is this unit, as a whole, that would have the function of a determiner in relation to the noun.

It is hardly surprising, in the light of such a simple example, that although the term 'determiner' has been in common use for nearly half a century, there is no consensus in detail, especially among recent authorities, either as to what words should be assigned to such a part of speech or, if categories and functions are distinguished, what the units are that have a 'determining' function. This is true both intensionally, of the features by which determiners have been defined, and extensionally, of the range of individual words included. If the indeterminacy is genuine, it is one that

Denison has shown, in a perceptive survey, to have persisted in the history of the language. In successive periods there has been, in his account, a 'stepwise movement' from one category to the other: from that of adjectives, which are modifiers, to that of the demonstratives, which we may see as the only 'determiners' in Old English, of the articles, and so on. Such movements, or reanalyses, have not ended. Therefore the evidence may 'point' now, as it would have in the past, to 'fuzzy boundaries' (Denison 2009: 301).

How linguists have described determiners

5.3 How far, though, have the problems been manufactured by the assumption of linguists that there is a major boundary, between parts of speech or different functions that they are thought to have? For many or most readers, it is an assumption that may seem uncontroversial. It has been the stuff of textbooks for some decades, and the only doubt that may appear to persist is whether determiners are heads. But in a longer perspective they are an innovation of, in particular, the early 1960s. It may therefore be salutary to look back at the ways in which the finding, supposed or real, has come to be established. The idea was, in the beginning, very simple: that demonstratives and articles, in particular, go together. But other words could be seen, in one way or in another, as partly like them. One way, however, was not always like another, and likeness, as always, can be a matter of degree. There has never, accordingly, been a single criterion by which determiners in a more general sense have been identified. Analyses have conflicted from the beginning, and although most textbooks in particular never let on, the conflicts have become more complicated and not less.

The simple idea was originally Bloomfield's. In the classification inherited from antiquity, an article had been one part of speech and a demonstrative, as in *these children*, was an adjective. In English, however, they have the same place in a noun phrase, in relation both to units that come before them, as in *all the children* and *all these children*, and those that follow. Nor do demonstratives combine with articles: one cannot, for example, say *the this child*. It was therefore natural for Bloomfield that they should be classed together. Both were in his account a type of adjective, and in a phrase such as *a happy boy* two adjectives, in succession, were both 'attributes' or 'modifiers' of a head. But while adjectives such as *happy* were 'descriptive', those that came before them had a meaning he identified as 'limiting'. Of these some, such as *all*, were 'numerative'; likewise *other* in *the other children* (Bloomfield 1933: 205–6). Others were 'determiners', and for Bloomfield these included articles and demonstratives, plus 'possessive adjectives' such as *my* in *my child* and, as he described it, *John's* in *John's child* (1933: 202–3).

In later treatments a determiner is one part of speech and an adjective is another. Central, however, to all the analyses of English that have used this term is the idea that the articles and demonstratives belong together. It is to Bloomfield too that we can trace a layered analysis, as shown in (5), of phrases. An adjective such as, as he classed it, *the* can be distinguished from one such as *happy* 'by the circumstance', in his words, 'that when adjectives of both these classes occur in a phrase, the limiting adjective precedes and modifies the group of descriptive adjective plus noun' (1933: 202). He therefore took for granted that in a phrase such as *a happy boy*, the noun heads a 'group', or smaller constituent, *happy boy*:

(8) [a [happy boy]]

which for Payne and Huddleston is again a 'nominal' combining as a whole with *a*. In *all happy children* a similar group would be preceded and modified by a 'numerative':

(9) [all [happy children]]

and so on.

5.4 The next important contribution is by Long, nearly three decades later. In *this boy*, for example, *this* is no longer, in his account, an adjective. It is instead a pronoun, of a class he called 'determinative', and it has the function of a 'determinative modifier' (1961: 40, 46). Such pronouns were in turn divided into three subclasses (46–7). One included the cardinal numeral in, for example, *three boys* and a 'determinative of totality' in *all boys*. These, with others, were 'determinatives of number and quality'. The articles and demonstratives were 'determinatives of identification'; this class also included determinatives of 'universality', such as *every*, or of 'negation', such as *neither*. Finally, there were words that Long described as 'partial determinatives of identification'. These were ones on which a 'full' determinative could be, as he put it, 'superimposed'. *Same*, for example, was a partial determinative which would form a 'fully determined' unit when a determinative such as *the*, in *the same boy*, is added to it. Other partial determinatives include the ordinal numerals: thus in *every second boy* a determinative of universality would be superimposed on *second*.

Five decades later, this analysis may seem to have been forgotten. Long's grammar was referred to in the first of those by Quirk and his colleagues (1972: 1088), but not in the bibliographical notes to chapters on the noun phrase (228, 934). It is not listed in their second grammar (1985); nor in Huddleston and Pullum's skeletal bibliography (2002). Long's treatment is significant, however, for two reasons. First, he talks both of 'determinatives' as a category and of the 'determinative' function that they have in larger units. In, for example, *this tall boy* the demonstrative is distinguished in both ways, as a determinative with the function of a determinative modifier, from the adjective *tall*, which has the function of an 'adjectival modifier'. The terms imply that types of modifier are distinguished by the categories corresponding to them. But there is at least the logical possibility, exploited widely in more recent treatments, that it might not always be so.

A second reason is that Long's determinative pronouns form a larger and more varied category than the determiners as Bloomfield had defined them. Bloomfield's criterion was in part as we have seen: that units belonged together if they had the same place in a larger unit. They had also, however, to have some kind of meaning in common. Thus his determiners had similar distributions, as we have seen, within larger units headed by nouns. But they also shared a meaning which was 'roughly', as he put it, that of '*identificational* character of specimens' (Bloomfield 1933: 203). The words that Long classed as determinative have more varied meanings, of which 'identification' was implicitly just one. They can also form a sequence. Thus in *all the three boys*, a determinative of number, or specifically of totality, is followed by a determinative of identification, which is followed in turn by another determinative, but of a different kind, of number. We are not yet talking of a separate part of speech. We need to ask, however, what unites these units. What distinguishes a determinative modifier, which represented the 'basic use' (Long 1961: 46) of a determinative pronoun, from an adjectival modifier? Or are there other properties, perhaps of meaning, by which determinative pronouns can be distinguished from both adjectives and other pronouns?

Attempts to answer the first question lead directly to the problem, in Payne and Huddleston's terminology, of dividing determiners from nominals. Long's terminology is different; but in an example given earlier, a full determinative would in his view have been superimposed on *same*. *Same* could therefore form a unit with it, as shown earlier in (7):

(10) [[the same] children]

which as a whole would be the determiner of *children*; not part of a nominal *same children* (5.2).

The second question is about determinatives as a category, in abstraction from their function or functions. It is therefore crucial, in particular, for linguists who do not see functions as established independently of parts of speech and syntactic structures composed of them.

5.5 A familiar answer is that determiners have a 'grammatical' meaning. This links them with pronouns, as in Long's analysis and others much more recent; but distinguishes them especially from adjectives. In one analysis, which has crept into textbooks, adjectives are one of a set of 'lexical' categories. Verbs, for example, are another. 'Determiners' are instead one of a set of 'functional' categories: see accounts by Radford (1997: 45–8), or by Radford and his colleagues (1999: 151). Conjunctions such as *and*, for example, will belong to another.

The foundation for this is not always wholly made clear. In the tradition of English grammars, however, the most important criterion has been that a unit with grammatical meaning enters into a closed set of contrasts. In a grammar by Strang, whose first edition was published a year after Long's, the 'adjuncts', as she called them, of a noun could be divided into two main classes. One was of 'open-class items', which were adjectives. The other was that of 'closed-system items'. These were the determiners, and included both the articles and the demonstratives; 'noun-phrase initiators', as she called them, such as *all*; numerals and words such as *few*; and all others seen as entering into a fixed set of oppositions (Strang 1968: 124–33). *Same* is not among the words that she discusses. But it would be a determiner, in this light, if it too was seen as forming part of a closed system. It might, for example, be opposed specifically to *other*. It would be an adjective if classed more generally, with *happy*, *nice*, and others, in a set which has no fixed bound.

For Quirk and his colleagues, in the second of their grammars, determiners are similarly one of six word classes that are closed; adjectives one of four that are open (1985: 67, 71–2). There are problems, however, when 'determiners' in this sense are compared with Bloomfield's 'limiting adjectives'. By Bloomfield's criteria, *my* in *my child* was again like *the* in *the child*: there are no phrases such as *my the child* or *the my child*, and a possessive adjective, as he called it, also identified a 'specimen' or 'specimens'. Another such adjective was the form in *-'s* in *John's child*; and, although *John's* is itself a word, it cannot easily be separated from a phrasal modifier like *my brother's* in *my brother's daughters* or *that awful couple's* in *that awful couple's offspring*. But of the 'adjuncts' in these examples, only *my* can be said to enter into a closed system of contrasts. By Strang's criterion, as we may call it, even *John's* will not be a determiner, since there is no bound to the set of names that form such units.

One remedy that by now, at least, is obvious will be to insist on a difference between categories and functions. The article in *the child* has what may be called a 'determining function'. So too does *my* in *my child*; and in both phrases the unit that has this function has what is called 'grammatical meaning'. As such it is a member of, let us say, a 'determiner category'. In *John's child* or *my brother's daughters* a phrase in *-'s* has a determining function; and as a function, in the construction of a larger unit, this need be no different. But where phrases have this function they are 'determiners' in that sense only, and do not belong to the 'determiner category'. The concept of a construction is again one in which any syntactic function may be shared by units of quite different syntactic classes (**2.8**).

Any class of units may in turn have different functions in a range of different constructions. *Few*, for example, was one of Bloomfield's 'numeratives', and is assigned by Strang to one group of 'determiner pronouns' (1968: 130–1). In this view, however, categories are one thing and their functions are another. We could say, in principle, that *few* is, as it is traditionally, an adjective. Therefore it is not a member of the determiner category. But in *few children* it too has the determining function, which it shares with the article in *the children* or the demonstrative, as another member of the determiner category, in *these children*.

This remedy is obvious, and indeed is tempting. The problem, however, is that it makes possible many alternative solutions, and it can be hard to say which ought to be preferred.

5.6 The first grammar by Quirk and his colleagues, or the first version of their grammar, appeared four years after Strang's, to whose analysis of the noun phrase it referred (1972: bibliographical note, 228). In their account too, units called 'determiners' formed 'a set of closed-system items'. They were also, however, 'mutually exclusive with each other, *ie* there cannot be more than one occurring before the noun head' (137). They were therefore distinguished from adjectives by Strang's criterion, and by Bloomfield's original criterion from a set of other units called 'closed-class premodifiers'. These included *all* in, for example, *all (of) the meat*; this was called, from its relation to determiners, a 'predeterminer' (140–1). They also included 'ordinals', such as *first* or *next*, and 'quantifiers' such as *few*. Of these the ordinals were glossed, perhaps prophetically, as 'post-determiners', and the quantifiers were 'mutually exclusive with', and had the same place in phrases, as cardinal numbers (143). This protreptic study is now no longer much referred to. But such is the analysis, in embryo, that is elaborated and reformulated in the second and definitive version, published more than ten years later.

The term 'determiner' is first used of a word class (1985: 67). This appears, for Quirk and his colleagues, to have been an innovation: in their earlier grammar, articles and demonstratives were different parts of speech, separate from each other, among a set of six closed classes, as both were from, for example, pronouns (1972: 45). But the change from the traditional classification is one of those claimed, in a passage cited earlier, to be 'well-motivated for modern English' (2.2; 1985: 73). A few pages earlier, Quirk and his colleagues also distinguish what they call 'determination', as a 'broad' function separate from modification and complementation. This is the function, as they put it, 'of words and (sometimes) phrases, which, in general, determine what *kind of reference* a noun phrase has' (64, their italics). One kind of reference is, for example, 'definite (like *the*)'; another 'universal (like *all*)'. An article, therefore, has this function; and, among the units that can have it, belongs to a category of units that are specifically 'closed-class items'. Other members of this word class include the demonstrative *that* and, for example, *every* (67). Other units that have such a function include phrases, and might, by implication, include words that would belong to other classes.

This is cited from an introductory 'survey of English grammar' (Quirk et al. 1985: ch. 2). For further analysis, we may turn to a chapter on 'nouns and determiners', and in particular to a section headed 'determinatives' (253–64). This term refers to units with the function of determination: a 'DETERMINATIVE element' (their capitals) is thus 'the item which "determines"' a noun phrase, on which again its 'kind of reference' depends. Crucially, however, in a phrase like *half the first book*, it will be a function not just of the article, but also of the units, formerly called 'closed-system premodifiers', that precede and follow it. *Half* is what had already been called a 'predeterminer', which comes before what is now a 'central determiner'. *First* is instead a 'postdeterminer'; and all three, together, implicitly 'determine' *book.*

To be precise, all three terms are said to refer to categories. Thus the determinative function, in general, 'is typically realized by a set of closed-class items, or DETERMINERS' (253, again their capitals), and determiners in this sense are of 'three classes'. Of these, the central determiners include '*eg*: the articles'; the predeterminers '*eg*: *half, all, double*'; the postdeterminers '*eg*: cardinal and ordinal numerals, *many, few*'. There is however, at first sight, a puzzle in that the 'determiners', as so defined, include some items that were not determiners in the introductory survey. The numerals, in particular, had been treated not as determiners, but as forming a class 'additional' to that and to the other main word classes. They were distinguished 'by virtue of the difficulty', as Quirk and his colleagues perceived it, of classifying them as either a closed or an open class (1985: 73). If we may presume, however, to interpret their analysis, we may say that in, for example, *the month* a member of a closed class of determiners (D) has a 'determining' function, also called that of a 'determiner', in construction with a head noun:

(11) $_{D}$[the] $_{N}$[month]
DETERMINER HEAD

In *half the month*, the category of *half* might again be that of a determiner, but its function is that of a 'predeterminer':

(12) $_{D}$[half] $_{D}$[the] $_{N}$[month]
PREDETERMINER DETERMINER HEAD

In *half the first month*, a numeral (Num) has the further function of a postdeterminer:

(13) $_{D}$[half] $_{D}$[the] $_{Num}$[first] $_{N}$[month]
PREDETERMINER DETERMINER POSTDETERMINER HEAD

which, though realized by a unit whose word class is not the determiner category, is also, as a function, 'determinative'.

If these distinctions are drawn, a determinative function can straightforwardly be realized, as Quirk and his colleagues say, by phrases. The most common function of expressions like *John's* or *my brother's* is to fill, as they explain elsewhere, 'a slot in the noun phrase equivalent to a central determiner such as *the*' (1985: 326). The function of a postdeterminer is not only that of numerals, which may themselves be more than one word, but also of an 'open class of phrasal quantifiers' (264). An example is *large number of* in *a large number of students.*

5.7 Fast forward seventeen years and we return to the analysis of Huddleston and Pullum. Throughout their grammar a distinction between categories and functions is maintained explicitly and resolutely, and in the chapter on the noun phrase, signed by Payne and Huddleston, the analysis is also resolutely layered. In a phrase then whose constituents we may represent as follows:

(14) [both [the [two [red flowers]]]]

the questions to be answered are of two kinds. Which dependents, at which levels of constituency, have the function of a modifier, and which have instead what we are calling the 'determining' function? Which, independently, are members of the 'determiner category', and which are adjectives?

The answers for *the* agree with those that are generally accepted. On the one hand, articles belong to a determiner category: this is the 'lexical category' which Huddleston and Pullum, in a reversal of the terms distinguished by Quirk and his colleagues, call that of a 'determinative' (2002: 22). On the other hand, *the* has the function of a 'determiner', which is distinguished in broad terms, as by Quirk and his colleagues, from that of a modifier and a complement (2002: 24). This may again be called the 'determining' function.

The answers for *red* are equally straightforward. It has the function of a modifier, and forms with its head the unit distinguished earlier as a nominal (5.1). Its category as a word is again that of an adjective. For neither, however, of the other dependents does the analysis proposed by Payne and Huddleston match categories and functions in a one-to-one way. Both are 'determinatives' (Payne and Huddleston in Huddleston and Pullum 2002: 356). They are members, that is, of the determiner category. But the functions of both, in this example, are as types of modifier.

To be precise, the role assigned to *both* is as a modifier which will form a larger noun phrase from a smaller noun phrase. The smaller phrase is formed, as illustrated earlier, by the combination of *the* with the nominal *two red flowers*:

(15) $_{\text{NP}}$[$_{\text{D}}$[the] $_{\text{Nom}}$[two red flowers]]

To this structure may be added what in their analysis is again a 'predeterminer', to form a phrase of which (15) becomes the head:

(16) $_{\text{NP}}$[$_{\text{D}}$[both] $_{\text{NP}}$[the two red flowers]]

As a modifier, *both* is of a type that is said to be 'external': external, that is to the smaller 'NP' (compare Huddleston and Pullum 2002: 331, with tree diagram).

The function of the numeral is instead 'internal': internal, that is, to a nominal. The structure of (15) can thus be further analysed as follows:

(17) $_{\text{NP}}$[$_{\text{D}}$[the] $_{\text{Nom}}$[$_{\text{D}}$[two] $_{\text{Nom}}$[$_{\text{A}}$[red] $_{\text{N}}$[flowers]]]]

with *two* a modifier of, in general, the same kind as *red*. To be precise, it is in Payne and Huddleston's account an 'early modifier', whose 'default position is before any other modifier' (Huddleston and Pullum 2002: 452). The adjective in *red flowers*, which comes later, is instead what is called a 'residual modifier'.

If we ask why *two* is assigned to the determiner category, the answer seems to be that, in the analysis that Payne and Huddleston propose, a cardinal numeral can begin a noun phrase. In, for example, *I picked red flowers* a modifying adjective does not. It is instead part of a nominal, within a noun phrase which has no determiner:

(18) $_{\text{NP}}$[$_{\text{Nom}}$[red flowers]]

Such noun phrases, in their terminology, are 'bare' (Huddleston and Pullum 2002: 355). But in *I picked two red flowers*, the object is in their analysis not 'bare'. It is instead determined by the numeral, just as in *I picked these red flowers* it would be determined by a demonstrative. It does not follow from this that *two* must also be, in their term, a 'determinative'. It could, in principle, be an adjective which, in this use, would have a 'determining' function. Let us assume, however, that if words can have this function they are ipso facto members of the determiner category. In this light, a cardinal numeral will also belong to it:

(19) $_{\text{NP}}$[$_{\text{D}}$[two] $_{\text{Nom}}$[red flowers]]

and naturally belongs to the same category, though its function is different, in (17).

Take finally, for comparison, an ordinal numeral. In, for example, *the second red flower*, the function of *second* is also said to be that of an early modifier, within a nominal that is in turn determined by *the*. But ordinal numerals do not begin noun phrases: one cannot say, for example, *I picked second red flower*. By the same logic, ordinal numerals do not belong to the determiner category. In Huddleston and Pullum's terminology, they are not 'determinatives'. In comparison, therefore, with (17), the structure of *the second red flower* is as follows:

(20) $_{\text{NP}}$[$_{\text{D}}$[the] $_{\text{Nom}}$[$_{\text{A}}$[second] $_{\text{Nom}}$[$_{\text{A}}$[red] $_{\text{N}}$[flower]]]]

where *second*, like *red*, is classed as an adjective.

5.8 The ingenuity and thoroughness of Payne and Huddleston's analysis is breathtaking. If we compare it, however, with that of Quirk and his colleagues, against the background of 'determiner phrases' and other proposals over the past half-century, it is clear that there are both broad and narrow views of what we are calling the 'determining function'. In all accounts demonstratives and articles are determiners in *this flower* or *the flower*. That is again the simple idea Bloomfield began with. In all accounts, the adjective in *the red flower* is a modifier. But in the structure of other phrases, especially in places intervening between an article and a descriptive adjective, there are units whose functions remain controversial. In a narrow view none are determiners: thus the numeral is not a determiner, for Payne and Huddleston, in *the second flower*. In the broadest view all might be. For Quirk and his colleagues, *second* was a postdeterminer: the determining function was that of the article and numeral together. For Long, the article in phrases like *the same flower* was superimposed on *same*, which was a 'partial determinative'. We may link this treatment with a recent article by Breban (2010), who argues that *same* too has 'postdeterminer uses'.

Why divisions can be uncertain

5.9 Why should the boundary between determiners and modifying adjectives vary from one account to another? An answer can be formulated, in the abstract and in concrete instances, fairly easily. It points, however, to types of structure that many linguists have been trained, effectively, either not to notice or not to represent straightforwardly for what they are.

Let us begin again with the simple case of, for example, *a happy child*. The adjective depends on *child* and so, in one view, does the article. The structure of the whole can thus be shown schematically as follows:

(21) Dependent Dependent Head

Add layering:

(22) [Dependent [Dependent Head]]

and we posit three syntactic relations, between the head and the first dependent, between the head and the second dependent, and between the first dependent and the unit that Payne and Huddleston call a nominal. In another view (5.1) the schema is instead as follows:

(23) [Head [Dependent Head]]

and the relations we posit are, mutatis mutandis, those of a dependent to the second head, of the second head to the first, and of the first head to the larger unit which includes the second. Crucially, in (22), we posit no specific relation between one dependent and the other dependent; likewise no specific relation, in (23), between *happy* as a dependent of *child* and *a* as a head at a higher level.

Either analysis accords beautifully with the model of tree structures, of constituency analysis, or of phrase structure grammar, that has dominated discussion of syntax since the middle of the last century. Words form constituents where they are linked by some relation: thus *happy* plus *child*. Where there is no link they do not.

Hence there is no constituent *a* plus *happy*. Let us suppose, however, that in some instances a unit like *a* and a unit like *happy* do stand in a separate relation. Then in (21), if this analysis may be considered for the sake of argument, each unit would be linked to each of the others: both dependents to a head and a dependent at a lower level to a dependent at a higher level. But a question would arise at once as to whether the layering in (22) is still valid. Would a constituent formed by the second dependent and the head be any more justified than one formed by the two dependents together?

The problem with *same* is precisely of this kind. In one view, *the same children* would have a structure like that of *the happy children*. But while *same* may depend on the head noun, it is also related, by specific restrictions, to the article that comes before it. *These same children* is also normal; but not, for example, *each same child* or *every same child*; or, if the noun is plural, *both same children*. Nor does *same* form a 'bare' phrase, as it would, if the sentence were possible, in *I talked to same child*. *Same* is in effect 'restricted', as Huddleston and Pullum describe it, 'to definite NPs' (2002: chapter signed by Huddleston, 1138). If we insist that the words are related as in (22):

(24) [the [same children]]

it is natural to take a narrow view of the determining function, as developed by Payne and Huddleston. But we discount the relation between *same* and *the*. If *children* combines instead with a constituent *the same*:

(25) [[the same] children]

it is more natural to take a broad view of the function, as developed in different ways by Quirk and his colleagues and by Long before them. But we discount a specific relation of dependency between *same* and *children*. It is reasonable to ask if we have any grounds to discount either relation, other than an engrained assumption, central to most forms of constituency analysis, that any sequence of three or more units ought to be divided somehow.

Part of a 'stepwise movement', if we may borrow Denison's term, could involve a change, in the history of the language, from a structure [*X* [*YZ*]] to a new structure [[*XY*] *Z*] (Denison 2009; 5.2). At any stage however, which will naturally include the present, there may be evidence that on its own would justify either.

5.10 Let us explore some variants on this theme, where a relation between successive dependents, as they would be in the schema of (22), can be established.

In an extreme case words that are otherwise independent form a single lexical unit. *Another*, for example, is historically from *a*(*n*) plus *other*; and as independent units, in *a child* or *some other child*, its members are classed respectively as an article and an adjective. Let us imagine however, for the sake of argument, an analysis which would represent them as still separate. In *an other child*, as we could then write it, *an* alone, in Payne and Huddleston's system, might be a determiner, and *other* could be a modifier within a nominal:

(26) $_{\text{NP}}$[$_{\text{D}}$[an] $_{\text{Nom}}$[other child]]

But this would lead to a problem where the noun is plural. *A*(*n*), on its own, will be straightforwardly excluded: there is no phrase *a children*. Add *other*, however, and although there would be no phrase *an other children*, a plural would be possible if, as in *an other three children*, we also add a cardinal numeral. *A three children*, in comparison, is again excluded. The obvious solution, which any actual treatment implicitly takes for granted, is that *another* must be one word and no longer two. It has become a compound; and, as a lexical unit different from *a*(*n*), it enters into its own relations, as a whole, more widely.

For Payne and Huddleston it is, more precisely, a 'compound determinative'. As a 'determinative', in their terminology, it is lexically a member of the determiner category, and in this example has the function of determining *three children*:

(27) $_{\text{NP}}$[$_{\text{D}}$[another] $_{\text{Nom}}$[three children]]

The argument, so far, appears straightforward. We may anticipate, however, that a change in which two units become one may involve historically a stage of indeterminacy. In the case, moreover, of *another* we are still not wholly out of the wood. For as the determiner in (27) depends on the nominal, so the nominal in turn, still following Payne and Huddleston's analysis, would be headed by *children*. The noun should therefore be the unit that, in the terms of Huddleston and Pullum's definition of headship, 'plays the primary role in the distribution' (Huddleston and Pullum 2002: 24) of the nominal. But it does not. It is not, that is, by virtue of the plural *children* that *three children* can be determined by *another*. If that were so, *another children* should also be possible. It is by virtue of the numeral *three*; which, in the schema proposed in (22), would be a dependent at the lower level.

This might suggest, as an alternative analysis, that *children* is determined by *another* plus *three*:

(28) [[another three] children]

with the functions that for Quirk and his colleagues were those of a central determiner and a postdeterminer. The relation between them would hold for any cardinal numeral; therefore it is syntactic and not within an even larger lexical unit. But *three* remains related to *children*, through the restriction that excludes *another three child*. The structure is instead one where, if we are prepared to consider it without prejudice, successive units form a network of relations, which each of (27) and (28) represents in part only.

5.11 Where a relation holds for a single pair of words, or for just a few that go together similarly, a change may be completed if they join to form a lexical unit. This may be a word, such as *another*. But Payne and Huddleston also speak of combinations of words that belong to a lexicon as wholes. In, for example, *a little money*, the role of *little* is historically that of an adjective. But *a* plus *little* has a meaning of its own, and combines as a whole with a noun which is uncountable, as *a* on its own tends not to. For Payne and Huddleston, it too is a lexical unit and a member of what we are calling the determiner category. Yet it is not a compound. It is therefore among a set of lexical units that they call 'complex determinatives' (chapter in Huddleston and Pullum 2002: 392; see earlier, 356).

One case where they hesitate, which Denison picks out as of current interest, is that of *a* plus *certain*. As an adjective in general, *certain* is of the 'default' type (1.10): compare its uses in predicative position, in *The result was certain* or *I am certain they are coming*. The use, however, that concerns us is as in, for example, a line from Browning:

> There was a certain bold young handsome priest
> (*The Ring and the Book* 3.839)

where *certain* is distinguished by its place in a sequence from the three adjectives that follow. In citing an example from the nineteenth century, we must remind ourselves that there are dangers in projecting present uses onto earlier periods. But *certain* could be read now as less prominent in the intonation of the whole than, in particular, both *bold* and *handsome*. Like *same*, moreover, it restricts, but in a different way, the units that come before it. One could say, for example, *There are certain handsome priests*, where the noun is plural and the phrase it heads might be described, in Payne and Huddleston's term, as 'bare'. One would not say, however, *these certain priests* or *all certain priests*, unless the meaning of the adjective, and most probably the intonation, were different. The priests referred to might be distinguished, perhaps, as definitely in orders. Nor would one say, where a singular noun is prominent, *the certain* PRIEST or *that certain* CLER*gyman*. Where *same*, for example, is said to be restricted to definite phrases, this use of *certain* is restricted to indefinite.

In another chapter, signed by Pullum and Huddleston, *certain* is classed with *main* and, for example, *particular* as a 'particularising attributive'. Its function is implicitly that of an 'early modifier' (5.7; Huddleston and Pullum 2002: 452–3):

(29) $_{\text{NP}}$[$_{\text{D}}$[a] $_{\text{Nom}}$[$_{\text{A}}$[certain] $_{\text{N}}$[priest]]]

The role, however, of such an attributive is 'to pick out a specific member or group of members of the set denoted by the head' (Huddleston and Pullum 2002: 558). This is surely very like, in particular, the role of a demonstrative. In an alternative analysis, which will now be obvious, the role in the singular could be that of *a certain* as a whole. In *a certain priest* the nominal would be *priest*, and would be determined by a lexical unit:

(30) $_{\text{NP}}$[$_{\text{D}}$[a certain] $_{\text{Nom}}$[$_{\text{N}}$[priest]]]

which, however, would again be 'complex' not 'compound'.

Payne and Huddleston in fact stand on the brink of saying so. In a phrase like *certain priests*, they talk of *certain* as among the 'somewhat marginal members of the determinative category'. They are marginal in being 'less clearly distinct from adjectives than most' (Huddleston and Pullum 2002: 392). Where the noun, however, is in the singular, there is a 'strong association' (393) of *certain* with *a*. It 'may be best', they say, 'to treat *a certain* as a complex determinative'.

How strong is the argument for this? Payne and Huddleston themselves observe that in, for example, *This gave her a certain authority*, 'we could not omit *certain* and retain *a*'. Compare, as they mark it, #*This gave her an authority* (393). By '#' they mean 'semantically or pragmatically anomalous' (Huddleston and Pullum 2002: prelims, xii). What seems, however, to be the anomaly would also be achieved by omitting, for example, *real* from *a real authority* or the relative clause from *an authority she had never had before*. If there is further evidence it might lie, therefore, not in the relation of *certain* to what precedes it, but in restrictions that *a certain* might as a whole impose, like *a little* or like *another*, on what can follow it. *Another* is not the only unit that selects, in Payne and Huddleston's words, 'a single or a quantified plural head' (Huddleston and Pullum 2002: 353). So, as they point out, do *a further* or *an additional*: compare *a further priest* or *an additional five bishops*. On this evidence, though they are not compounds, they too could be identified as 'complex determinatives'. As one cannot say *a further priests* or *an additional bishops*, so *a certain priests* is also excluded. Can one say, however, *a certain five priests*? Judgements may differ, and that is perhaps the most convincing symptom of indeterminacy. If *certain*, however, was a modifier, and was still in every way an adjective, we would expect that, just as *certain priests* can be a referring expression, so could *certain five priests*. It could be the object in, for example, *I know certain five priests*. Compared with that, a phrase in *a* does seem more likely.

5.12 A complex determinative fits straightforwardly, as a unit, in a structure of progressive layering. As *some red wool*, for example, would have an initial layer that is formed by *some*:

(31) $_{\text{NP}}$[$_{\text{D}}$[some] $_{\text{Nom}}$[red wool]]

so *a little red wool* would have one formed by the single unit *a little*:

(32) $_{\text{NP}}$[$_{\text{D}}$[a little] $_{\text{Nom}}$[red wool]]

But other relations, like that of *another* to a cardinal numeral, may hold for all members of a class. If they hold for units that are otherwise dependents, as again in the schema represented in (22), boundaries between constituents are again cast into doubt.

Take, for another example, a phrase like *every third child*. This could mean 'every child who is a third child to be born to given parents'; and, in that case, a layered analysis is straightforward. *Third* modifies *child*, and *every* could have, independently, the same role as the article in *a happy child*:

(33) ${}_{\text{NP}}$[every ${}_{\text{Nom}}$[third child]]

But such phrases also have another meaning. Some children could instead be standing, for example, in a line-up, and the reference would be to all those at intervals of three. A meaning like this may in many cases be more obvious than the other: compare *every tenth man*, in the Roman practice of decimation. A difference in the way the phrase is understood might then be thought to reflect a difference in syntax. As *third child* is determined in (33) by *every*, so in a contrasting structure *child* could be determined by a unit *every third*:

(34) ${}_{\text{NP}}$[[every third] ${}_{\text{N}}$[child]]

which would have its own internal structure.

But the *every* of (34) can be seen as entering, like *another*, into two distinct relations. On the one hand, it has a relation to *third* that is also specific to it: there is no similar use of, for example, *each* in *each third child* or of *all* in *all third children*. This relation, in passing, is one it would also have with *other*, where *every other child* is understood similarly. On the other hand it restricts, as in (33), the number of the head noun: *every third child*, not *every third children*. It is perhaps worth noting that in Long's analysis (5.4) an ordinal numeral was, like *same*, a 'partial determinative'. Another unit could thus be 'superimposed', as a 'full determinative', on it (Long 1961: 6–7). The full determinative can then be seen as entering simultaneously into two constructions. Into one it enters as itself: thus *every* as a determiner of a head noun. In the other it enters as a unit 'superimposed', in a combination that is determinative as a whole. In whatever way, however, we try to conceive of such a structure, it may be helpful to start by thinking in terms of a sequence, of simple *every* plus *third* plus *child*, rather than to begin by positing divisions between constituents.

Given any partial sequence, the range of words that can be added to it, either before or after, is variably restricted by those that are already there. Before *three young children*, in the types of sequence that concern us, we can add, among others, *another* or *all*; but not, for example, *every* or *a*. A sequence *these other* can be extended to, for example, *these other young*, and that in turn to *these other young children*. But there is no sequence *these other young child*. In seeking to explain why, we of course class *these* as a demonstrative and *child* as a noun, and establish a rule of agreement. This implies a unit, which is in one account a noun phrase, within which the rule operates. But it implies nothing about any smaller divisions within it.

This way of talking reflects a basic insight of information theory, which has been familiar since the 1950s. If we ask, moreover, at what point in sequences such as these the transitions from one word to the next are least restricted, the answer, it seems clear immediately, is between such words as *these*, *another*, *three*, *same*, or *third* and the adjectives, such as *young* in *young child*, that Bloomfield (5.3) called descriptive. This is the boundary in Payne and Huddleston's analysis between determiners and 'early modifiers' and what in their term are 'residual modifiers' (5.7). For Quirk and his colleagues, it is between the 'constituent parts' that they describe, in a later chapter on the noun phrase, as a 'determinative' and a 'premodification' (1985: 1238–9). In one view, as the terminology implies, the major division in a noun phrase is between determiners and the 'nominals' they determine. Within nominals, there is a subsidiary division between two kinds of modifier. It is this major division, however, that is most problematic and the subsidiary division that appears uncontroversial.

Are determiners a part of speech?

5.13 In phrases such as *a happy child*, where the distinction between a determiner and a modifier is clear, it can be seen in the first instance as a distinction between functions. Even, however, for linguists who see functions and categories as independent, the words which typically have a determining function also belong to a determiner category. This is the part of speech that in most accounts is that of 'determiners'; for Huddleston and Pullum (2002), it is again of 'determinatives'.

Its members are said to include articles, demonstratives, units often described as 'quantifiers', and others that vary. Each of these subclasses is in itself quite clearly defined. *This* and *these* have functions very similar at least to those of *that* and *those*, and both demonstratives are inflected for number. The articles have partly different distributions, but no authority disputes that they belong together. There is no doubt, too, as to what we mean by a cardinal numeral. Where linguists disagree, it is over the part of speech as a whole. Are numerals, for example, determiners, or are they adjectives? Or are they a category on their own? If cardinal numerals are determiners, is that also true of ordinal numerals? Or are ordinal numerals, but not cardinal numerals, to be classed as adjectives?

Even where there is no controversy, determiners of different subclasses have a different range of functions. Demonstratives, for example, can form phrases on their own, as in *This is better* or *The best are* THOSE. Articles, with which they have been classed since the outset, do not. In practice, therefore, a grammar will often talk not of determiners in general, but of a subclass with, as it might be distinguished in a lexicon, a feature [+ Demonstrative]; another with a feature [+ Article]; often simply of the indefinite article or the indefinite, or of *a*(*n*) or [səm]. Similarly, as was remarked in an earlier chapter (2.2), we will tend to talk in one context of full verbs and in another of modal or of other auxiliaries, more than of verbs generally.

In this way we are lumping together units that are quite heterogeneous. It does not follow that the part of speech cannot be justified. But it is worth asking the same question, crudely, as for any other: as to what exactly it is for.

5.14 In the early days of generative grammar, Postal argued forcefully, in tune with work by Chomsky, that syntactic functions were not independent of categories (Postal 1964; compare, for subjects and objects, Chomsky 1965: 69). The units that were beginning to be called determiners were at the time no more than a marginal topic. It is assumed, however, by many of Chomsky's current followers that *the child* has a structure:

(35) $_{DP}$[$_{D}$[the] $_{NP}$[$_{N}$[child]]]

This is a representation purely of phrase structure. Having said that *the* is a member of the category 'D', what can we gain by saying, in addition, that it has a 'determining' function? That would be, as Postal might have put it, a mere duplication.

In the light, however, of arguments since the 1960s it is obvious that this is a sword that can be turned the other way. We say that in *the child* the article has a determining function. So does the demonstrative in *this child*; so too do others, such as in one view the numeral in *one child*. Having said that, what do we gain by saying, in addition, that all are members of a determiner category? Is that itself any more than a gratuitous duplication?

Huddleston and Pullum draw the clearest distinction between functions and categories. If we ask, however, what distinguishes the units assigned to the 'determinative' category (2002: 356) from adjectives and other parts of speech in general, the answer is simply that, whatever functions they may have in other constructions, all and only these can have what they describe as the determining function. All and only these can combine with a 'nominal' to form a 'noun phrase'. Is the term 'determinative' any more, in this light, than a covering label? The function is that of several different kinds of unit: articles, demonstratives, cardinal numerals, and others, plus a few odds and ends. To achieve an illusion of unity we may say instead that it is the function of a determiner category, where the members of this category are articles, demonstratives, cardinal numerals, and so on. It is a category, however, that may not be relevant as a whole in any other context.

For other linguists the motives may be as they have been since antiquity, to establish a system of 'parts of a sentence' (2.4) that is exhaustive and distinguishes as few classes, at the highest level, as possible. Some, such as adjectives or verbs, can be justified directly. While they are real, however, they are not exhaustive. A class of 'determiners', in comparison, may be at best factitious.

... in the early days of generative grammar, that a grammar ... syntactic ... were ... [illegible] ... Postal ... Chomsky 1965 ... The units that ... [illegible]

[illegible]

[illegible]

6

Relations between premodifiers

6.1 In *a bold young handsome priest*, three adjectives intervene between the article and the noun. Each is a modifier, and in Payne and Huddleston's analysis (in Huddleston and Pullum 2002) a 'residual modifier' (5.7). Their order can in principle vary: compare *a young bold handsome priest* or *a handsome bold young priest*. Each too could modify *priest* on its own: *a bold priest, a young priest, a handsome priest*. Do we need to say more than that the meaning the phrase has as a whole will reflect the intersection of the meanings each modifier will have separately?

The received assumption, or at least one very widespread, is that the 'stacking' (4.5) of premodifying adjectives implies layering. In the system of Payne and Huddleston, which we may continue to take as a basis for discussion, the last adjective forms a nominal with the noun:

(1) $_{\text{Nom}}$[$_{\text{A}}$[handsome] $_{\text{N}}$[priest]]

This as a whole is a head which is modified, within a larger nominal, by *young*:

(2) $_{\text{Nom}}$[$_{\text{A}}$[young] $_{\text{Nom}}$[handsome priest]]

and this larger nominal, as a whole, is a head within another that is larger still:

(3) $_{\text{Nom}}$[$_{\text{A}}$[bold] $_{\text{Nom}}$[young handsome priest]]

The largest nominal is a head, as a whole, in relation to a determiner. If this is right, then at each level of constituency, a unit can be said to have a meaning determined by its parts. A priest is distinguished, at the level of (1), as handsome. This handsome priest is said, at the level of (2), to be, in addition, young. At the level of (3), this priest who is both young and handsome is further distinguished as being, in addition, bold.

There are phrases whose meaning such an analysis fits perfectly. In *a tall marine biologist*, a classifier (4.6) combines with *biologist* to form a unit that denotes a specialist in a certain field; and, in addition, this marine biologist is said to be tall. One is unlikely, instead, to say *a marine tall biologist*, even *a* MARINE *tall biologist*, with the adjectives in the opposite order. A structure, however, which may be appropriate for some phrases may not be appropriate for all. *A huge black animal*, though the order of adjectives is constrained, refers more obviously to one of a class of animals perceived as huge and black than to one of a class of black animals that, in addition, is huge. *A nice large sofa*, as distinguished from *a* NICE *large sofa*, will more obviously refer to a sofa that is nice in being large. One natural question, which will be addressed in particular in the next chapter, is whether there are arguments which justify analyses like that of (1)–(3) above. But we may also ask how far the model of layering may raise problems, in some sequences of adjectives at least.

Sequences and coordination

6.2 Let us begin, however, by inserting a coordinator. In many sequences it is at best difficult: one is unlikely to say *a tall and marine biologist* or, with the structure required in predicative position (1.5), *a nice and large sofa*. But in, for example, *a bold and handsome priest* two adjectives again modify the noun, and the meaning, with *and* or without it, will be similar. Are the structures of such phrases also similar? Or is the 'stacking' of premodifiers different from coordination? These questions may at first appear naïve, or maybe forgetful. For in my own introduction to syntax, which is now more than thirty years old, coordination and modification are quite different. Coordination is a symmetrical relation between units neither of which depends on the other. Modification is a relation of dependency and thus asymmetrical (Matthews 1981: chs. 8 and 9). In reality, however, the distinction is not nearly so straightforward.

What exactly, to begin with, is the nature of coordination? As Marouzeau defined it, in his dictionary first published in the 1930s, it consists in the 'arrangement at the same level' ('disposition sur le même plan') of terms either juxtaposed or joined by a conjunction (1951: 63). By 'sur le même plan' we may understand 'at the same level of subordination'. In, for example, *They like children and animals*, the verb has as its objects two words which, though one is closer, are equally subordinate to it. In *a bold and handsome priest*, or in *large and fluffy animals*, the adjectives are equally subordinate to *animals*. Remove *and*, and the adjectives are juxtaposed. But they could be juxtaposed in exactly parallel relations to a head noun. In *large fluffy animals*, as in *a bold handsome priest*, one adjective cannot but be closer to it. But their functions need not be seen as different. With or without the coordinator, a head N has two modifiers A_1, A_2. The meaning of the whole can again be reduced to the intersection of the meanings of $A_1 + N$, $A_2 + N$.

The structure implied is not only compatible with this view of coordination, but is one that Jespersen, a century ago, seems to have taken for granted (1914: 2–3; 1924: 97). His system of syntax is of a kind most linguists are no longer used to, and much of his terminology, which was partly his own, is now obsolete or has been recycled. But in *large fluffy animals*, where *animals* would now be called a head, it was in his account a 'primary'. It was a word to which others were subordinate, and as 'secondaries' or 'adjuncts', at what we may call an immediate level of subordination, *large* and *fluffy* both stand in a direct relation to it. The same held for other units which in later theories of dependency grammar, in the tradition of Tesnière (1959) and Hays (1964), depend directly on nouns. Thus in *much good white wine*, which was one of Jespersen's own examples, the adjuncts of *wine* were equally *much*, *good*, and *white*. Each can relate to *wine* on its own: *much wine*, *good wine*, *white wine*. In the sequence *much good white* each is a secondary; they are related to *wine* at the same level of subordination; and if coordination is defined in this way, they too are coordinated. *Large fluffy animals* has a structure different from *large and fluffy animals* merely in that in one the adjectives are joined by a conjunction. In the other they are 'simply', in the terms of Marouzeau's definition, 'juxtaposed'.

A more specific criterion for coordination, as Dik put it some decades later, is that members should be 'equivalent as to grammatical function' (1968: 25). In both that book, which is still the best-informed discussion of coordination, and in the theory of grammar that he went on to develop (1979), functions and categories were independent. We might argue in this light that *much* in Jespersen's example has the function of a determiner, and therefore cannot be coordinated with the adjectives, which are modifiers. A demonstrative is likewise a determiner in *these large fluffy animals*; if there is coordination, therefore, it may only be of *large* and *fluffy*. They, however, will still meet the definition perfectly.

6.3 Jespersen's remarks were brief, and in a more general context, and may largely have been forgotten. He went on, however, to make a point that from this viewpoint is a crucial insight: that where words form a sequence, any element in it may form a more specific connection with the ones that come before or after. In *a nice young lady*, which is another of his own examples, the adjuncts are not joined by a connective, and, as 'often', there is 'a specially close' relation between the final adjunct and the primary. Together, as he put it, they form 'one idea, one compound primary (*young-lady*)' (1924: 97). Jespersen did not say so, but in *much good white wine* we may see a similarly close connection between *white* and *wine*.

This insight makes sense in its context, in a system of grammar where words relate to other words directly, at successive levels of subordination. But for many and perhaps most linguists, Marouzeau's 'at the same level' will now mean 'as part of the same constituent'. It is therefore tempting to see Jespersen's account as incoherent. If there is a connection between *young* and *lady*, it implies that there is a constituent *young lady*:

(4) [nice [young lady]]

If *nice* and *young*, however, are coordinated they form a constituent *nice young*:

(5) [[nice young] lady]

and (4) and (5) cannot both be right.

If this view were justified, the criterion for coordination could again be that the units have equivalent functions. But for Bloomfield, whose account has long been very influential, a constituent formed by coordination was instead of the same 'form-class' (1933: 195) as each of its members. For 'form-class' we may read 'syntactic category'. Thus, in *large and fluffy animals*, there is not only a constituent *large and fluffy*. Not only are *large* and *fluffy* what we may call 'adjective phrases':

(6) [$_{\text{AP}}$[large] and $_{\text{AP}}$[fluffy]]

but if the construction of (6) is coordinative, the whole is also an adjective phrase:

(7) $_{\text{AP}}$[$_{\text{AP}}$[large] and $_{\text{AP}}$[fluffy]]

Remove the coordinator, and in *large fluffy animals*, to establish that the structure is not coordinative, we must argue either that there is no constituent *large fluffy*; or, if there is such a constituent, that it is not, as a whole, an 'adjective phrase'.

The argument that there is no such phrase relies implicitly on a criterion of distribution. A form-class is at first defined by Bloomfield in terms of 'a given position'. This is also the definition of a 'function' (1933: 185). The position, then, that *large* has in *large animals* or that *fluffy* has in *fluffy animals*, is the same that the coordination has in *large and fluffy animals*. It is also that of the sequence in *large fluffy animals*. We must therefore look beyond this 'given position', at the distribution that such units, if they are all units, have in other positions. The coordination *large and fluffy* has again the same place, in *They were large and fluffy*, as the single adjectives in *They were large* and *They were fluffy*. This confirms that all three can be classed as adjective phrases. But one would not say, with reference to the same two separate properties, *They were large fluffy*; nor, in another predicative structure, *She likes them large fluffy*. In the logic of constituency analysis, larger units are assigned to the same category only if their distributions overall are similar.

6.4 The assumption that coordination forms constituents has long held the field. If there is no constituent, therefore, like *large fluffy* or like, in our earlier example, *bold young handsome*, it follows that the adjectives are not coordinated. It does not follow, without further argument, that they form layers. A structure, however, in which modifiers are related in a sequence to a head noun:

(8) [bold young handsome priest]

may be distinguished in principle from one in which a noun is modified by a coordination:

(9) [[bold young and handsome] priest]

How thoroughly, in practice, can such structures be distinguished?

It is clear at once that 'stacking' and coordination can be complementary. Take, for example, a pair of adjectives like *red* and *yellow*. They stand in the sense relation that Lyons called 'incompatibility' (1963: 59–61; 1977: 242): what is red cannot be yellow and what is yellow cannot be red. The reference, therefore, of *a red and yellow carpet* must be to a carpet which is in part one colour and in part the other. But with the same adjectives, as Quirk and his colleagues point out, a sequence without *and*, as in *a red yellow carpet*, is excluded (1985: 961). The same holds for many at least of the units Malkiel (1959) called 'irreversible binomials'. In *a rough and ready answer*, the 'binomial' *rough and ready* has a meaning not matched, in regard to *rough* especially, in *a ready and rough answer*. In that sense it is 'irreversible'. Neither would one normally say *a rough ready answer*.

In other cases, structures like (9) would be in turn unlikely. In the predicative position, adjectives of size, for example, and of colour can be joined quite readily by a coordinator: *The carpet is big and yellow* or, since their order is not constrained, *The carpet is yellow and big*. But in that position coordination is the only option. In the attributive position, *big* plus *yellow* can as readily form a sequence: *a big yellow carpet*. Their order follows the principle that applies in general (4.6). It is unlikely, however, that one would say *a big and yellow carpet*. Is it possible, therefore, that the structures of (8) and (9) may be distinguished by their meanings? In saying *a large fluffy animal* a speaker will indeed refer, it might be suggested, to the intersection of two properties. The animal is simply, as it happens, large and it is simply, as it happens, fluffy. But in saying *a large and fluffy animal*, one would refer not just to an animal with both properties, but to one perceived as belonging to a class that has them. It is natural, that is, to see animals which are large and fluffy as in general different from another class whose members are large but without fur, or another distinguished as fluffy but small. The reason, it might be then suggested, why one would not say *a big and yellow carpet* would be that no natural class of carpets is perceived as different from others in that they are big and yellow.

Appeals to how things are perceived by speakers, or to how they think of the world around them, are one of the oldest expedients to which linguists have traditionally been driven. The problem, of course, is that they can easily become self-verifying. But another form of complementarity is far less slippery. In, for example, *a very big white carpet* the first adjective takes an intensifier, and forms a unit which to that extent is phrasal. The structure of (8), however, is in other respects that of a sequence of single adjectives. Add an adverb to another adjective and a coordinator will be normal: thus *a very big and dazzlingly white carpet*. Delete *and*, and the most likely pattern will be one in which the intonation is broken (4.7): *a very* BIG, *dazzlingly* WHITE *carpet*. The order too is freer. *A dazzlingly white, very big carpet* may be no less acceptable than, with a conjunction, *a dazzlingly white and very big carpet*. It is at least less constrained than, or not constrained in the same way as, *a white big carpet*. It may be dangerous to make comparisons across languages or across categories. But the difference between the stacking of adjectives and the coordination of adjective phrases is in part like that of a serial verb construction and the coordination of verb phrases.

The intonation can be broken both where adjectives take modifiers and where they do not. Is this, in general, simply an alternative way in which coordination can be realized?

6.5 For Quirk and his colleagues, a phrase whose intonation they mark thus: *a dis*HÓ*nest*, LÁ*zy* STÙ*dent*, illustrates 'the possibility of replacing *and* by asyndetic coordination' (1985: 961). The pattern is implicitly like that of, in a predicative structure, *He was* BÒLD, YÒUNG, HÀND*some*. Asyndetic coordination, or coordination realized with a broken intonation, might in that light be distinguished, with or without a similar pattern of constituency, from the stacking of single adjectives, whether or not it involves layering, which is restricted to attribution. Let us return, however, to a line from Shakespeare cited in an earlier chapter:

I spy a black suspicious threatening cloud

It is sometimes printed with commas (4.7), and whatever distinction may or may not have been possible four centuries ago, the phrase can now be read in ways that range from one where hearers may perceive a pause between successive adjectives—*a* BLÁCK, *sus*PÍ*cious*, THRÉA*tening* CLOUD—to a continuous rhythm in which *cloud* alone is maximally prominent. But can such variation also imply a difference in syntax?

A clear distinction may in the end elude us. In his recent study of the order of premodifiers, Feist (2012) develops in detail an analysis proposed by Quirk and his colleagues (1985: 437, 1338–41), in which lexical units are assigned to a succession of 'zones'. Across zones, modifiers will form sequences. *Big* plus *yellow*, as in *a big yellow carpet*, can therefore be a sequence in which an adjective which is lexically of one zone comes first and an adjective which is lexically of another zone comes later. But modifiers are instead seen as coordinated, 'phonologically' or by commas and conjunctions, if and only if the zone they are assigned to is the same (Feist 2012: 156; 'phonologically', 146). If *stupid* and *idle*, for example, can be coordinated, as in *a stupid and idle student*, it is in this account because the same zone includes both. Delete the conjunction, and in *a stupid, idle student*, which would normally be written with a comma, they would again by implication be coordinated. 'Phonologically', this too could have a broken intonation: *a* STU*pid,* ID*le student*. If Feist's argument is, however, as I have understood it, stacking and coordination will be strictly complementary. If one can say *a bold and handsome priest*, the adjectives must be in the same zone. Therefore in *a bold handsome priest*, where *and* has been removed, they are still coordinated. That its phonology, or its rhythm, is the same as that of *a big yellow rug* is not, if I have followed the logic correctly, an objection. In *a huge inedible dinner*, the adjectives are in an order we can explain in principle by assigning them to different zones; but only, it would seem, if we can exclude the coordination in *a huge and inedible dinner*, which would assign them to the same zone.

We can insist that a distinction must be drawn. It seems possible, however, that after a period of five hundred years, over which the stacking of premodifiers has become a separate construction, its differentiation from coordination may not be wholly complete.

Combinations of premodifiers

6.6 If stacking is not coordination, it could still be as in (8), without layers. In, for example, *a large yellow carpet* the adjectives might combine with *carpet* in a nominal which has no smaller nominal within it:

(10) $_{\mathrm{NP}}$[a $_{\mathrm{Nom}}$[$_{\mathrm{A}}$[large] $_{\mathrm{A}}$[yellow] $_{\mathrm{N}}$[carpet]]]

If so, we might expect that in such phrases as *a tall marine biologist*, or in Jespersen's example of *a nice young lady*, a final modifier could stand in a close relation to the head noun. For Jespersen, however, there could also be relations among specific modifiers; or, in his term, adjuncts.

An illustration similar to one he gave would be of the adjectives in *a scorching hot day*. Both *a hot day* and *a scorching day* are possible; and in Jespersen's analysis, together as separately, they are adjuncts. Compare, however, *a very hot day*. *Very* is in origin an adjective, and is still classed that way in some uses. It would modify, for example, *image* in *He is the very image of his father*. But *very* has evolved, in other uses, into an intensifier; as such it is subordinate, in *a very hot day*, to *hot*; and the two together can be said to form an adjective phrase:

(11) $_{\mathrm{NP}}$[a $_{\mathrm{Nom}}$[$_{\mathrm{AP}}$[very hot] day]]

which as a unit modifies *day*. This is not the case with *scorching*, which in Jespersen's analysis would remain an adjunct. Its use is similar, however, in that the idea expressed, as he might have said, is of heat to an intense degree. A word subordinate to an adjunct is in his terminology a 'subjunct'. In phrases, therefore, like *a scorching hot day* 'the first of two adjuncts tends to be subordinate to the second'. In that way, it 'nearly becomes a subjunct' (Jespersen 1924: 97).

When Jespersen was writing, the development of constituency analysis and phrase structure grammar lay well in the future. But let us suppose, with Huddleston and Pullum and with many other authorities, that such a phrase is layered. In a schema, therefore, which we can repeat from the last chapter:

(12) [Dependent [Dependent Head]]

a relation in (13) between the adjectives:

(13) $_{\mathrm{NP}}$[a $_{\mathrm{Nom}}$[$_{\mathrm{A}}$[scorching] $_{\mathrm{Nom}}$[$_{\mathrm{A}}$[hot] day]]]

is between dependents at a higher and a lower level. Compare *the* and *same* (5.9) in *the same day*.

It does not follow, if such a relation is established, that the layering in (13) is wrong. The crucial question is the one deferred to the next chapter, as to whether there are any arguments for it. It is important to ask, however, if in particular instances there are also arguments against it.

6.7 Let us begin with an illustration that may seem, at first sight, to belong in the last chapter. In, for example, *any priest* we take *any* to be a determiner. This term is used, as Huddleston and Pullum use it, of a function; and in, for example, *any old priest* the unit determined could be a straightforward nominal:

(14) $_{\mathrm{NP}}$[any $_{\mathrm{Nom}}$[old priest]]

The meaning would be 'any individual who is a priest and is, in addition, old'. But a phrase that would be written the same way has another meaning, which is normal with a rhythm in which *any* is prominent. Thus in ANY *old priest will* DO, the sense of *old* is no more than affective. A priest is called for, but whether an old priest or a young priest is immaterial. All that matters is that he or she should be in orders. Where the phrase, then, has that meaning, is its structure still as in (14)? Or does *old* form a unit with *any*:

(15) [[any old] priest]

which as a whole is the determiner?

Compare *a* plus *certain* (5.11), or *every* plus an ordinal numeral (5.12). The connection is specific, on the one hand, to *any*. *Every old priest*, for example, would refer straightforwardly to all priests who are old: it has no meaning 'all priests whatever'. The connection is also specific, on the other hand, to *old*. *Any young priest*, for example, will mean 'any priest who is in addition young'; *any new hammer*, as in *Just bring me* ANY *new hammer* will refer to a hammer that is new; and so on. If another adjective is inserted, either it too is affective or *old* is less so: compare, if they are likely, ANY *good old priest* or ANY *kind old priest*. As *a certain*, for example, can be a 'complex determinative' (Huddleston and Pullum 2002: 393), so in principle can *any old*. If so, it would be a lexical unit. Alternatively, it might be a syntactic phrase whose head is *any*. In ANY *priest* the head would stand alone; in [[ANY *old*] *priest*], the adjective would modify it.

This use of *old* can be compared with others, where it follows another adjective. In, for example, *Some poor old* CYC*list was knocked over*, *poor* plus *old* is what we may call an 'affective combination', which is likely to express as a whole no more than sympathy. The cyclist referred might in fact be young and well-off; all that is relevant is what has happened to them. In a line of Betjeman which we may repeat from an earlier chapter:

And my silly old collarbone's bust

there is no implication, similarly, that the speaker's collarbone is either silly or is perceived as not new. Such uses are again specific to *old* and to the words that *old* combines with. Replace *poor* in *some poor old cyclist* with, for example, *careless* and the cyclist referred to is either physically old or might be perceived as careless in the manner of old people. Replace *old* in the line from Betjeman with *new* and the girl who is represented as speaking, who has fallen off her pony, might be thought to blame the collarbone for getting broken.

The problem, as always, is how far a relation implies a unit. If *poor* plus *old* were to form a single modifier:

(16) $_{\text{NP}}$[some $_{\text{Nom}}$[[poor old] cyclist]]

we could describe it as a phrase whose head, as in the case of *any old*, is its first member. Compare *some poor* CYC*list*, without *old*, which could also be affective. But if *poor old* is not a unit, and the structure were layered:

(17) $_{NP}$[some $_{Nom}$[poor $_{Nom}$[old cyclist]]]

a dependent would be related to a dependent, within nominals, in the same way as it might across the boundary between nominals and determiners.

6.8 The affective uses of *old* have been explored with insight, on the evidence of largely written material, by González-Díaz (2009). The intonation, however, of such phrases is worth noting. Make *old* prominent and its meaning is no longer affective. Compare *any* OLD *priest* or *some poor* OLD *cyclist*; and, if there exists a context in which it makes sense to say it, *my silly* OLD *collarbone*. In the uses that concern us a legato rhythm (4.8) will instead be usual. In *some póor old* CYC*list* the rhythm of an affective combination can be seen as more like that of compounds, such as *dead-drunk* in *some dead-drunk driver*, than of, for comparison, *some táll blónd* CYC*list* where the adjectives have meanings independently.

The rhythm of noun phrases is a topic that has often been passed over, even in the best accounts of English syntax. But for Hill, in the 1950s, successive adjectives could normally have what he described as secondary stress. In the sequence *tall blond cyclist*, this would be shown in his notation by successive circumflexes: *tâll blônd cýclist* with a primary stress, marked by an acute, on the noun. Compare *flât whîte róck* (Hill 1958: 184). This pattern was distinguished from that of, for example, *fôrty-òdd bóoks* where *odd* has instead a tertiary stress, marked by a grave. The phrase would have a different meaning, as Hill pointed out, if *odd* too had a secondary stress—*fôrty ôdd bóoks* and was thus an independent modifier.

The *odd* of *forty-odd*, with the meaning of some number 'in the forties', is for Payne and Huddleston an affix (Huddleston and Pullum 2002: 431n). If so, it is a unit separate from the adjective *odd* in, for example, *a few odd stragglers*. Whatever the pros and cons of that analysis, it would be harder to separate an *old* that would be purely affective, as in, in Hill's notation, *a pôor òld príest* from another *old* in uses where age will be relevant. Compare *a kînd òld príest* or, as is also possible, *some câreless òld cýclist*. It is tempting, nevertheless, to treat affective combinations as if they were a different kind of unit. They have a pattern of stress which is similar, again, to that of many compounds. One possible solution, it might seem, is that they are themselves compounds. If so, in *some poor old cyclist*, the noun is modified by a single lexical unit:

(18) $_{NP}$[some $_{Nom}$[$_{A}$[poor old] cyclist]

just as it would be, by a different lexical unit, in *a poor cyclist* and *an old cyclist*. *Silly* and *old* would form another compound; *good old*, as in *good old Bill*, a third; and so on.

If we were tempted by this solution, no dependent would be related syntactically to another dependent, and the 'interface' between phonology and grammar, as Hill might have put it if he had been writing a few decades later, is as straightforward as it can be. There are perhaps two reasons, however, why accounts of compounding in English do not include such units. First, they would have an internal structure unlike that of other compounds. That of *dead drunk*, for example, can be compared to a syntactic structure in which *drunk* is a head and *dead* a modifier. Compare *clean-shaven* or *cold sober*; or, where the first member is a unit other than an adjective, *punch-drunk* or *ice-cold*. But it is hard to see *old* as the head of *poor old*; if anything the relation is the opposite. Nor is its stress pattern like that of a dvandva compound: compare, for example, *a silly clever suggestion* or *the North-South divide*. A second reason is that, if these forms were single adjectives, they would as a class be only attributive. One can say *The driver was dead drunk* or *The water was ice-cold*. As compounds these can naturally be predicative. But one would not say, for example, *My collarbone is silly old*. One simple explanation is that *silly* plus *old* forms a sequence, and sequences are again restricted to attribution.

For many linguists, (18) and, for example, (17) represent the only alternatives. *Old* could combine syntactically with *poor*, under assumptions that go back to Bloomfield, only if they are members of a coordination. But these assumptions may reflect the logic of constituency analysis better than they accord with the evidence.

6.9 This may seem a lot of argument to hang on a handful of examples. The more, however, we turn to others the more such connections are syntactic and not merely lexical.

Huddleston and Pullum describe one construction (their term, not mine) that might be linked to that of *scorching* plus *hot*. In, for example, *a tiny little bird* they take for granted that the adjectives are stacked in layers. The structure, therefore, as they see it is again that of a smaller within a larger nominal:

(19) $_{\text{NP}}$[a $_{\text{Nom}}$[tiny $_{\text{Nom}}$[little bird]]]

But the sense, implicitly, is not just that the bird is little and, moreover, that this little bird is tiny. The example illustrates instead the second of two 'intensificatory constructions'. The first is that of 'intensificatory repetition': thus of *long*, for example, in *a long, long way*. That of (19) is instead of 'intensificatory tautology'. There is a 'sequence', that is, 'of two adjectives with identical or near identical meanings', which is 'interpreted' as if a modifier were intensified. The meaning of the phrase is that of 'a very little bird' (Huddleston and Pullum 2002: chapter signed by Pullum and Huddleston, 561–2).

Exactly what, though, is the nature of their relation? The term 'construction' is defined, in Huddleston and Pullum's introductory chapter, in reference to syntactic units (2002: 23). If *little bird* is one such unit, as in (19), it is one construction; if *tiny little bird* is a larger unit, it is a larger construction. But the term can also be used, as grammarians have traditionally used it, of the structure of a unit in general. If (19) is right, the phrase would have a construction in which *tiny* stands to *little bird* in a relation of dependency; more precisely, one of modification; yet more precisely, of intensification; more precisely still, of intensification through tautology. The meaning, however, that is intensified, or the meaning expressed tautologically, is not that of a unit *little bird*. It is simply that of the adjective. If there is a unit, therefore, which has this construction it is more plausibly the sequence *tiny little*. In, for comparison, *a very small bird*:

(20) $_{\mathrm{NP}}$[a $_{\mathrm{Nom}}$[$_{\mathrm{AP}}$[very small] bird]]

the intensification would be similarly within the unit *very small*, between Jespersen's subjunct and his adjunct (**6.6**); and as *bird* is modified by this, so, by implication, it can be modified by the intensified unit, or what Huddleston and Pullum would call the construction, *tiny little*.

Compare, among their other examples, *a great big hole*. Nothing is said, at this point, or in the earlier chapter on noun phrases, about the intonation that would be normal for such sequences. But there is an obvious difference, in that respect, between intensificatory tautology and 'intensificatory repetition'. In *a tiny, tiny bird* each adjective might have a separate falling tone: *a* T*ìny*, T*ìny* BIRD or, if the intonation is continuous, they would be equally prominent. But in *a tiny little bird* a legato pattern would at least be normal. That of *great* plus *big* could be similarly like that of the affective *poor* plus *old*: in Hill's notation, *a grêat bìg hóle*. Alternatively, it could be like that of the adjective phrase in, for example, *a quite big bird*: thus, as Hill himself recorded it, *a grèat bîg bóy* (1958: 185). Hill's judgements were restricted, cautiously, to his own 'idiolect' (13) of American English. Compare, however, in the same notation and with a use observed at least in American speakers, *a lìttle tîny pérson*. The order of adjectives in this last example is queried, in passing, by Givón (1990: 470). But neither there, nor in a phrase where *tiny* would come first, is *little* likely to be more prominent. One is not likely to say, for example with emphasis, *a tiny* LITT*le bird* or *a* LITT*le tiny person*.

6.10 The construction is, as Huddleston and Pullum rightly make clear, a construction. In an earlier essay (2009) I put up as a straw man a naïve alternative, in which the functions of *tiny* and *little* would be as separate as those of any other modifiers. In modifying therefore, *bird* by *little* a speaker would be saying that the bird is of small size, and in modifying *little bird* by *tiny*, if we may assume for the sake of argument a layered structure, the speaker would be adding to this, redundantly it might seem, that this bird of small size is of small size. The explanation, we might be tempted to propose, is not syntactic but 'pragmatic'. In quasi-Gricean terms, the speaker violates a maxim of 'manner' (in the sense of Grice 1989: 27), which enjoins one to say no more than is needed. There has to be a reason why it is flouted; this is to communicate, we would propose, what would in a Gricean account be an implicature, that the bird is very, very small indeed.

A linguist who would argue like that may indeed be no more than a straw man. It is important to emphasize, however, that we are dealing with specific details and not, or not only, with a general principle. The construction as Pullum and Huddleston describe it is 'found with a very narrow range of adjective meanings' (2002: 562): chiefly, as in the examples given, of size. It is further restricted to specific adjectives, in specific orders. *Tiny* combines with *little*; but less readily, at least, with *small*. Neither *a tíny small* BIRD, with a legato rhythm, nor *a small tiny house*, with either the same rhythm or that of *a quite tiny house*, would be likely. Nor does *small* combine readily with *little*; still less, for example, *minute* with *tiny*, or *small* with *diminutive*. *Great* combines with *big* as in *a great big hole*. But while that order is normal, one is less likely perhaps to say *a big great hole* or *some big great lorry*. Combine *great* with *huge* and the order is likely to be the opposite: *a huge great mountain*, rather than, preserving still the legato rhythm, *a great huge lorry*. Pullum and Huddleston also cite *enormous* plus *great*, as in *an enormous great house*. But with adjectives denoting large size the relation has again its limits. As *small* tends not to form such combinations, neither does *large*. One is less likely to say *a great large hole*; still less *a large big lorry*. There is doubtless scope for variation among speakers, and my own judgement is at times taxed. The relation is nevertheless between specific lexical units, in a construction which, whatever it may be, is in that respect distinguished from others.

Of the adjectives with which Huddleston and Pullum illustrate it, *great* and *little* both call for more comment. In many uses, as in *a great wine* or *The mountains were great*, the first more normally means 'pre-eminently good' or 'wonderful'. Examples are in *The Oxford English Dictionary* from the early nineteenth century onwards; and, as Huddleston and Pullum remark, it is no longer 'much used for expressing "largeness"'. 'One of the places', however, where it 'retains' this sense is as in *a great big hole*. The intonation would have to change for this to mean 'a big hole which it is wonderful to experience'. Delete *big* and it could again mean 'very large': thus *The entrance is blocked by a great* LORry. But its use would be affective whereas that of *big*, in *a big* LORry, would not be. The sense of 'large' might also be excluded if *great*, on its own, is prominent: compare, for example, *There was a truly* GREAT *hole in the road*.

The use of *little* is in turn affective, and can be linked to others whose development González-Díaz (2009) has compared to those of *old*. An example may be cited at random from the 1890s:

She lives in her precious little Aggie
(Henry James, *The Awkward Age*, ed. Edel 1967: 44)

where the phrase would now, at least, be read with the same legato intonation—*her précious little* AGgie—as, with the same number of syllables, *a tiny little insect*. Elsewhere in the novel, which is a masterly representation of conversation, James writes the hypocoristic *ickle*. The use of *tiny little* can also be compared to that of the echo-formation *teeny weeny*. Neither is an expression purely of small size.

6.11 In *a great big hole* the pattern of stress, as represented by Hill, can be different. He did not see it, however, as that 'of two adjectives' (1958: 185): not, as we might put it now, that of two independent modifiers. One possibility, which he briefly mooted, was to describe *great* as a modifying adverb: the phrase as a whole would therefore have the structure of *a very big bird*, as illustrated earlier in (20). One 'criterion', however, was that '*great* with tertiary stress seems limited to occasions when the following form is *big*'. In his light it seemed 'preferable' to call their combination a 'fixed adjectival phrase'.

If the noun phrase were analysed into constituents, this would have to be a unit that, as a whole, would modify the head noun. It could be headed, as an adjective phrase, by *big*, but its structure could differ from that of *very big* in that the dependent, *great*, would also be an adjective:

(21) $_{\text{NP}}$[a $_{\text{Nom}}$[$_{\text{AP}}$[$_{\text{A}}$[great] $_{\text{A}}$[big]] hole]]

In that way, *great* and *big* would form a unit. There is, as Jespersen might have said, a specially close connection between them. But the meaning of *great* is still not quite that of a 'subjunct', or a pure intensifier, such as *very* or *quite*. Compare now, for a fresh example, the use of *dirty* in *a dirty great lorry*. Its meaning, in this combination, is no longer 'not clean', and the phrase as a whole can again have a legato rhythm. Reverse the order, and *a big dirty lorry* will refer instead to a lorry that is literally dirty. Its rhythm will also change: thus in Hill's notation, if it remains continuous and not broken, *a bîg dîrty lórry*. *Dirty* can also be used, in the same affective or intensifying sense, with *great*: compare, with the meaning 'very large', *We have to cross a dirty great river*. But it is not used in this way with, for example, *large*; still less with adjectives of other semantic types. Compare *a dirty old house* or, if it might be said, *a dirty bad dinner*.

Delete *dirty*, and *big* in *a big lorry* will stand on its own. Delete *big*, and *dirty*, in *a dirty lorry*, has its usual meaning. On that evidence, the combination would be another headed by *big*. If *dirty* remains an adjective, the structure would again be as in (21).

Modifiers and submodifiers

6.12 Does *dirty*, however, remain an adjective? *Pretty*, for comparison, is an adjective in *a pretty house*; also, with a legato rhythm, in *a prétty little* HOUSE. It is a modifier of a noun, in the construction, for Huddleston and Pullum, of a nominal. In *a pretty lárge* HOUSE, with *large* relatively prominent, an adjective is modified by a word whose form is the same. It can be seen, however, as a different lexical unit, and the category it belongs to, traditionally as one kind of adverb, is that of, for example, *quite* in *quite large* or *dreadfully* in *dreadfully small*. Is *dirty* any different? As a modifier of a noun, as in *a dirty lorry*, it remains an adjective:

(22) $_{\text{NP}}$[a $_{\text{Nom}}$[$_{\text{A}}$[dirty] $_{\text{N}}$[lorry]]]

but the same form might in this view realize an adverb which can modify an adjective:

(23) $_{\text{NP}}$[a $_{\text{Nom}}$[$_{\text{AP}}$[$_{\text{Adv}}$[dirty] $_{\text{A}}$[big]] $_{\text{N}}$[lorry]]]

In Jespersen's terms, both *dirty* and *pretty* would have evolved in this view into 'subjuncts'.

In the transition from Old to Middle English (**4.2**), the inflections that distinguished adjectives from the words called adverbs were, as we have seen, lost. But a distinction in syntax persists, and in some cases, such as that of *fast*, we may posit conversion (**2.8**). This might be another such case, or conversion might be distinguished from a split into two separate lexical units. But differences like that between one '*pretty*' and another '*pretty*' have developed historically, and it is not surprising that where such a split may be suggested, the evidence, as with *dirty*, can pull either way.

One obvious criterion is that of lexical meaning. *Pretty* as an adjective has one meaning, from which its meaning as an adverb cannot be predicted. It is broadly that of an intensifier; but in, for example, *That was a* PRĚT*ty nice house, certainly*, with a fall-rise in my own speech, it can imply a qualification which *very*, as what we might call a pure intensifier, would not. That too does not follow from the uses of the adjective, literal or figurative. Another criterion might be that intensifiers, such as *very*, should not restrict the range of words that they intensify. *Pretty* as an adverb 'can occur freely', as Hill pointed out, before all units of certain general kinds (1958: 184). In a paper we will return to in a moment, Adamson (2000) cites in particular its use as in *a pretty ugly house*, where it modifies an adjective whose own meaning would entail 'not pretty'. In the light of these criteria, an adverbial *pretty* depends straightforwardly on an adjective that heads an adjective phrase. But *great big*, by the same criteria, might remain an adjective plus an adjective. The meaning of *great*, as we would argue, is the one it also has in, for example, *huge great*, and its use as a putative intensifier is limited to the tautological construction and the other adjectives that enter into it.

These criteria can, however, conflict. As *dirty* can combine with *big* or *great*, so *dead*, for example, can combine with *straight*, as in *a dead straight road*, or *easy*, as in *a dead easy solution*. It too has the meaning of an intensifier: the road is absolutely straight, the solution to a problem as easy as it can be. Delete the adjectives which follow and the meaning of *dead*, like that of *dirty*, is different. *A dead road* might be used, perhaps, of a road that is no longer used; *a dead solution* of a solution that has been abandoned or discredited. Yet *dead* too is restricted, though less narrowly, in the adjectives it can combine with. *A dead big lorry* or *a dead fast road* are not normal; nor would one say, unless it might be in word play, *a dead crooked road*. In *a dead live animal*, it might have again the meaning of 'not living', and would plausibly modify a combination of *live* with *animal*. Has *dead* in this light split into an adjective and an adverb, or is it still no more than an adjective?

A natural criterion is that if a unit is an adjective phrase, we might also expect it to be predicative. One can say, for example, *The house is pretty large*; so too *The road ahead is dead straight* or *The solution was actually dead easy*. The criterion by which these are phrases would be the one, in part, by which a word like *dead-drunk* (**6.8**) is a compound. Some forms might thus be adverbs but with a very limited range of uses. *Precious*, in *They had précious little* MO*ney*, has a meaning it does not have in, for example, *a precious diamond ring* or in James's *her precious little Aggie*. This meaning is unlikely with other adjectives; the crucial evidence, however, that it is an adverb would be that one can also say *The money they had left was precious* LITT*le*. Other intensifiers may, like *pretty*, be used very widely. *Bloody*, for example, would modify *good* in *a bloody good dinner*, *awful* in *that bloody awful lecture*, and so on. It could also be an expletive on its own, as in *a bloody dinner* or *some bloody driver*. But the crucial evidence is that one can also say, for example, *Dinner was bloody good*.

In Payne and Huddleston's system, the function of *pretty* in *a pretty úgly* HOUSE is one of 'submodification' (Huddleston and Pullum 2002: 447). Like Jespersen's 'subjunct', it is the modifier of a modifier. One would not say, however, *The lorry blocking the entrance is great big*, or *The river we have to cross is dirty great*. By this last criterion, therefore, *great* and *dirty* are not submodifiers. If the criterion is seen as necessary, they cannot form 'adjective phrases', whether as adverbs, as in (23), or adjectives, as in (21); and for Huddleston and Pullum their function would remain that of *tiny*, as they describe it, as a modifier alongside, for example, *little* ((19) in **6.9**).

6.13 Or is there, since criteria conflict, an indeterminacy? *Pretty* is one of a group of words identified by Adamson, in the paper already referred to, as having 'dual function', as both an adjective and an intensifier (2000: 54). In its intensifying use its function can be that of a submodifier, and represents, from an historical viewpoint, what for Adamson is the end-point of a process. But it is the end-point of a 'cline', along which other uses are to varying degrees intensifying and can be to varying degrees affective. If she is right, it is not surprising that a change in function should be less clear in some combinations than in others. In a phrase like *pretty ugly* the process is complete. We may add that *pretty* is no more affective than, for example, *quite* is in *quite ugly*. An intensifying use of, for example, *dirty* meets some of the criteria that *pretty* meets. Our problem is precisely that it does not meet all.

The starting-point of Adamson's analysis lies in the use of adjectives with an evaluative meaning. *Lovely*, which is her leading example, denotes beauty in, for example, *She has a lovely face*: in the typology of semantic types proposed by Dixon (2010 and earlier) it would, I take it, be an adjective of 'physical property'. This meaning of *lovely* has been normal since the later Middle Ages. But from the seventeenth century onwards (Adamson 2000: 48), an evaluative meaning is increasingly attested: compare, for example, *It was a lovely dinner*. The development of *great*, as we have seen, has been more complex. Its dominant sense, however, is now evaluative: *It was a great dinner* is no longer likely to mean that the dinner was very large. Other adjectives, such as *nice*, are now rarely other than evaluative. But with a change of meaning there can also come a change in how an adjective is placed in a sequence. In an example of mine which Adamson cites from Matthew Arnold:

Through the cool lovely country follow'd you
('Empedocles on Etna', 45)

lovely again means 'beautiful' and comes after *cool*. The adjectives will also be read with equal prominence: in Hill's notation (**6.8**), *the côol lôvely cóuntry*. But in *a lovely cold beer*, or *a lovely hot bath*, the sense of *lovely*, in Dixon's typology, is that of an adjective of 'value'. As its semantic type has changed, it has historically, as Adamson points out, moved 'leftwards'.

Is the syntax of an evaluative adjective always that of an independent modifier? If so, the structure of a *lovely hot bath* could again fit Huddleston and Pullum's template:

(24) $_{\text{NP}}$[a $_{\text{Nom}}$[lovely $_{\text{Nom}}$[hot bath]]]

The meaning, however, is not simply that the bath is hot and, in addition, it is lovely. It is lovely precisely in that it is hot. As Dixon argued, in a paper Adamson refers to, an adjective of value can have the role of 'qualifying' not a head noun, but an adjective that follows it (1977 [1982: 25]). He did not address the issue of layering, and it might seem tempting to say that, as implied in (24), the evaluative relation is of *lovely* to the whole of *hot bath*. Compare, however, *a nice warm new hat*. The hat could be nice in that it is warm; that it is new might be incidental. The relation is between the adjectives, not of *nice* to the whole of a nominal in which *warm* is included.

It does not follow that *nice* plus *warm*, or *lovely* plus *hot*, has to be a syntactic unit. But the relation between the adjectives is, in part, like that of an intensifier to an adjective in, for example, *a very hot bath*. Between these relations, as poles, lies the cline as Adamson identifies it. At its starting-point, there is already an asymmetry. If either adjective were subordinate, it would be the adjective of value that 'qualifies', as Dixon put it, the one that follows, not the opposite. In such a use it can easily be thought of as intensifying: *a lovely large garden*, for example, would be said of a garden pleasingly, and thus especially, large. The meaning of *lovely* may thus be described, with Adamson (2000: 54), as that of '*very* plus approval'. Such words are seen as undergoing 'varying degrees of semantic bleaching'; and at a later stage of their history, or of the conceptual shift that is taken to underlie it, the category of an intensifier can change, as Adamson implies, to that of an adverb.

6.14 Adamson's concern is with the process she describes, whose end-point is a unit headed by its second member. She does not discuss examples of 'intensificatory tautology', whose origin does not involve value adjectives. Nor does she discuss the intonation of phrases, whose role, if any, in the historical change of modifiers to submodifiers cannot be recovered. If there is a problem, however, of indeterminacy it is one that arises in general wherever, in the schema repeated from **5.9**:

(25) [Dependent [Dependent Head]]

a dependent at a higher level is related to a dependent at a lower level. If we are to believe that there is layering, the process, for example, by which *very* has become a submodifier has involved a drastic reconstruction in which not only has its category changed, but the construction has flipped from one in which it was a modifier at a higher level:

(26) $_{\text{Nom}}$[$_{\text{A}}$[very] $_{\text{Nom}}$[ ]]

to one in which its role is fundamentally different:

(27) $_{\text{Nom}}$[$_{\text{AP}}$[$_{\text{Adv}}$[very] $_{\text{A}}$[ ]] $_{\text{N}}$[ ]]

Could it be plausible that, with other units, there should not be intermediate structures?

Beyond this there is still, of course, the wider question we have yet to address, as to whether layering, as assumed in (26), is itself justified.

7

Linear and layered dependency

7.1 Functions and hierarchies. 7.2 The principle of binarity.

Is there evidence for layering? *7.3 Arguments from the ordering of dependents. 7.4 From 'anaphora'. 7.5 From coordination. 7.6 Constituents as units of meaning. 7.7 Compositionality.*

Linking within sequences *7.8 Minimal and maximal constituency. 7.9 As competing explanations. 7.10 Adjectives used together. 7.11 Modifiers linked in meaning. 7.12 Restrictions involving determiners.*

Links to a head *7.13 Distinguished from compounds. 7.14 Arguments from 'idioms'.*

7.1 The alternative to a layered analysis of noun phrases is one in which all elements other than the head noun depend equally on it. In, for example, *all these huge ugly lorries outside* five other units would depend on *lorries*. As the phrase would be described, for example, by Quirk and his colleagues, *all* and *these* have a determining function (5.6); *huge* and *ugly* are premodifiers; *outside* is a postmodifier. The sequence would in that way be divided into four 'constituent parts' (1985: 1238–9), which are labelled and ordered as follows:

(1) Determinative + Premodification + Head + Postmodification

These are 'parts', however, defined by the functions of their members. They do not imply a hierarchy in which *huge ugly*, for example, is a syntactic unit; or is assigned to a class of what are called 'premodifications'; or either does or does not combine directly, in a larger syntactic unit, with *lorries.*

Payne and Huddleston distinguish a similar but more elaborate sequence (Huddleston and Pullum 2002: 452). *All*, in the same example, is a 'pre-head external modifier' ('external' as for *both* in 5.7) and as such comes before *these* as a determiner. *Huge* and *ugly* are each 'pre-head internal modifiers', and their place is further distinguished (5.7 again) as 'residual' rather than 'early'. 'Post-head' dependents are in turn divided into internal, such as *outside* in this example, and external. These too are divisions among functions, and elements form sequences accordingly. The divisions are married, however, to a layered structure of nominals and noun phrases, in which the post-head modifier could, for example, form a nominal with the head:

(2) $_{\text{Nom}}$[$_{\text{N}}$[lorries] outside]

and the pre-head modifiers would form two layers above that:

(3) $_{\text{Nom}}$[huge $_{\text{Nom}}$[ugly $_{\text{Nom}}$[$_{\text{N}}$[lorries] outside]]]

At each level in the hierarchy, a dependent combines with a head: *outside* with *lorries*; *ugly* with *lorries outside*; *huge* with *ugly lorries outside*. As constituents they are ordered; thus a sequence as a whole is further detailed in that way.

For most linguists, the division of phrases into constituents is uncontroversial. An obvious question, therefore, will be how far, if at all, a representation of functions can add insights that will go beyond what is implied by, or can be defined on the basis of, a hierarchy of categories. Many will cleave still to the view of Chomsky and of Postal in the 1960s (5.14), that functions are not independent. Once more, however, the question could be quite the opposite. Let us take for granted that noun phrases have a head, which in this example we identify as *lorries*. Let us take for granted that dependent units have specific functions in relation to it. They have them, too, in a specific order: *huge* and *ugly*, for example, precede *lorries* in their function as premodifiers. Given that relations within phrases can be distinguished in that way, what insight do we add by speaking of a hierarchy of categories as well?

7.2 The origin of constituency analysis has been explored by Percival and others (Percival 1976; see also Matthews 1993). It was developed by Bloomfield and his followers, and for Chomsky, from the beginning, was the received or customary mode of representing syntax (1957: 26). From then on few authorities, whatever their other differences, have called it into question. Any sentence will be analysed exhaustively into a hierarchy of smaller and smaller units; and at all points, or at least wherever possible, divisions must be binary. For Bloomfield, in the 1930s, a larger form could 'rarely' be divided into more than two constituents (1933: 169). But for many of his successors the principle of binarity is absolute. See, for one instance, a very lucid exposition, by Hornstein, Nunes, and Grohmann, of the 'minimalist' theory of phrase structure (2005: ch. 6).

Let us assume, for the sake of argument, that it is so. In the example that we have taken for illustration, therefore, a first division could be between *all* and everything that follows. This second constituent is for Payne and Huddleston a smaller noun phrase:

(4) $_{\text{NP}}$[all $_{\text{NP}}$[these huge ugly lorries outside]]

and, within it, nominals will form three layers. The largest will combine in their analysis with *these*:

(5) $_{\text{NP}}$[these $_{\text{Nom}}$[huge ugly lorries outside]]

but there are then three ways in which it might be subdivided. The smallest nominal could, as in (3), be *lorries outside* and the next layer would be formed by *ugly*:

(6) $_{\text{NP}}$[$_{\text{Nom}}$[huge $_{\text{Nom}}$[ugly $_{\text{Nom}}$[lorries outside]]]]

Alternatively, the smallest nominal could be *ugly lorries*; and, if so, the next layer might be formed by either *outside*:

(7) $_{\text{NP}}$[$_{\text{Nom}}$[huge $_{\text{Nom}}$[$_{\text{Nom}}$[ugly lorries] outside]]]

or by *huge*:

(8) $_{\text{NP}}$[$_{\text{Nom}}$[$_{\text{Nom}}$[huge $_{\text{Nom}}$[ugly lorries]] outside]]

Payne and Huddleston allow explicitly for 'structural ambiguities' like that between (6) and (7) (Huddleston and Pullum 2002: 446–7). All three analyses assume, however, that postmodifiers and premodifiers both form 'nominals'. We may therefore consider yet another possibility, that *outside* forms instead a noun phrase:

(9) $_{\text{NP}}$[$_{\text{NP}}$[these $_{\text{Nom}}$[huge $_{\text{Nom}}$[ugly lorries]]] outside]

with, as shown, a smaller noun phrase formed with the premodifiers only.

An analysis on the lines of (9) appears to have been the received solution, for some linguists at least, at one time. Compare Hockett's representation, in an equivalent diagram, of *all this fresh milk on the table* (1958: 188–9):

(10) [all [[this [fresh milk]] [on the table]]]

and also an analysis in which Bolinger talks of 'inner' and 'outer' noun phrases (1968: 197 [1975: 141]). For Payne and Huddleston, the postmodifier has instead the function of an 'internal post-head modifier': internal, that is, to a nominal. (9) would be valid only if it could be 'external'. But is there any real evidence that bears on these issues? We can agree that *huge*, *ugly*, and *outside* are modifiers. The reference of the phrase, in keeping with this, is to lorries that are perceived as huge; and are perceived as ugly; and are outside some place that can be identified. Since *outside* follows *lorries* it might or might not combine directly with it. But would the structure in (9) have implications for the meaning of the whole any different from those of any of the others? If (9) is excluded, there is no clear argument for rejecting any of (6), or (7), or (8). Thus the analysis forces us to see the phrase as structurally 'ambiguous'. But can we justify an 'ambiguity' in syntax that may explain no real ambiguity (Matthews 2007b: 124–5), in the way the phrase is used?

A possible answer is that phrases must have a constituency analysis and the binary principle must be preserved. Have we any reason, however, to accept that, other than the say-so of innumerable authorities, often parroting what other authorities have said before them, over the past half-century or more?

Is there evidence for layering?

7.3 A layered analysis can be traced, as we have seen, to Bloomfield (5.3). In *this fresh milk* a word that he classed as a limiting adjective both preceded *fresh*, as a descriptive adjective, and modified a head, *fresh milk*, in which *fresh* was included (Bloomfield 1933: 202). The 'form-class', moreover, of 'descriptive adjectives' was in turn 'divided into several types by features of order'. Speakers 'say', in his words, '*big black sheep* and never **black big sheep*, *kind old man* and never **old kind man*, and so on'. The asterisk was used here, maybe for the first time in the history of linguistics, to indicate not reconstructed words, but 'forms whose existence the writer is denying' (Bloomfield's note, 516). It is because, it seems, one cannot say **fresh this milk* that, in *this fresh milk*, the limiting adjective is taken to modify the whole of *fresh milk*. Neither would one say **black big sheep*. Therefore, in *big black sheep*, the first descriptive adjective, *big*, implicitly modifies the whole of *black sheep*.

What Bloomfield left implicit was spelled out by Hockett in the 1950s. 'Complex expressions', as he explained, 'are often built up by a series of attributive constructions, one nesting within the other'. Thus, in the phrase whose build-up was shown earlier in (9), *fresh milk* represents a construction nested within that of [*this* [*fresh milk*]]; this is nested within the construction of [[*this fresh milk*] *on the table*]; and that in turn, at a still higher level of constituency, is nested within the construction of [*all* [*this fresh milk on the table*]]. Not only, however, is there a hierarchy. 'The presence of certain attributive constructions in the nesting' specifically 'precludes the presence of certain others at a more inclusive level'. So, to paraphrase what Bloomfield had said in the 1930s, *fresh milk* can be nested within *this fresh milk*. But *this milk* cannot equally be nested within *fresh this milk*. Hockett did not use Bloomfield's asterisk, which was seized on instead by Chomsky and his followers. But similarly, as he put it, 'we can say' *little white house* 'but not *white little house*'. If that is right, the construction of *little house* cannot be nested, at one level of layering, within a construction in which the attribute, or modifier, could be *white*.

Thus Hockett (1958: 188–9), in a passage which many beginners in linguistics must have pored over as carefully as he, as a student two decades earlier, must have pored over his copy of Bloomfield. The argument as a whole has since become part of the way the subject is taught, and appears to hang together beautifully. If we examine it, however, without prejudice it is clear that the layering of constituents represents a premise more than a conclusion.

A demonstrative, we agree, will come before a descriptive adjective; an adjective of size before an adjective of colour; and so on for as many categories as we have grounds to distinguish. These are statements simply about relations between words. But any relation in syntax, as Bloomfield saw it, was between 'linguistic forms' which were part of a larger 'linguistic form'; therefore between units in a hierarchy. In *this fresh milk*, there are two kinds of relation. One is of subordination, and, in such a relation, *fresh* is subordinate to *milk*. This implies that there is a linguistic form, or unit, *fresh milk*. The other is that of order, and, as *fresh* comes before *milk* so, in another such relation, *this* comes before *fresh*. There cannot, however, be a linguistic form *this fresh*, as one unit in a hierarchy, if there is already a linguistic form *fresh milk*. The natural reconciliation is that *this* both comes before, and is subordinate to, the form *fresh milk* as a whole. In *a big black sheep*, there cannot be constructions which unite both *big* with *black* and *black* with *sheep*. A similar solution is to say that *black* and *sheep* are united by one construction, which forms a linguistic form *black sheep*. *Big* is then subordinate, in another construction, to the whole of that.

The terms 'construction' and 'linguistic form' are the ones that Bloomfield might himself have used, had he thought it necessary to spell out this reasoning. The argument takes for granted, however, that syntactic relations are between adjacent units in, as they might now be represented, a tree structure. This led directly to the principle of binarity, and it is by this straightjacket that so many students of syntax, seven decades later, seem to be constrained.

7.4 One man's straightjacket is, of course, another man's theory. We have to ask if there are arguments that independently support the structures such a theory leads to.

Payne and Huddleston offer two kinds of 'syntactic evidence' for the layering of modifiers, 'from coordination and anaphora' (Huddleston and Pullum 2002: 446–7). Their arguments are not entirely spelled out, but can be linked to a tradition, in textbooks especially, of devising 'tests' for constituents. The justification for any analysis lies in the end, as Huddleston and Pullum make clear in their introductory chapter, in 'the whole of the rest of the grammar' (2002: 21). The idea, however, is one that can be traced back to the 'methods' developed by Zellig Harris in the 1940s (1946, 1951): that by performing certain operations on the sentences and phrases before us, we can diagnose divisions and relations in ways that are likely to prove right. They are tests that take for granted either a stronger or a weaker version of the binary principle. If they are successful, however, it is tempting to claim that they confirm it.

Let us begin with the evidence from what is called 'anaphora'. In *some blue cotton blankets*, which Payne and Huddleston take for illustration, *blankets* is the head, in their analysis, of a constituent *cotton blankets*; this constituent is in turn the head of a constituent *blue cotton blankets*; and that in turn is a head in relation to *some*. Any of these three heads 'can be the antecedent', in their words, 'for various kinds of anaphoric expression'. Thus in a sentence *I prefer those blue cotton blankets to these*, with which they illustrate the point they are making, '*these* can be interpreted as "these blankets", "these cotton blankets", or "these blue cotton blankets"'. The argument implied is that the antecedent of an 'anaphoric expression' must be a constituent. Therefore each of *cotton blankets* and *blue cotton blankets*, as well as *blankets* itself, must be a constituent.

The question may at first appear pedantic; but what exactly is the relation they call 'anaphora'? The term is used traditionally where a pronoun, as a referring expression, 'refers back' to an antecedent which will also have the form, at least, of a referring expression. In, for example, *My sister said she was coming*, the pronoun *she* is a referring expression which is anaphoric, in one meaning that this sentence can have, to *my sister*. But there is no such relation, in Payne and Huddleston's example, between *these* and any of the 'antecedents' *blankets*, *cotton blankets*, or *blue cotton blankets*, which are themselves no more than parts of a referring expression. In a more traditional account, *these* is instead an expression that is incomplete. Its meaning, as it were, is 'these X'. What X is has, it is said traditionally, to be 'understood'. A better parallel, therefore, is not with anaphora, but with a similar understanding, in a similar context, of *these ones*. In many accounts, though *one* is not a pronoun, it is, more generally, a 'pro-form'. As such it 'stands for', in another traditional expression, some 'X', and in an example similar to Payne and Huddleston's, what X is might again be given by what, for them, is an antecedent nominal.

As a demonstrative can combine with *ones* so, in Payne and Huddleston's example, it can be seen as combining with a zero or null pro-form. This would be different only in that it is not overtly realized. But in either case the X a pro-form stands for, or the X to be understood in place of zero, can be understood from earlier in a sentence. The argument, therefore, is that an X can only be supplied by units that are constituents in a layered structure. But this imposes no constraint that cannot be explained more simply. If *these*, in Payne and Huddleston's example, is an incomplete referring expression, we can represent X by a sequence of words that will complete it. If it is to complete a noun phrase it must, first, include a head: thus, in the simplest case, *these blankets*. The head may also form part of a larger sequence, whose members will be continuous: thus *cotton* plus *blankets* in *these cotton blankets*, or *blue* plus *cotton* plus *blankets* in *these blue cotton blankets*. Now it is true that, if a phrase is layered as Payne and Huddleston propose, any sequence like this will be a constituent. But it does not need to be described as such. On the face of it, it is no more, precisely, than a sequence. A possible X consists of a head noun plus or minus any one unit, any two or more units, and so on, that precede or follow it.

7.5 Is the argument from coordination any more convincing? In phrases like *a big black sheep*, a determiner (D) again combines, in a layered analysis, with a nominal; within the latter a head (H) combines with one modifier to form a smaller nominal, which combines with another modifier. The structure of the whole can thus be shown schematically as follows:

(11) ${}_{\text{NP}}[\text{D}\ {}_{\text{Nom}}[\text{M}\ {}_{\text{Nom}}[\text{M H}]]]$

The evidence, therefore, that Payne and Huddleston are claiming is of constraints on sequences of words that can be coordinated, which they explain by divisions among sequences, as this schema proposes.

Their illustration is again of the constituents, as they see them, of *some blue cotton blankets*. At the lowest level, *blankets* could be coordinated with, for example, *sheets*:

(12) [some [blue [cotton [blankets and sheets]]]]

This is an instance of the coordination of head nouns. In *some blue cotton blankets and silk sheets*, the units coordinated could be nominals at the next higher level:

(13) [some [blue [[cotton blankets] and [silk sheets]]]]

The reference, accordingly, is to blankets and sheets that are both blue. In *some blue cotton blankets and white silk sheets*, the coordination would instead be of two larger nominals:

(14) [some [[blue [cotton blankets]] and [white [silk sheets]]]]

'We can have coordination', accordingly, 'at any of the three levels' (see again Huddleston and Pullum 2002: 446). Payne and Huddleston do not say that other sequences cannot be coordinated. But textbooks often rush in where grammarians who respect the evidence are more cautious. One 'test', accordingly, for constituency has been based on a constraint 'suggested', for example, by Radford and his colleagues (1999: 299): that coordination can be only of 'like constituents'. This entails that 'non-constituent strings cannot', in the term that they are using, 'be conjoined'.

If that, however, were the argument, it would be rather easy to knock down. Let us imagine, as an alternative, an analysis in which there are no nominals at all. The structure, therefore, of *a big black sheep* is one in which a noun phrase is formed by a sequence of four elements:

(15) ${}_{\text{NP}}[\text{D M M H}]$

distinguished only by their functions. This is supported, we would argue, by the evidence that in such examples any smaller sequence can be coordinated with another like it. Such a sequence might be of a modifier and a head:

(16) $_{NP}$[D M [M H] and [M H]]

as in the example whose layered analysis is as in (13), or of two modifiers and a head, as represented similarly in (14):

(17) $_{NP}$[D [M M H] and [M M H]]

But sequences coordinated could also consist of a determiner plus the first modifier:

(18) $_{NP}$[[D M] and [D M] M H]

Compare, for example, *some big and some small black sheep*, referring to sheep that are variously big and small but are all black. They could also consist of two successive modifiers:

(19) $_{NP}$[D [M M] and [M M] H]

as in *the white silk and blue cotton sheets*; or of a determiner plus both the modifiers:

(20) $_{NP}$[[D M M] and [D M M] H]

Compare *some small white and some enormous black sheep*.

Objections to the test as it is often peddled are not new (see, for example, Matthews 1981: 203). In the form presented, it will either point to multiple ambiguities (Matthews 2007b: 172–3) or it will simply take for granted the constituents it is designed to establish. It might be argued, however, that some patterns of coordination, as in (16) and (17), apply more generally, with fewer or no specific restrictions. The principle may therefore hold, not for coordination in general but for what Huddleston and Pullum see as 'basic coordination' (2002: chapter signed by Huddleston, Payne, and Peter Peterson, 1348). One definition of a basic coordination would be as a coordination of constituents. If noun phrases, therefore, have a layered structure, with constituents like those shown schematically (11), the coordination in, for example, *a blue sheet and white blanket* would be basic. But the pattern in *a black and a white blanket*, with a meaning complementary to that of *a black and white blanket*, would be non-basic.

That is not, however, the only definition possible. We have assumed, with Huddleston and his colleagues, that elements are distinguished by their functions: in the schema in (11), as in (15), one is a head and its dependents are a determiner and two modifiers. The question we have raised is whether there are arguments for adding an analysis into binary constituents, as again in (11), to it. If we ask if there is anything that distinguishes the patterns in (16) and (17) from those of (18), (19), and (20), the obvious answer is that the sequences of words coordinated include the unit whose function is as a head. They are the kinds of sequence that, again, can 'stand for' *one* or *ones*, or can be 'understood', as linguists have traditionally put it, as completing an incomplete referring expression. Have we any reason, in the present context either, to distinguish them as more than sequences, which naturally are continuous, and of which the 'ultimate head' of a noun phrase (Huddleston and Pullum 2002: 330) is the centre?

7.6 The ball, at this point, can perhaps be left on Huddleston and Pullum's side of the net. An appeal, however, to what is called 'syntactic evidence' implicitly allows for evidence that is not syntactic: in particular of meaning or, more strictly, of no more than meaning.

For Bloomfield a 'linguistic form' was a 'phonetic form which has a meaning'; the task of grammar, of which syntax is part, was that of telling 'what meanings are attached' to forms phonetically identified (1933: 138). Take, for example, a sentence *I bought one red blanket*. The whole is a linguistic form, and so would be any of the constituents that might be posited within it:

(21) [I [bought [one [red blanket]]]]

In this analysis *red blanket* has a meaning, which would be determined by the 'lexical meanings' of the noun and adjective and a 'grammatical meaning', in the sense in which this term was used by Bloomfield, of the construction that combines them. *One red blanket* has in turn a meaning which would follow in part from that assigned already to *red blanket*. The meaning of *bought one red blanket* would be determined by those of *bought*, of the construction of a verb with a direct object, and, as given already, *one red blanket*. It would in turn determine, in part, that of the sentence as a whole. A criterion, accordingly, for establishing layers of constituency is that each constituent should have a meaning that will be a distinct part of the meaning of a larger constituent.

For Bloomfield's treatment of meanings see my own commentary (Matthews 1993). But the idea was redeveloped, thirty years on, in what was in its day a famous article by Katz and Fodor (1963; comments in Matthews 2001: 133–4). 'Semantics' was by then conceived as separate from 'syntax'. But syntactic structures were projected onto representations of meaning, and a natural criterion was that they should correspond as simply as possible. If there is a semantic unit, for example, that we may represent as 'blankets which have the property of being red', then, all else remaining equal, there is a syntactic unit *red blankets*. Therefore a level of constituency, as in (21), is established by them.

How far can hierarchies be justified in that way? The strongest case is for constituents that combine straightforwardly with others, but have meanings that are not themselves determined by the meanings that their parts have elsewhere. The model implied by Bloomfield or by Katz and Fodor has in that light to be qualified. But this is because, among the constituents established, some have meanings that can only be assigned to them as wholes.

Take, among many examples of a familiar kind, *a juvenile green woodpecker*. The last word is a compound, which is modified by *juvenile* and *green*. The phrase, however, is most likely to refer not simply to a woodpecker that is green, but to a member of the species *Picus viridis*. It is, more precisely, a juvenile member; and if *juvenile* were the only modifier, a meaning 'woodpecker that is a juvenile woodpecker' would be formed straightforwardly. But the meaning '*Picus viridis*' is not sufficiently determined by the meanings *green* can have in other combinations. *Green woodpecker* therefore represents at least a unit of meaning. If it is not a larger compound, it would instead be a syntactic unit modified as a whole within a larger syntactic unit:

(22) [juvenile [green woodpecker]]

As described by Payne and Huddleston, both would be nominals.

In some cases we are dealing with what are traditionally 'idioms'. *Red herring* would be a syntactic unit, if again it is not classed as a compound, in *an ingenious red herring*, or *white elephant* in *another ridiculous white elephant*. In *a green woodpecker*, the noun has its normal meaning and *green* alone does not. The adjective has a role, however, which may be compared to those of *criminal* in *a criminal lawyer* or *marine* in *a marine biologist*. As a classifier (**4.6**), *green* too is a part of a larger unit whose denotation is of the whole. But in, for example, *a beautiful green bird*, both adjectives are epithets (in the sense again of **4.6**), each with its own denotation. If (22) is right, it does not follow that a level of layering as in:

(23) [beautiful [green bird]]

is right also.

7.7 The argument is similar for a classifier and a postmodifier. Thus for Burton-Roberts, whose discussion of layering is very helpful, *the nuclear scientist from Germany* has a structure in which *nuclear scientist* forms what for him too is a smaller nominal. Adding the postmodifier forms a larger nominal (Burton-Roberts 1997: 169):

(24) [[nuclear scientist] from Germany]

as would adding a premodifier such as *handsome*. It does not follow, however, that in *a handsome scientist from Germany* either

(25) [[handsome scientist] from Germany]

or:

(26) [handsome [scientist from Germany]]

has more justification than the other. 'In the case of some NPs', as Burton-Roberts himself remarks, it does not matter much which analysis we give' (1997: 168).

So why should we give either? Units like *green woodpecker* in (22), or *nuclear scientist* in (24), are justified on the grounds that their meanings are not 'compositional'. The term is drawn from another tradition, but reflects an insight similar to Bloomfield's, that the meanings of sequences of words will in general reflect the meanings of words individually. Let us return then to *a beautiful green bird.* If *green bird* were a unit, as shown in (23), its meaning would be said to reflect those of its constituents *green* and *big,* and the meaning of *beautiful green bird,* those of *green bird* as a whole and *beautiful.* Add the meanings that Bloomfield called 'grammatical', and one would be saying of the bird that it is green; and, furthermore, it is a green bird that is beautiful. Alternatively, if there is no unit *green bird,* the meaning of *beautiful green bird* would reflect the meanings of all three words directly. One would be saying of the bird that it is beautiful and that it is green. The properties of the bird referred to are no different: as in arithmetic, $x + (y + z)$ comes to the same as $x + y + z$. The principle, therefore, which appears to be assumed, if it is not directly that of binarity, is one of maximizing levels of compositionality. Wherever a meaning assignable to a whole can be analysed into a hierarchy of meanings, on the model of $x + (y + z)$ or $(x + y)$, it must be so analysed. The relation of semantics to syntax will again be simpler if syntactic units are established correspondingly.

The argument would rely, in short, less on the evidence than on prior philosophical assumptions. If such a principle, however, could be taken to justify the layering in [*a* [*beautiful* [*green bird*]]], could it also justify that of the adjectives in, for example, [*a* [*great* [*big hole*]]]? This is one case where Huddleston and Pullum, though it would be unfair to foist a similar philosophy on them, are explicit (2002: 561; **6.9**). Or are such examples a warning that meanings and syntactic units are not abstractions coupled one to the other as Bloomfield, for example, saw them?

Linking within sequences

7.8 If functions are distinguished independently, the argument changes. In one view, they are defined by structures in which constituents are assigned to categories; therefore there must be such structures. The alternative, however, is that the structure of certain kinds of unit, such as noun phrases, is in the simplest case of functions alone.

This is a form of analysis developed by, above all, Halliday (1985: section on the 'nominal group', 159–75). In *a young criminal lawyer,* the functions of *young* and *criminal* are again those of an epithet and a classifier (**4.6**). The function of *a,* which precedes them, is in his use of the term that of a 'deictic'; that of *lawyer,* which we are calling the head, is of a 'thing'. Add, for example, *particular* and in *a particular young criminal lawyer* its function would of 'a second' deictic element, or 'post-deictic'. It is worth noting that for Huddleston and Pullum *particular* was distinguished, with *main* and others, by a 'picking out' role, as a 'particularising attributive' (2002: 558; **5.11**). In, for example, *the same two trains,* the function of *same* is also that of a post-deictic, and is ordered before that of *two*, which is distinguished as a 'numerative'. In *the same two lovely long trains* they are followed by two epithets, of which the first is distinguished as 'attitudinal' and the second as 'experiential'. Successive functions are characterized by meaning, in Halliday's analysis, within what he calls, more generally, an 'experiential structure'; and within this structure sequences, as can be seen from these examples, are then 'largely fixed'.

Functions do not, however, define constituents. Halliday's analysis is cited by Feist, in his recent partitioning of premodifiers into zones (2012; **6.5**). But layering across zones is for Feist, as for many textbooks, a 'basic syntactic fact' (2012: 76). Halliday, in contrast, was proposing no more than a minimal bracketing of clauses and phrases. A noun phrase, or nominal group, is a syntactic unit as a whole, as is a larger unit in which it may have a function. But in Halliday's 'ranked constituency analysis' (1985: 22) a sequence is a constituent only if, as a whole, it does have such a function. A phrase may therefore include smaller phrases: *very old*, for example, could have as a whole the function of an epithet, within a larger phrase such as *a very old train*. But as an epithet it simply follows a deictic and is followed by the head or 'thing'. In *those two splendid old electric trains*, which Halliday himself gives as an illustration, there are no smaller phrases; the constituents are simply six words with six separate functions:

(27) [Deictic Numerative Epithet Epithet Classifier Thing]

and the whole has no other internal structure.

In a 'maximal bracketing', the same example would have the constituents proposed by Payne and Huddleston:

(28) [those [two [splendid [old [electric trains]]]]]

(compare Halliday 1985: 23) and, if that were our starting-point, functions would again be within binary units. That of the classifier would be relative to [*electric trains*], that of the second epithet to [*old* [*electric trains*]], and so on. The choice, as Halliday presented it, is between two models of explanation. If bracketing is maximized, as in (28), the concept of constituency is taken 'as a powerful explanatory device', and 'as much of the grammar as possible is explained by it'. If its use is minimal, as in his own analysis, the notion of constituency will 'take us only a limited way in the explanation of grammar, and no further' (1985: 24–5). Explanation through functions then takes over.

Payne and Huddleston's description of the noun phrase is more clearly of the first type. Constituency and the classification of constituents is maximized; but, since that alone is not sufficient, functions are also distinguished. It seems possible, however, that explanation of some things might be easier if constituency is minimized.

7.9 Let us return to the pattern of *her precious little Aggie* (**6.10**). The use of *little* may be affective, but we have no reason not to see it as a modifier separate from *precious*. In a layered structure a first adjective would therefore modify a constituent that included a second:

(29) [precious [little Aggie]]

Compare, however, a sentence from a story by Kipling:

> About two in the morning, . . . , a wise little, plain little, grey little head looked in through the open door.
>
> ('The Maltese Cat', ed. Gottlieb 1994: 496)

The example is literary, of course. But it exploits a relation between *little* and an adjective before it which is closer than between successive adjectives in general. Compare *her précious little* AGgie, with a legato rhythm distinguished as in **4.8**, with *her précious gólden* HAIR; or *a wise little head*, in which for Kipling *little* may already have been less prominent, with, if the order is reversed, *a little wise head*. Exactly how then are the modifiers and the head related? The adjectives themselves may be said to form an asyndetic coordination:

(30) [[wise little], [plain little], [grey little]

each of whose members is a modifier plus another modifier. Yet if structures such as (29) are right, the constituents in (30), when they are not coordinated, are parts of a larger structure in which *little* combines with the noun, and is layered separately, as in:

(31) [wise [little head]]

from the adjective before it.

If constituency is minimized, two modifiers and a head are basically a sequence: *wise* + *little* + *head*, like *big* + *black* + *sheep*. One link, however, in a sequence may be seen as closer than another. To say that *wise* has such a link to *little* is not to say that they are a constituent:

(32) [[wise little] head]

That would imply a function of *wise little* as a whole, like that of the adjective phrase in *a very wise head*. In *a great big black sheep* there is a different relation between *great* and *big*, in which they are closer than either is to *black*. It does not follow that *great* is a submodifier (**6.12**), any more than that it modifies the whole of *big black sheep*. As a sequence, however, *great big* could be coordinated, in a pattern where the other member could be a constituent: thus *a great big and completely black sheep*.

The point is one made over a century ago, as we have seen, by Jespersen. In his account, the dependents of a head noun were throughout related by coordination

(6.2); but if sequences are distinguished, successive modifiers such as *great* + *big* or *scorching* + *hot* may remain parts of a longer sequence while the first again, in Jespersen's words, 'nearly becomes a subjunct' (1924: 97). The 'flip' (6.14) from a modifier to a submodifier is less drastic than it appears if layering is maximized, but there can similarly be intermediaries. In the case of *wise* + *little* the first adjective would not be subordinate; but compare *poor* + *old* (6.7).

7.10 In what ways may a link develop? A straightforward noun phrase has a head, we are assuming, on which other units are equally dependent. In, for example, *three black sheep* the numeral, which might be distinguished by the function 'numerative', has the same relation to *sheep* as it would have in *three sheep*. Insert another modifier, and in *three black wild sheep*, where *wild* could be distinguished as a classifier, *black* has the same relation to *sheep* as in *black sheep*. The functions of dependents accounts in large part for their order: *three* before *black*; *wild*, with this function, after *black*. These are the kinds of relation we expect in any phrase of this type. Where there are complications, therefore, they arise where dependents are related to a head in ways not wholly independent, or where they are themselves related by something other than their order.

A minimal complication, if we may so call it, is where successive adjectives tend to be used together. In *an angry young man*, the first is related to the noun as in *an angry man*; the second as in *a young man*. Compare, however, *an irritable young man* or *a yóung ángry* MAN. The last phrase is perfectly possible, and might be used to refer to someone young who, on a specific occasion, was angry. Reverse the order, and the likely reference is to someone characterized in general by two properties, of being a young man and of being by disposition angry, that implicitly go together. In *a long hot summer*, the adjectives are related to *summer* as they would be in *a long summer* and *a hot summer*. Compare, for example, *a short scorching summer* or *a long cold winter*. But *a long hot summer* is used routinely to refer to summers in which high temperatures, and their persistence over a longer period, together make them disagreeable, liable to provoke rioting in cities, and so on.

It does not follow that the modifiers stand in a syntactic relation. It is worth remarking, however, that both phrases may have a legato intonation. Take for comparison a line by Browning:

These hot long ceremonies of our church
('Bishop Blougram's Apology', 10)

in which the reference is to ceremonies which are simply hot and simply long. We may have no evidence to suggest that a poet writing in the 1850s needed to avoid the order *long hot*. But for a modern reader *hot* plus *long* both makes clear that the modifiers are independent, and ensures an intonation where each has its own weight. The rhythm would thus be straightforwardly continuous (4.7): *these hót lóng*

CEremonies, as it would be in *a táll hándsome* PRIEST or, with the same pattern of syllables, *those húge brówn* DROmediaries. In Hill's notation in the 1950s, *hot* and *long* would both have secondary stress: *these hôt lông céremonies*, not *these hôt lòng céremonies* (Hill 1958; **6.8**).

In *a long hot summer* the second adjective will often be less prominent: in the notation for a legato rhythm (**4.8**), *a lóng hot* SUMmer. That is also true of, if we may switch for comparison to Hill's notation, *an ângry yòung mán*. It is impossible, as always, to be sure about past periods in the history of a language, but in *a certain bold young handsome priest*, in the line cited earlier from *The Ring and the Book*, the metrical ictus falls on *bold* and *han(d)-*. This allows at least a reading in which *young*, following *bold*, is less prominent. If what is possible now was already possible in the mid-nineteenth century, a line with *young* before *bold*:

There was a certain young bold handsome priest

could perhaps have been metrically less apt.

The adjectives in *an angry young man* can combine freely in other sequences. Compare *an intelligent young woman*, or *an angry middle-aged customer*. There may therefore be no closer link between them. But in other cases we can establish relations closer at least to a syntactic construction. These may involve words that in a broad view are determiners: thus *every* and an ordinal numeral (**5.12**). They can also involve adjectival modifiers: thus the tautological construction, as Huddleston and Pullum describe it, of *tiny* plus *little* (**6.9**).

7.11 Take, for a fresh example, the phrase *a perfect Elizabethan house*. The modifiers could at a pinch be independent: the house, as a house, is perfect and it happens to date from the late sixteenth century. A more likely meaning, however, is that it is 'perfectly' of that period. The style of architecture is characteristic, and the building has never been modernized in a way that has significantly changed it. There is no evidence that the adjectives form a single unit: one is less likely to say, for example, *The house is perfect Elizabethan*. But there is a relation between them partly like that of an adjective of value, in a phrase such as *a nice hot bath*, to one denoting a property that is valued. This was, for Adamson, a first point on a cline whose end-point is an adjective phrase, like *pretty ugly*, formed with an adverb (Adamson 2000; **6.13**).

Where modifiers stand in such relations, it is natural that what goes with what may also tend to be restricted. *Good*, for example, is an adjective of value in *a good hot bath* or *a good sharp shock*. But it may not perhaps be used as generally as some others. One could say, for example, *Give it a nice gentle push*; but is *a good gentle push* as likely? One could say *It was a lovely long film*, and mean, though it is not the only meaning possible, that the film was lovely in being long. But *a good long film* might be more likely to mean that it was good and, also, it was long; or that it was good in spite of its length. It is tempting to say that *good* is, in a term that Adamson uses, less 'bleached'. But the evidence may be no more than that its collocations, in the relevant role, are more restricted.

In other kinds of relation, as we have seen, the restrictions are clear at once. One reason to talk of a 'construction', linking the adjectives in *a tiny little bird*, is that neither combines as freely with, for example, *small* or *diminutive* (**6.10**; Huddleston and Pullum 2002: 561–2). *Dirty* goes with *great*, or with one of its senses, in *a dirty great lorry* (**6.11**); but not, with the same role, in *a dirty new car*. It is at this point that we can begin to talk of one term as subordinate in meaning to another. In *a perfect Elizabethan house*, a link between the adjectives would be one in which *Elizabethan* might be seen as 'head-like'. In, for example, *a lovely big lorry* we might argue that, if *lovely* is deleted, the relation of *big* to *lorry* is not affected. But if *big* is deleted, *lovely* is more likely, on its own, to have a sense of 'physically attractive'. The more a modifier can be seen as qualifying or intensifying one that follows, the more it tends, as Jespersen would have described it, to the status of a 'subjunct'. Accordingly the more its role begins to resemble, in Adamson's cline, that of the intensifier in *a very big lorry*. We have no reason to expect, however, that a modifier may not equally be 'head-like' in relation to one that follows it.

Connections with *old* are an obvious illustration. In *a silly old woman* the modifiers are no closer than in, for example, *an angry young man*. A determiner (D) is followed by a two modifiers (M) in a sequence that ends with the head (H):

(33) D M M H

and the meanings of the modifiers are independent. Note, though, the legato intonation in *a sílly old woman*. But in *a rotten old dinner*, the use of *old* is likely to be affective, in a way it would not be in *an old dinner*. That of *rotten* is as it would be in *a rotten dinner*: compare *some poor old cyclist* and *some poor cyclist*. The modifiers are connected more clearly to each other:

(34) D M-M H

in a pattern in which the second, now, is more plausibly subordinate.

7.12 Other connections could involve words that are usually, at least, determiners: thus the affective *any* plus *old* (again **6.7**). The more usual relations, however, of determiners can be at a distance, and potentially within a network. In *the same child*, for example, *same* could be regarded as a modifier; but with a link to a definite article or a demonstrative (**5.9**):

(35) D-M H

that can also be established when, as in *this very same child*, they are not adjacent. We may compare too, for a trickier example, the traditional inclusion of *the* in a superlative. It is easy to argue that they are not a unit: in phrases like, for example, *the three oldest children* a numeral comes between them. A superlative can also follow a possessive, as in *her best novel*; and in, for example, *She is the person happiest with what is happening* it would head on its own what Huddleston and Pullum call a superlative phrase (2002: chapter signed by Huddleston, 1168–9). Compare, however, the comparative. In *the older children*, the article can readily be deleted: *They look after older children* or *Older children are more interesting*. But a noun phrase *oldest children* would normally be excluded. A comparative also combines straightforwardly with *every*, as in *every older candidate*; with *all*, as in *all larger gardens*; and more widely. It is hard, however, to imagine circumstances in which one might say *I interviewed every oldest candidate*, or *All largest gardens are too much trouble*.

In *the oldest children*, the noun may not be modified by the traditional superlative *the oldest*:

(36) [[the oldest] children]

But the article and superlative are related, and would again be, at a distance, in *the three oldest children*.

Links to a head

7.13 There is no necessary link between successive modifiers, and in most phrases their relations to the noun they modify remain independent. But both determiners and modifiers are of their nature related to a head. A closer connection, or a more specific relation between them, would therefore be a closer relation of the same kind.

It could in principle involve a determiner. One old chestnut, of the place of *the* in the traditional superlative, may remind us of another, of its use with names of, for example, rivers. The problem again is that they cannot strictly form a unit, such as *the Danube*, where others intervene, as in *the upper Danube*. But Jespersen's example, of *young lady* in *a nice young lady*, is more interesting. He talked, as we have seen, of 'one idea, one compound primary' (1924; **6.3**). This might be taken to imply a single noun (Jespersen's '*young-lady*'), which *nice* would modify just as, in *a nice girl*, it would modify *girl*. But a compound was, as he conceived it, a semantic unit (1909–49, 6: chapter 8), and as in the example of *green woodpecker* (**7.6**), a compound in a narrower sense may be distinguished by other criteria from a larger unit whose meaning is not wholly determined by its parts. We may compare then, in particular, a legato intonation in *a níce young* LA*dy* with the different rhythm of, say, *a nice* TEA*lady*. This makes clearer what appears to have been Jespersen's point: that between a phrase in which a modifier depends freely on a head:

(37) D M H

and one that can historically develop from it, where the modifier has become part of a single lexical unit, there may be phrases with a structure:

(38) D M-H

that is neither straightforwardly one nor straightforwardly the other. In, for example, *a little old lady*, again with a legato rhythm *a líttle old* LA*dy*, it would then be tempting to see a structure:

(39) D M-M-H

with three words connected similarly.

7.14 An objection is that such words form, more loosely, 'idioms'; and, in analyses that maximize constituency, idioms form syntactic units. 'There seems to be a constraint', as one authority puts it, 'that only a string of words which form a unitary *constituent* can be an idiom' (Radford 1997: 322). Where a modifier might stand in a close relation to a head, on the grounds that the two together have a meaning that transcends those they have separately, it is easy to argue that, in this view, they form a syntactic unit. The structure of the phrase need not be represented as in (38), but is simply layered:

(40) [D [M H]]

by virtue of a semantic relation within it.

Assuming still that we must maximize constituency, it is tempting to slide from the constraint as Radford words it into a more general principle that, where there are idioms, other 'strings of words' whose syntax is similar, but are not idioms, must also be constituents. *Red herring* is an idiom in *an ingenious red herring*. Ergo it is a constituent. *Black insect* is not an idiom in *a big black insect*. But *black* modifies *insect* as, in abstraction, it might be argued, from relations of meaning, *herring* is modified by *red*. Ergo *black insect* is also a constituent.

This brings us back, however, to where we began. The crucial assumption is that constituency must be maximized, and it is not clear why it should be.

8

Adjectives in extended predicative positions

8.1 Enough has been said about attributive adjectives and their place in the structure of noun phrases. The problems that remain are mostly those of adjectives whose functions are in clauses. Finally however, in Chapter 10, we will return to phrases where they are 'postpositive'.

The predicative position is traditionally one where adjectives combine with *be*. The same adjectives, however, can combine with *seem* or *become*, and other verbs, like *sound* or *smell*, in senses that have developed over the Modern period (4.10). One central issue, as we noted at the beginning, is whether the adjective in, for example, *The children were happy* has a function any different from those in *They seem happy* or *The answer sounds obvious*. Does *were* take *happy* as a complement, as one tradition sees it? Or is it no more than a copula (1.6)?

Let us reserve this issue for another chapter. But whether *be* is like them or not like them, these other verbs do take a complement. It is with them specifically that the construction is possible, and the adjective in, for example, *They seem happy* cannot be deleted. But it also stands in some relation to the subject, which is confirmed by what for Chomsky in the 1950s (3.4) would have been selectional restrictions. Therefore it has often been called a 'subject complement'. Beyond that, however, we run into further controversy. If *happy* is 'predicative' in *They seem happy*, it is also predicative in, for example, *That made them happy*. In one account *them* is the object of *made* and the adjective is an 'object complement' which stands in a similar relation to it. This parallel was seized on and developed by Quirk and his colleagues (1985: 53–5), and is central, as we will see in a moment, to the analysis by Huddleston and Pullum (2002).

But another account is widespread. In the same example *happy* again stands in a relation to *them*. But take, for comparison, *That ensured that they were happy*. The verb here combines with a clause as a whole:

(1) [$_V$[ensured] [that they were happy]]

and *happy* is related, within the clause, to *they*. Can *happy* not be related to *them* within what will also be a clause:

(2) [$_V$[made] [them happy]]

whose structure is reduced to just these units? This is what is often called a 'small clause': see, among many treatments, a textbook edited by Fromkin (2000: 133).

These accounts appear to exist in parallel universes. Each has been familiar for some decades; yet scholars who accept one often do not mention the other, let alone say why they think it might be wrong. We will therefore have to reconstruct some arguments which are at best implicit.

Predicative complements

8.2 Let us begin, without prejudice, with the broader analysis as developed by Huddleston and Pullum (2002). Their chapter on the complements of verbs is signed by Huddleston, and echoes an earlier treatment (1984: 177–226), which explains in particular his choice of terminology. Briefly, however, the function of a verb is as a 'predicator' (compare Matthews 1981: 101), and its 'complementation' includes functions that are specifically taken by it. As *her* is a complement in *They saw us*, so *happy* is a complement, as Huddleston sees it, in *They are happy*. But they are complements of different kinds. The function of *us* is again that of an object. That of *happy*, which for Quirk and his colleagues is a subject complement, is 'predicative'.

The object in *They saw us* is, to be more precise, a direct object (O^d). As a predicator (P) the verb is also related to its subject (S), and the pattern of complementation can be represented as follows:

(3) S P O^d

(Huddleston and Pullum 2002: 219). Other objects are indirect (O^i), and in the pattern of, for example, *He gave me a biscuit*:

(4) S P O^i O^d

the verb takes both. Compare (3) and (4), however, with the patterns we are now concerned with. With *seem* or with this sense of *make* the adjective has a function that could also be that of a noun phrase: *He seems the leader*, or *They made him the leader.* Unlike, however, the object in (3), or the second object in (4), it cannot be a separate referring expression. For Huddleston and Pullum, it is instead related 'semantically', as an adjective can also be related, to a 'predicand' (2002: 217). In *He seems happy* or *He seems the leader*, the predicand will be the referent, whoever it may be, of *he*. In *They made him happy* or *They made him the leader*, it will similarly, in this analysis, be the referent of *him*.

Take *him* to be a direct object, and an 'object complement' is once more parallel to a 'subject complement'. The function of either is as a 'predicative complement' (PC), and in equivalent terminology such a function can be either 'subject-oriented' (PC^s) or 'object-oriented' (PC^o). In a third pattern of complementation:

(5) S P PC^s

a complement of, for example, *seem* is thus in a semantic relation to a subject. In a fourth pattern:

(6) S P O^d PC^o

a complement like *happy* in *That made him happy* is similarly in a semantic relation to an object.

The symmetry is certainly seductive. Is it right, however, to see relations such as these as no more than 'semantic'? They make a difference in syntax: thus, where the complement is a noun phrase, between *He seemed a genius* and *He hired a genius*; or between *That makes me your enemy* and *They brought me your enemy.* Each complement has a syntactic relation to the verb as predicator. Why is its other relation, to a subject or an object, not syntactic also?

8.3 A grammar is a grammar, and a distinction between 'syntax' and 'semantics', in or out of inverted commas, raises issues in the philosophy of linguistics that are not its primary concern. One reason, however, why Huddleston and Pullum see this as they do may lie in the constraints imposed by theories of phrase structure. *They saw us*, for comparison, will be assigned a structure in which *saw us* forms a smaller constituent:

(7) [they [saw us]]

and the functions of *saw* and *us*, as a predicator and an object, will be in relation to that. 'To specify the function of a constituent', as Huddleston and Pullum put it in their introductory chapter, 'is to say what its relation is to the construction', which is defined as a larger constituent, 'containing it' (2002: 25). The function of *they*, as the subject in the pattern of (7), is similarly in relation to the larger constituent *they saw us*. We may in addition go on to talk, perhaps derivatively, of a relation between functions. *Us*, for example, is the 'object of' the predicator, and *they* is the subject in relation to the traditional predicate. But these too are relations within a smaller and a larger 'construction', as shown in (7).

Take then, in this light, *They seem happy*. The sentence can be divided similarly:

(8) [they [seem happy]]

and *happy* has a function, as a complement, in relation both to *seem happy*, as one construction, or, we can say, to *seem*. The function of *they* is similarly, in one perspective, in relation to the whole of *seem happy*. There is no construction, however, which 'contains' just *they* and *happy*. Therefore the complement and the subject stand in a relation which cannot be syntactic, and must be semantic, as we might say, only.

The pattern in (6) is more complex. But in *That made them happy*:

(9) [that [made them happy]]

the second unit might in principle be divided into *made* and a smaller constituent *them happy*:

(10) [made [them happy]]

That would, in the competing analysis, be a small clause. It is only, however, if (10) is right that the functions of *happy* and *them* are in relation to the same construction. Alternatively, *made them* is divided from *happy*:

(11) [[made them] happy]

or *made*, *them*, and *happy* are three separate units. But if the same constraints apply the predicative complement can form no more than a 'semantic' relation with the object to which it is 'oriented'.

What is clear at least is that Huddleston's 'predicative complements' are independently both complements and predicative. As complements they are related to verbs as predicators; in that way they are like the objects in (3) and (4). But units other than complements may also be related to 'predicands'.

Take the adjective in, for example, *We arrived exhausted*. It has a predicand, still in the same sense, in the people referred to by *we*. It does not follow, however, that it is also a complement of *arrived*. If it were, we might distinguish further patterns of complementation, which would include the function of a locative, in *We will get to the top exhausted*; or of an unrelated object, in *I will finish the work completely worn out*. In *They found us exhausted*, the object in turn refers to a predicand. But it does not follow that the pattern of complementation must be as in (6); or that we must distinguish a further pattern in, for example, *They left us in the car asleep*.

Such units are among those for which most linguists now use the term 'adjunct'. They are 'predicatives', as in the title of Huddleston and Pullum's section 5.3, in that they are related to predicands (2002: 261). But they are not complements in relation to a predicator. Take then, for a trickier example, *They have painted the wall blue*. *Blue* could, in one analysis, be an object complement: a predicative complement, as Huddleston describes it, that is object-oriented. It could, in a competing analysis, be part of a clause in which it is related to a subject. Alternatively, it too could be an adjunct. Another aspect, therefore, of our problem is to make clear, if we can, how predicative adjuncts are to be distinguished.

8.4 The most obvious criterion is that adjuncts can be deleted. One can say *We arrived exhausted*, but also *We arrived*; *They found us exhausted*, but also *They found us*. The adjective in *They seem happy* cannot be deleted; therefore, as a unit whose function is obligatory, it is a complement. The role of *happy* is also obligatory, if this term is suitably qualified, in *That made them happy*. It is obligatory, that is, in that its omission leads, in Huddleston and Pullum's formulation, to 'an unsystematic change of meaning' (2002: 221). *Drive*, for comparison, will have one sense in *She drives me mad* and another in *She drives me*. *Make*, in turn, has a different meaning in *That made me*; *get* has different meanings in *They got it ready* and *They got it*. These changes are not 'systematic', but must be described for each verb individually.

But complements, as most authorities accept, can be optional. There are therefore other criteria (as discussed in Matthews 1981: 123–36), and it is to one of these that, in distinguishing complements in general, Huddleston particularly appeals.

A complement is, to repeat, part of a pattern of complementation, which is specific to a class of verbs (Huddleston and Pullum 2002: 219) or verbs in certain senses. By each member of this class it is, as Huddleston describes it, 'licensed'. With other verbs, or other senses of the same verbs, it is instead not licensed. Let us return then to *They have painted the wall blue*. The adjective can be deleted, and the meaning of *painted the wall*, with or without it, need be described no differently. In that light, *blue* could be an adjunct. *Painted*, however, cannot be straightforwardly replaced with, for example, *covered*. The reason, we might argue, is that *cover* does not license a predicative complement. It takes, as would traditionally be said, an object only. But *paint* can be said to take, or license, two alternative patterns of complementation: one with and one without a complement such as *blue*. Therefore, like the *happy* of *That made them happy*, whose function would be licensed by one sense of *make*, *blue* is a complement and not an adjunct.

To be licensed is 'the most important property', in Huddleston's words, 'of complements in clause structure'. In, for example, *She thought him unreliable* the function of the adjective is obligatory, and that could in itself establish that it is a complement. But the crucial argument, as he presents it, is that '*think* licenses O +

PC^{o}'. *Say*, in comparison, does not: there is no sentence *She said him unreliable* (see again Huddleston and Pullum 2002: 219). A moment's thought, however, makes clear that the argument is not so simple. In *She found him exhausted*, the adjective can be deleted and on these grounds *find* might take an 'O' but no 'PC^{o}'. Yet *found* too cannot be replaced by *said*. The reason might be that *say* does not license objects like *him*, which is a definite referring expression. But that would also be sufficient to exclude *She said him unreliable*.

The difficulty, evidently, is that since an adjunct is not subject to licensing, no verb in principle excludes one. Let us therefore look more closely at the adjective that can follow *They have painted the wall*. It could be, as we have seen, an adjective of colour. But compare, for example, *They painted the wall wet*. The meaning here is that the wall was painted when it was wet; and, with a similar meaning, one could also say *They covered it over wet*, *They buried everything in the garden wet*, and so on. If an adjective is an adjunct when it is added to *They found us*, it could also be an adjunct here. But in *They have painted the wall blue* the meaning, at least, is different. The wall had not been blue beforehand, and became blue as a result of the painting. Yet *blue*, like *wet*, is optional. If *blue* then is to be seen as 'licensed', it seems crucial to the argument that this difference in meaning should not be in meaning only. If it is also a difference in syntax, the function of *blue* can be distinguished as syntactically resultative. That function, we would argue, is part of a pattern of complementation licensed by *paint*. But in *They painted the wall wet* the function of *wet* would not be syntactically resultative. If an adjective is possible, with the semantic role that *wet* has, it need not be because, as a complement, it is licensed. It is simply that, as an adjunct, it is not excluded.

8.5 In either structure a 'predicative' is related to a 'predicand', and can be either obligatory or optional. In *This got me furious* (Huddleston and Pullum's example (26)), the adjective is a complement which is both resultative and obligatory. In *They have painted the wall blue*, it is resultative but optional; and a predicative which is optional could, in principle, be an adjunct. There are 'grounds' however, in Huddleston's view, 'for saying' that such a unit is also a complement. 'Resultatives', that is, 'are either obligatory . . . or else need to be licensed by the verb' (Huddleston and Pullum 202: 262). *Smooth*, for example, would be another optional complement, seen as licensed by *polish*, in *I polished the stone smooth*; *dead* licensed similarly, by *shoot*, in *They shot it dead*.

If a predicative is not resultative, it is in Huddleston and Pullum's term 'depictive'. *Exhausted* is thus depictive and optional in *They found us exhausted*; as is *raw*, in their set of examples, in *He ate the steak almost raw*. *Wet* too would be depictive in *They covered it wet*. In comparison, however, with an optional resultative, optional depictives are 'less restricted in their occurrence'. In the same cautious terms, then, there are 'grounds' for saying that they are adjuncts. It is in that light, as we can now see it, that they would not be 'licensed'.

Other 'depictives' are obligatory; they include, for example, the adjectives in *She thought him unreliable* or *I believed the lot of them dishonest.* In one perspective, therefore, this analysis establishes a perfect symmetry: whether resultative or depictive, a predicative in such a structure can be either optional or obligatory. But it can also be either a complement or an adjunct. If Huddleston is right it is an adjunct, or there are grounds for seeing it is an adjunct, only if, as set out in Table 8.1, it is both depictive and optional:

8.1 Object complements and adjuncts

	Obligatory	*Optional*
Resultative	Complement	Complement
Depictive	Complement	Adjunct

In *They ate it cold*, if we may take a fresh example, the adjective would in that case be an adjunct (A):

(12) they (S) ate (P) it (O^d) cold (A)

in no way licensed by *eat.* But a predicative which is optional is a complement, or there are grounds for seeing it as a complement, if it is resultative. Compare, for example, the construction of (12) with that of *They froze it solid.* Whatever is referred to became solid through being frozen; therefore *solid*, albeit optional, would be a complement:

(13) they (S) froze (P) it (O^d) solid (PC^o)

just as *ready* would be in, for example:

(14) they (S) got (P) her (O^d) ready (PC^o)

where it is resultative and obligatory.

It is fundamental, however, to this line of reasoning that (13), where the predicative is resultative, has a syntactic structure distinct from that of (12), where it is depictive. What then is the function of an obligatory depictive? It could stand, as a complement, in the same relation to the verb as either an obligatory or an optional resultative. If so, the structure of *She thought him unreliable* would be as in (13) and (14):

(15) she (S) thought (P) him (O^d) unreliable (PC^o)

Is it plausible, however, that depictives should be distinguished from resultatives only when, as in the structure of (12), they are optional?

8.6 One obvious suggestion, which we will come back to in a moment, is that *him* and *unreliable* form a 'small clause'. The pattern of complementation could thus be different from that of both (13) and (14), in that *think* would take a single complement where *freeze* or *get* takes two. But it would also be different from that of (12), since in (12) the predicative remains a unit that has no direct relation to the object.

In other sentences, as we have seen, a predicative would, if a complement, be 'subject-oriented'. In some cases, it would again be obligatory. But in *He died young*, which is another of Huddleston's own examples, the adjective is optional; and, since it is also depictive, it could instead be an adjunct:

(16) he (S) died (P) young (A)

In *The pond froze solid*, as in *They froze it solid*, it is resultative; and, though optional, it too could be a complement. As the pattern in (12) is to that of (13), so that of (16) would be to that of:

(17) the pond (S) froze (P) solid (PC^{s})

which would also be licensed by *freeze*. That structure would accordingly be the same as in, for example:

(18) the boss (S) got (P) angry (PC^{s})

where *angry* is resultative but obligatory.

Here too there remains a fourth case, where the predicative is obligatory but depictive. An adjunct, in the logic of this analysis, will always be depictive. In (16) it has a subject as its predicand, as too, to take another of Huddleston's examples, in *They served the coffee blindfold.* This is a 'construction', as he puts it, that 'is not possible with resultatives' (Huddleston and Pullum 2002: 262). It is not obvious, however, how the function of a complement, when depictive, could be seen as different from that of the resultatives in (17) and (18). Compare Huddleston's example:

(19) they (S) look (P) fantastic (PC^{s})

or, once more, *The children seem happy.*

Object complements or small clauses?

8.7 An object-oriented predicative complement (PC^{o}) has the function that for earlier writers, including Quirk and his colleagues, was that of an 'object complement'. It is the function of both *ready* in *They got her ready* and *unreliable* in *She thought him unreliable*, and is symmetrical in this analysis with that of a subject complement, or PC^{s}. In the 'small clause' analysis, both *ready* and *unreliable* stand instead in a syntactic relation to a subject, and a unit within which they are related combines as a whole, in either case, with *got* or *thought*. A small clause can thus be taken by verbs with different kinds of meaning. In terms borrowed from the textbook edited by Fromkin (2000: 133), the *get* of *They got her ready* would be a verb of 'causation'; the *think* of *She thought him unreliable* would be a verb of 'perception'.

In the heyday of deep structures (3.7), there was a solution which seemed to allow us to have our cake and eat it. At an underlying level, verbs of either kind were described as taking a subordinate sentence. In abstraction, therefore, from the tense and other details, one underlying structure can be represented as:

(20) [she think [he be unreliable]]

and another as:

(21) [she make [he be unhappy]]

It was assumed at the time that the meanings of sentences were 'determined' by their underlying syntax. Those determined by (20) and (21) would therefore be the same, except that individual words are different. Thus *think* and *make* have lexical meanings of, again, perception and causation.

At a level of 'surface' syntax, the *he* of (20) could remain the subject of a subordinate clause:

(22) [she [thought [that [he was unreliable]]]]

and, for some verbs, that would be the only possibility. An example cited earlier would be that of *ensure*, whose meaning might be lexically of causation, in *ensured that they were happy*. But (20) can also be realized, at the surface level, with the structure of *She thought him unreliable*. In this no verb corresponds to *be*, and the pronoun that would otherwise have been its subject is *him* and not *he*. On that ground at least it was an object, and in a surface structure that we may represent as follows:

(23) [she [thought him [unreliable]]

was 'raised' from the subordinate unit, by a syntactic process relating deep and surface structures, into a direct relation with *thought*.

Where an underlying (20) could be realized in either way, an underlying (21), with *make*, could be realized through raising only:

(24) [she [made him [unhappy]]]

Replace *be unhappy*, in the underlying structure, with, for example, *move house*:

(25) [she make [he move house]]

and a 'surface' object would be followed instead by a non-finite *to move house*:

(26) [she [made him [to move house]]]

and so on. An object that had been raised was then in other respects like any other. In particular, it could form the subject of a corresponding passive: *Everyone was made to move house*, or *Your friend is thought unreliable.*

8.8 The process of raising was a solution 'ex machina' developed in the 1960s, and defended at length in a famous book by Postal (1974). I hope I may refer, without too much presumption, to a brief comment on its detractors (Matthews 1982: 10–11). But the theory of deep and surface structures had become a zombie at best by the end of the 1970s. Therefore this account had no foundation, and an analysis into constituents could focus on one aspect of these constructions only. One obvious focus could be on the relation of predication represented in (20), (21), and so on. What was essential, therefore, was that in, for example:

(27) [she [made [him happy]]]

him was a subject. There was no reason why, among other things, a subject pronoun should be *him* and not *he*. It simply was, through what was called in the trade 'Exceptional Case Marking' (Fromkin, ed. 2000: glossary, 694–5). This may have appeared at the time, to linguists committed to a generative solution, to be the sole solution remaining.

The alternative would have been to focus on *him* as an object, in the structures represented in (23) or (24). This leads to the analysis already developed, in another tradition, by Quirk and his colleagues (1972: 37–8). But the problem then is how an object complement, in their terminology, relates to an object, if that relation is also one of syntax. Linguists supporting either analysis have difficulty with, and in effect discount, the insight central to the other.

They have nevertheless two things in common. First, they assume that we are dealing with a uniform construction: that a verb like *think* has the same pattern of complementation, to put it in Huddleston and Pullum's terms, as one like *make* or *get*. A distinction between a resultative and an obligatory depictive, or a verb of causation and a verb of perception, is in meaning only. That had also been taken for granted by advocates of raising. A second assumption is that the construction is determinately of whichever type has been proposed. We cannot say in any instance that a sentence has one structure if it is looked at in one light, but another if it is looked at differently. One way of looking has to be straightforwardly wrong.

Let us reflect, however, on the kinds of meaning that might be represented. That a certain man is, for example, honest is a possible state of affairs, which may or may not hold. If someone thinks or believes that it does, it may be expressed by a clause like *He is honest.* But that too is expressed, it can be argued, in *I believe him to be honest.* The meaning is not that the man himself is believed: that he is believed, for example, when he asserts of himself that he is honest. The same is true if *to be* is deleted. The semantic role of *him* is therefore like that of a subject; and in the 'small clause' analysis, which chimes neatly with this meaning, *him* is syntactically a subject. Compare, however, a sentence like *He drove her crazy.* This expresses something that has been done, to one person, by another person. So too does a simple sentence like, for example, *He annoyed her. Her* has a similar semantic role; and, if seen as a unit separate from *crazy*, is syntactically, in either case, an object. This chimes instead with an analysis in which the adjective is a second complement. Or is someone being crazy, as it might be objected, simply another state of affairs? The sentence might then be said to describe a process by which it has been brought about. Does *I judged him dishonest*, if we may take another example, express a judgement of an individual, that he is dishonest? Or is the judgement simply that a proposition, that this individual is dishonest, is true?

Constructions, it will be said at once, cannot be distinguished on the basis of meanings only. Our problem, however, is to evaluate alternative accounts of what, on either side, is taken to be a single structure. Other arguments, from the form of pronouns on the one hand or from the parallel with infinitives on the other, are not seen as decisive, and appeals to meaning may be all that we are left with. Neither of these shared assumptions may then be secure.

8.9 It is against this background of uncertainty that we can turn to an interesting and original analysis by Ferris. Where current grammars distinguish three main functions of adjectives in English, the attributive, predicative, and postpositive, Ferris divides their constructions into eight (1993: 36–7) One is that of, for example, *He considers the prosecution case hopeless*, where the position of *hopeless* is in his terms 'clausal'. But this is not the position of, for example, *clean* in *Ali rubbed the lamp clean*, which is instead 'adverbal'. These are examples where, in Huddleston's analysis (8.5 above), *clean* would be resultative, but *hopeless* an obligatory depictive. Ferris also distinguishes a third construction, as in, for example, *He brought his gun loaded. Loaded* we might see as an optional depictive, and for Ferris it is in the 'predicate qualifying construction'.

Ferris's analysis of constructions is at an 'intensional' level (1993: 4), at which 'property notions', many of which are realized by adjectives, are related in various ways to 'entity notions'. One basic relation is that of 'qualification': thus, for example, in the structure of *brought his gun* the object is the exponent of an 'entity notion' (E) which qualifies a 'property notion' (P), which is realized by the verb. This relation can be represented, in Ferris's notation, as follows:

(28) P ◀ E

In *brought his gun loaded*, (28) is qualified as a whole by a further property notion:

(29) [P ◀ E] ◀ P

whose exponent is an adjective in the 'predicate qualifying' position. If words may be supplied for clarity:

(30) [bring ◀ gun] ◀ loaded

its role can be seen as like that of, in another system of analysis, an adjunct.

In *The case is hopeless* a P, whose exponent is again the adjective, stands to an E in a different intensional relation, which Ferris calls 'assignment'. This is shown with an arrow:

(31) E ← P

and, as an E can qualify a P whose exponent is a verb, as in the structure of *He brought his gun*, so too, in the structure of *considered the case hopeless*, will the whole of (31):

(32) P ◀ [E ← P]

The structure, accordingly, of a 'small clause', as of the finite *that the case was hopeless*, is one in which, if words may again be supplied:

(33) consider ◀ [case ← hopeless]

the adjective stands, as in (30), in no direct relation to the verb; but, unlike in (30), in a direct relation to the noun.

The 'clausal' position of *hopeless*, in (33), is thus distinguished radically from the 'adverbal' position of *clean*, in *Ali rubbed the lamp clean*. The latter term implies precisely that the adjective, as the exponent of one P, is directly related to the verb, as the exponent of another. For Ferris this is a relation of 'qualification':

(34) P ◀ P

in which, again for clarity, we can supply the words as follows:

(35) rub ◀ clean

The structure in (34) is then qualified by an E:

(36) [P ◀ P] ◀ E

whose exponent is again a noun:

(37) [rub ◀ clean] ◀ lamp

Not only, therefore, is *clean* not predicated of *the lamp*, as *hopeless* is predicated of *the case* in (33). It is in more conventional terms a modifier in a complex verbal unit, *rubbed clean*, of which *the lamp* is the object.

8.10 This last analysis is the most original. In passing, however, Ferris compares an adjective in the adverbal position to the 'particle' in what are conventionally phrasal verbs (1993: 83–4). *Up*, for example, in *They drank it up* is similarly part, in one analysis, of a unit *drink up*, whose object would be *it*. One argument in favour of structures such as (37), though it would also support an analysis in the tradition of Quirk and his colleagues, is that, like the verb and an accompanying particle, a verb and adjective are often linked by quite specific restrictions.

Let us return, for illustration, to *He drove her crazy*. The verb is one of many which in this use will exclude a noun phrase: one would not say *He drove her a desperate woman*, as one can say, with *make*, *He made her the desperate woman she has become*. Neither would one say, for example, *It drove them helpless*, as one could say *It made them helpless*; or *She drove me busy*, like *She kept me busy*. With *set*, for example, one would say *I set the dogs loose* or *I have set things right*; but not *I set the dogs active* or *I have set things wrong*. The adjectives in these examples are resultative and, by Huddleston and Pullum's criterion (8.4) obligatory. But alongside verbs like these there are many others with which the construction is optional, 'usually', as Huddleston and Pullum point out, 'taking a small range' of adjectives . Among the 'small sample' they list (2002: 266), *shoot* would take *dead* in *I shot him dead*; but one would not normally say *She shot him wounded* or *I will just shoot it immobile. The lecture bored us stiff* is 'typical'; but not *It bored us asleep*. A few more, including our earlier examples *paint* and *freeze*, are listed by Quirk and his colleagues (1985: 1197–8); among these *polish*, for a fresh example, has a 'typical collocation' in *I polished the wood smooth*, but the collocation would not be normal in, for comparison, *I polished the wood shining*.

Links like these are natural if the adjective has a direct syntactic relation to the verb. This is so if it is either 'adverbal', as illustrated in (37), or has at least a separate function in a pattern of complementation. Similar restrictions would not be expected where an adjective is directly related, as in Ferris's 'clausal' position, to a noun. This is also true if it is part of a small clause; and indeed, in sentences such as *He considers the case hopeless*, or *I thought the builders honest*, the verb does not appear to limit the range of adjectives that would be possible.

Ferris does not himself address the issue in this way. But it is tempting to argue that, of the two received analyses, neither is justified in all cases. One may be in essence right for one class of verbs, with which the meaning will be resultative. But can the other not be right for another class of verbs, whose meanings are of perception?

8.11 How clear a line, though, can we draw between one and the other? The obvious alternative, in the light of what has been said already, is that we are dealing with a complex pattern of indeterminacy. There is neither a single construction, nor two or three distinct constructions. In some sentences, an adjective is linked more closely to the verb. In others, in particular, it is linked more closely to a noun or noun phrase of which it is predicated. But the criteria are no more than of degree.

At one extreme, for example, the order of a noun phrase and an adjective can easily be reversed: *They threw open the doors*; *We must set free the hostages*. This supports the parallel with phrasal verbs. But one is less likely to say *I drove crazy my neighbours* or *His lecture bored stiff the audience*; although by another criterion, as we have seen, the verb and adjective are linked closely. In *I made fast the* DOOR they form a unit whose meaning, as a whole, restricts the range of objects it will take. One is less likely to say *I made happy the* CHILd*ren*, where *make* and *happy* do not. Increase the length and complexity of the noun phrase, and it is well known that in many constructions it may come later: thus, in comparison, *He has driven crazy practically everyone he has ever worked with*. But this is a matter of degree, and can still be attested when, at another extreme, the adjective would be in Ferris's 'clausal' position. One would not say, for example, *She considered hopeless the case*; and that, so far as it goes, confirms that *hopeless* is not linked directly to *considered*. It might seem tempting to argue that one cannot invert the subject and predicate of a small clause, except that one could say, for example, *She has to my knowledge considered hopeless every case when it was first presented to her*.

Are other criteria more decisive? Ferris himself relies especially on evidence of how an adjective can be questioned. In *They ate it cold*, the position of *cold*, which in Huddleston's system is depictive and optional, is classed as 'predicate-qualifying'. Such adjectives can be questioned with *how*: thus *How did they eat it?*. Compare, for example, *They found us exhausted* with *How did they find us?*. The adjective is in the same position, as Ferris sees it, in *They found the prisoner guilty*; and indeed a corresponding question would be *How do you find the prisoner?* (1993: 63). In another view, however, it would be crucial that *guilty* is obligatory: the verb is not used in the same sense in *They found him*. In that respect it is like the *guilty* of *They thought him guilty*. But one would not ask *How do you think him?*, and in Ferris's account its position would be 'clausal'. Nor would, for example, *I believe him innocent* answer the question *How do you believe him?*.

When an adjective is in clausal position, the structure with which intensional relations are realized is represented as including, optionally, a form of *be*: compare *She considers the prosecution case to be hopeless*. A corresponding question would be as in *What do you believe him to be?* (Ferris 1993: 37, 69–70). But note that his example with *consider* is not a natural answer to *What do they consider the prosecution case to be?*. An optional *be* is not included in the representation of either of his other positions. Thus one would not say, with the kind of meaning that concerns us, *He brought his gun to be loaded* or *Ali rubbed the lamp to be clean*. Take, however, *I want the door open*. A corresponding question could be *How do you want the door?*, and by Ferris's criterion the position of *open* could be 'predicate qualifying'. But one could also say *I want the door to be open*. The function of the adjective could in principle be different. If it is 'clausal', however, why is a question *How do you want the door to be?* still an alternative?

When an adjective is 'adverbal' it forms a unit, in Ferris's analysis, with the verb and cannot be questioned separately. A question corresponding to *He drove her crazy* would be instead *What did they do to her?* (Ferris 1993: 82). Let us look, however, at the relations of adjectives to *make*. In *They made the coffee too strong* the function of *too strong* could, in one view, be an adjunct. The meaning would be simply that some coffee was too strong as certain people happened to have made it. The corresponding question would be *How do they make the coffee?* and in this case, if I have understood correctly, Ferris would see the adjective as 'predicate qualifying'. In other cases, an adjective with *make* is said to be 'adverbal': thus in one of Ferris's illustrations, *You should make the string longer* could answer the question *What should I do to the string?*. But what is the structure of, for example, *This will make him jealous*? A corresponding question could be *What will this* DO *to him?* or it could be, as for an adjective in 'clausal' position, *What will* THIS *make him?*. The meaning is in Huddleston's terms resultative, where the adjective in a sentence like *She thought him unreliable* is again depictive. But compare again the resultative in *He drove her crazy*, for which the question would not be *What did he drive her?*. Where resultatives are optional we can find a similar discrepancy. *They froze it solid* is not matched by *What did they freeze it?*. In Ferris's terms the adjective is 'adverbal'. But *Let's paint it blue* could be an answer to *What shall we paint the bathroom?*. Is this evidence that *blue* and other adjectives of colour would instead be 'clausal'?

There are explanations, no doubt, but they lead to further distinctions. Ferris's own are often subtle, and his criteria are clearly relevant. But while he may have shown successfully that there is no single uniform construction, it is not clear that there is a set of constructions that are neatly separate.

8.12 Indeterminate structures are, in general, nothing new. The term 'syntactic blend', which might be appropriate in this context, was coined by Bolinger (1961) in the early days of transformational grammar, in reaction to a famous analysis which multiplied ambiguities in the relation of adjectives to infinitives. The origins of blending in this instance, or of the problems in whatever way we see them, may be sought in the history of individual verbs; but may also reflect a more fundamental indeterminacy.

The pattern as such is early: examples with *make* are attested (*OED*, III.48) from the early Middle Ages. The chapters on syntax in *The Cambridge History of the English Language* (Hogg, ed. 1992–2001) do not therefore record innovations. It seems likely, however, that if specific uses were to be explored in detail, relations would be shown to have diversified as verbs with different patterns of complementation and different types of meaning were at different times attracted to it. That of *get*, for example, is attested from the late sixteenth century, and in an example from Spenser:

And knitting all his force got one hand free
(*Fairie Queene* 1.1.19)

the meaning is that of affecting, in some way, an entity referred to by *one hand.* But the entry in the *OED* notes especially a link of *get* in this construction with *ready*. Uses with restricted collocations may have developed on this model quite late in the Modern period: for *drive*, for example, the *OED* gives a citation from Shelley in 1813:

or religion
Drives his wife raving mad
(*Queen Mab* 5.113).

For *believe* an example is cited from 1513:

Who byleveth her chast

which may be an early instance where the adjective was depictive and obligatory. A similar use of *consider*, as distinguished from *consider . . . as . . .*, seems to have been established by the nineteenth century. But the pattern remains linked to a construction with *to be*, as in *I believe her to be chaste*, while the meaning of *get*, for example, in *I got her ready*, can be distinguished from the one it would have in *I got her to be ready.*

These are hints at best. Many years ago, however, Palmer pointed out that it is sometimes hard to 'distinguish semantically' between a statement about some individual and one about an event, for example, in which an individual is involved. The distinction is traditionally obvious: a verb, for example, may take an object referring to someone or something, or it may take a clause which realizes a subordinate predication. But 'the "obvious" distinction', as Palmer's paper suggested, 'is not always as obvious as it may seem' (1973: 21). Is, for example, *She found him ignorant* a statement of what one person discovers about another person, or of what one person discovers to be a state that another person is in?

Palmer's argument ranged much wider, and the indeterminacy may be basic to language generally. The problem, however, in this instance in particular is that linguists of different stripes have each assumed that the solution they are proposing must in every instance be exclusively right.

Subject complements

8.13 The construction of, for example, *He seems ignorant* is simpler. But subject complements, as they are called in one tradition, can in part be analysed similarly. In the days, for example, of raising, *ignorant* and *he* could be said to form a predication:

(38) [he be ignorant]

related as a whole, at an underlying level, to *seem*:

(39) [seem [he be ignorant]]

In a surface realization, as *him* in *She thought him unreliable* was raised to become the object of *thought* (8.7), so in either *he seems to be ignorant*:

(40) [he [seems [to be ignorant]]]

or with *to be* deleted, *he* was raised to supply a subject for *seem*. In Huddleston and Pullum's analysis, the same divisions can be made between obligatory and optional resultatives and obligatory and optional depictives, and there are once more 'grounds', as Huddleston argues, for seeing an optional depictive as an adjunct (8.5–6). The grounds indeed are stronger, in that it is significantly easier to find what would be an adjunct following what would be a subject complement. Compare, with the same system of abbreviations:

(41) They (S) proved (P) more useful (PC^s) alive (A)

or, in an example of Huddleston's, *They look even more fantastic naked.*

Finally, a verb and a resultative adjective can again be linked by very specific restrictions. None are imposed by *become*, which also combines freely, like *seem*, with noun phrases. But many verbs 'appear', in Huddleston's words, 'with such a limited range of PCs that the combinations are more or less fixed phrases or idioms'. One could say, for example, *The door flew open* or *We are growing old*; but hardly *Everything flew shut* or *We are growing unwell.* Where verbs are 'found with only one or two items', they are part of 'what are basically just fixed phrases' (Huddleston and Pullum 2002: 264). One example given is that of *break* plus *loose.* In Ferris's account, as a 'deverbal' adjective realizes a 'property notion' which qualifies another property notion, so does any adjective in what he calls a 'postverbal' position. The two together are 'assigned' to an entity notion:

(42) E ← [P ◀ P]

or, to supply words from his own illustration (1993: 36):

(43) crowd ← [remain ◀ angry]

8.14 In the second grammar by Quirk and his colleagues, the verbs that take a subject complement, and the structure itself, are 'copular' (1985: 54, 58–9; 'copular complementation', 1170). Where there is an object complement, they are 'complex transitive'. The second term is adopted by Huddleston and Pullum, in distinction from an 'ordinary' transitive construction, in which there is no predicative complement (2002: 217, 218). But verbs such as *seem*, and the construction they take, are correspondingly 'complex intransitive'. We have doubtless better things to do than argue about which terminology is more appropriate. In one view, however, the construction with *be*, as in *He is ignorant*, is implicitly as simple or 'ordinary' as that of, say, a transitive. In the same construction other verbs can naturally be substituted for it, in *He seems ignorant* or *He sounds ignorant*, just as in *He saw us*, for example, *saw* can be replaced with *heard* or *found*. In the other view, the construction is explicitly not 'ordinary': neither for *seem*, *sound*, and others; nor, since it too is a 'complex intransitive', for *be*.

The notion of 'complex transitivity' has its origin in the first grammar by Quirk and his colleagues, where it was applied to verbs of two types. One type took an object and an object complement; the other an object and a locative. Compare *put*, for example, in *They put the plate on the table* (1972: 343). Both were 'complex' as distinguished from transitives: either 'monotransitives', which take a single object, or 'ditransitives', which take two. In their definitive account, the term was extended to verbs which take an object plus an infinitive or participle. Compare *allow*, as in *They allowed me to take leave*, or *hear* in *I heard the rain splashing on the roof* (Quirk et al. 1985: 1203–8; earlier 1195). But the basic insight, if we may go back to their first treatment, is that the relation of an object complement to an object, in an example like *They proved him wrong*, is 'identical' (1972: 38) to that of a subject complement to a subject, as in *He was wrong*. 'Complex transitive complementation represents a fusion', as they put in another passage (1972: 850), of the monotransitive type of complementation and the type that they were later to call 'copular'.

The term 'complex intransitive' is originally mine, in a paper which responded in particular to this concept of a 'fusion' (Matthews 1980). In, for example, *The sky turned dark*, the adjective is a complement of, and thus stands in a syntactic relation to, *turned*. The relation is confirmed by restricted collocations. But *be* imposes no specific restrictions, and in one view, in *The sky was dark*, the adjective is directly predicated of the subject. If so, the term 'copular' could be limited to it, and the construction with a subject complement, of verbs other than *be*, would represent a fusion of the copular type of complementation, as so restricted, with the intransitive.

For Huddleston and Pullum, constructions such as the monotransitive are 'ordinary' in that complements, such as an object, are related only to the verb. But a predicative complement is also related semantically, in their analysis, to the unit that would refer to a predicand (**8.2**). Hence the constructions they stand in are complex, and where one is complex and transitive, the other is correspondingly complex and intransitive. Assume that in *The sky was dark*, the adjective is a complement of *was*. It is also semantically related to the subject; and, like *turn* or *seem* or *become*, *be* too is complex intransitive.

To be precise, however, the chapter by Huddleston also talks of a 'copular clause', as formed by *be* specifically. The term is 'based', as he explains, 'on the traditional idea of *be* as a copula', as 'a syntactic link relating' a predicative complement to a subject. 'In some cases', he continues, it 'has little semantic content but primarily serves the syntactic function of filling the verbal predicator position, and thus carrying the tense inflection' (Huddleston and Pullum 2002: 218). A separate term is useful, we are told, because 'distinguishable semantic and syntactic relations' are involved. But this way of talking provokes the thought, at least, that *be* might have a simpler construction, in which, unlike other verbs, it is not followed by a complement. In Ferris's analysis, an adjective would realize a property notion assigned directly to an entity notion:

(44) P ← P

as shown earlier in (31). It is then in 'ordinary predicative' position. Is it so clear, to put it in Huddleston and Pullum's terms, that the construction must be 'complex'?

9

States and occurrences

9.1 Many linguists who have addressed the syntax of predicative adjectives, in the sense of an adjective combining with a form of *be*, have proceeded as if their role was always that of *happy* in *The children are happy* or *tall* in *The chief is tall.* They are used in this way to ascribe what they denote to whoever or whatever is referred to by a subject, or to 'make a statement', in a formula with which we began, 'that something has a certain property'. The formula is Dixon's (1.1; 2010: 70), and is proposed as a criterion by which a class of adjectives may be distinguished, in a given language, from verbs, nouns, and so on. It is no more, however, than a criterion. It does not follow that every predicative adjective has this function, to describe a state, as we might also put it, in which people or things may be.

There have been sundry attempts to classify the 'situations', as Huddleston and Pullum call them, that a clause or sentence can be said to express (2002: chapter signed by Huddleston, 118). We have no reason to commit ourselves to their scheme rather than to any other, or to imagine that such typologies are of more than strictly practical interest. Compare, however, *They are stupid* with the progressive *They are being stupid.* The first sentence typically has a meaning like that of *They are stupid people*: a number of individuals are characterized, that is, by their stupidity. The role of the adjective meets Dixon's criterion, and the whole expresses a state, in Huddleston and Pullum's typology, that these individuals are in. Where the verb is progressive the adjective again denotes a property; but of what exactly? It could again be of the individuals *they* refers to; but, if so, it is one they are said to display on a specific occasion. There is no implication that they are not, in general, as intelligent as anyone else. It is a property evinced, moreover, by the way in which they are acting, or by a decision they have taken. Compare, with a verb and an adverb of manner, *They are behaving stupidly.* The situation that this last sentence would express is of a type that Huddleston and Pullum label an 'occurrence'. Can the one expressed by *They are being stupid* be classed any differently?

Many adjectives do not, or do not readily, form clauses with the progressive. One problem, therefore, which we will turn to in a moment, is to explain the circumstances in which, over the past two hundred years (4.11), its use has become normal. It is not only, however, when *be* is in the progressive that such a clause can express an occurrence, or a situation in which something happens, rather than a state of the world in which some property holds.

Compare, for example, *The bus was late.* The sense that *late* has here, in relation to what Huddleston and Pullum call a predicand, is different from the one that would be normal in *It was a late bus*, in relation to a noun as head of a noun phrase (1.3). The situation that this sentence expresses is instead one that might be expressed, with an intransitive verb and an accompanying adverb, by *The bus arrived late. Early* is used similarly in, for example, *The tulips are early.* The meaning is not that of *They are early tulips.* It is not that they are tulips which, as a variety, flower earlier in the spring than others. They might indeed be classed in horticultural catalogues as late tulips. The situation would instead be one in which the flowers, for example, have appeared significantly earlier than might have been expected: earlier perhaps than in a usual year, or earlier than the person who planted them intended.

We are talking of 'situations' that can be distinguished objectively. Against this there is always, of course, the time-honoured let-out: that whatever may be the reality a speaker is describing, they may perceive or 'think of' it, subjectively, in varying ways. The tulips blooming could be thought of by a speaker as an occurrence; and, if that is the situation as subjectively perceived, they might be expected to say, for example, *The tulips have come into flower a fortnight early.* But if someone says *The tulips are a fortnight early*, it is because, some linguists might be tempted to explain, the same reality is perceived differently, as a state like that expressed by *They are stupid* or *The hyacinths are pink.* If we ask for evidence for such perceptions, the answer would be, naturally, that it lies in the sentences themselves. If we eschew, however, this kind of circularity, it is reasonable to ask if what is said of the tulips is that they have a property of 'earliness'; or is it that they have behaved in a way described as 'being early'?

Which adjectives take the progressive?

9.2 First, however, we may concentrate on the progressive. Its extension to forms of *be* dates from the late Modern period, and it seems likely that its scope is still expanding. But, for the moment, it is usual with some adjectives only. Others besides *stupid* include *good* as in *The children are being good*; *conscientious* in *I was being* *especially conscientious*; or *serious* in *I am being serious*. Compare its use with a noun phrase in *You are being a bit of a fool*. With many other adjectives uses like these are at least less normal. One would not usually say, for example, *Their house is being large*, *The children were being red-haired*, or *I was being utterly amazed*. One problem, therefore, is to make clear the conditions under which the progressive is more normal; or what factors may, on the contrary, inhibit it.

An early paper by Givón took a use with the progressive as one of a set of 'test-frames' (1970: 831), by which adjectives could be divided into two main classes. *Stupid*, for example, fits it and by that criterion can be classed as 'active'. *Large* does not fit it and was classed as 'stative'. The difference lay simply in the way such adjectives are distributed, in this and other respects, in sentences. But Givón proposed a match between these classes and two forms of 'semantic structure'. An adjective such as *stupid*, that had one such structure, would fit this and other relevant test-frames, that define it as active. An adjective such as *large* was assigned a different semantic structure. Such adjectives would not fit this test-frame, and by that and other tests were stative.

Givón's analysis is more than forty years old, and of its period. In whichever way, however, the distinction is represented it depends in part on differences in lexical meaning. A natural temptation, therefore, is to claim that varying distributions, as revealed by test-frames, have a semantic explanation. It is because, that is, some adjectives have a certain type of lexical meaning that the progressive is, in a term now fashionable, 'licensed' by them.

To talk in this way is to risk circularity. To be conscientious, for example, or not conscientious can be seen as under someone's control. *Conscientious*, therefore, is semantically 'active'; and for that reason, we will argue, it is 'active' distributionally. *Good*, for example, will be said to have some senses in which it is semantically 'stative'; thus in *Dinner was very good* or *She is good at arithmetic*. Therefore, as we will see it, one does not say *Dinner was being very good*; nor, though the subject now refers to someone with a will of their own, *She is being good at arithmetic*. One can say, however, *The children were being very good*. Therefore, we will argue, *good* must have another sense in which, like *conscientious*, it is semantically 'active'. The progressive, we might propose, is possible under two conditions: first, that the subject refers to an individual capable of self-control; secondly, that the adjective has such an active meaning.

If *stupid* too is said to be semantically active, or to be active in one of its senses, the evidence is that one can say, for example, *They are being stupid*. There is no independent argument for it being so. A circular explanation can at times, however, be no worse than a misformulation of the truth. It is clearly relevant that in *The children were being good* the subject would refer to individuals perceived as able to control their actions or behaviour. It seems likely too that if one were to say this, it would be to make clear, as *The children were good* might not, that they were behaving well on a particular occasion. They would not be characterized as either good or not good generally.

9.3 Let us therefore begin, more carefully, with two points that both seem to be true. First, all adjectives that are used with the progressive are also used without it. As one can say *The children were being good* so one can say *The children were good*; as one can say *They are being stupid* or *They are being noisy* so one can say *They are stupid* or *They are noisy*; and so on. It is the opposite that, as with the progressive generally, does not hold.

The second point is that, where the progressive is used, it is with a narrower meaning. *The children were noisy* could express a situation, in Huddleston and Pullum's terms, in which children are making a row on a particular occasion. Compare, with the addition of an adverbial, *The children were noisy this morning.* With the meaning the sentence would have in that case the progressive, as in *The children were being noisy this morning*, is also normal. But *The children were noisy*, without the progressive, could also mean that some children were rowdy generally. Compare, with the adjective in attributive position, *They were noisy children.* This is a meaning the use of the progressive would not express.

The progressive is in both respects the 'marked' form in an opposition. The term in inverted commas carries with it a loose mass of philosophical baggage, even when it is defined as strictly as I am implying. We are concerned, however, only with the progressive as it is used with *be*, and with an adjective. What holds there need not hold for other clauses; still less are we assuming that the progressive has a basic meaning, or *Gesamtbedeutung* as conceived by Jakobson (1971: 73), to which all its uses can be reduced. On the strength, however, of its meaning with such adjectives as *noisy* and *stupid*, it seems possible that it is used in this construction not just where its meaning is appropriate, or under the conditions suggested earlier, but where, if it were not used, the meaning of a clause or sentence would be less explicit. With other adjectives, or with some senses of other adjectives, it would simply not be needed, since there is no meaning which it would distinguish.

It is possible, in large part, to reformulate this by distinguishing situations. In Huddleston and Pullum's typology, a sentence like *The children were noisy* will express a state as opposed to an occurrence (2002: 118). The situation is in that case 'static', and the adjective, as a word denoting a property, is, if I have understood their terminology correctly, 'stative'. *Noisy* would thus be lexically stative rather than, in a term apparently applied to situations and to words, 'dynamic'. A 'basically stative expression' can combine, however, with the progressive 'to yield a dynamic interpretation'. An example given is that of the progressive in *He is being tactful*, with the gloss, in brackets, 'agentive activity' (Huddleston and Pullum 2002: 167). Now an 'activity' is one type of situation classed, in their typology, as dynamic, and a sentence has a 'dynamic interpretation', if again I have understood correctly, when it is such a situation that it expresses. *Tactful*, therefore, is an adjective which can be used in the expression both of states and, with the progressive specifically, of situations that are dynamic. These are instead occurrences.

An adjective that does not combine with the progressive would instead be limited, in this view, in the situations it could be used to express. *He is being incorrigible* is a sentence Givón saw as excluded, and the adjective is distinguished in that way from, for example, *unreasonable* (1970: 833–4, (25) and (26)). Usage may well, of course, have changed since he was writing. In cases such as this, however, the distinction as he saw it was in underlying structures. *Incorrigible* was semantically, and in turn distributionally, 'stative'. Or was it that *incorrigible* had a meaning that precluded its use in sentences expressing 'dynamic' situations? *Unreasonable*, like *stupid*, could be used both in describing someone's character in general and in describing their attitude on given occasions. The latter meaning would be made explicit in, for example, *Your friends are being very unreasonable.* But *Your friends are incorrigible* may have seemed more clearly a statement of how people are by nature. If so no 'agentive', in the sense of Huddleston and Pullum's 'agentive activity', would be distinguished by *He is being incorrigible*, any more than by, for example, *He is being tall* or *The children were being heavy.*

To say, however, that one type of situation is not matched by another does not imply that this one type must be 'static'. Take the use of *early* with an animate subject, as in *She is early.* The sentence would express a situation that we might see as dynamic: someone being early is, objectively again, an occurrence. Crucially, however, it expresses that type of situation only. No different meaning, therefore, would be made clear if one were to say *She is being early*, as one might perhaps say, of what would be no more and no less a type of occurrence, *She is being on time.*

9.4 An active adjective, as Givón called it, is in this view one with a certain kind of meaning, with which alternative kinds of situation, as defined by Huddleston and Pullum, can be expressed. In Dixon's typology of lexical meanings, *stupid* or *tactful* are adjectives whose semantic type would be that of 'human propensity' (2010: 73). So might be, for example, the *good* of *good at arithmetic.* The progressive may thus be expected, as a marked alternative, when the propensity an adjective denotes can both characterize an individual, and be instanced or not instanced, potentially under their control, on one occasion or another. As Givón made clear, however, 'it is not enough to simply designate an adjective as stative or non-stative'. An adjective may be of the relevant semantic type in one meaning, or some meanings, only. *Big*, for example, is basically an adjective of, in Dixon's typology, 'dimension'. It is only in another sense that it will be used as in *He is being very big about it* (example from Givón 1970: 831–2). *Good* has another sense, as in *He is being very good today*, distinguished in *The New Shorter Oxford English Dictionary* (Brown, ed. 1993) as 'Esp. of a child'.

Dixon's typology of meanings is designed for other purposes (2010; Dixon and Aikhenvald, eds. 2004), which call for a high level of abstraction. At that level, the semantic type of *good* is one of 'value'. Where it is used with the progressive it would have instead what is traditionally a 'transferred' meaning, whose type is different. The entry for *good* in, for example, the *New Shorter OED* is divided into two main sections, both beginning with senses traced back to Old English. One early sense is as in *The cakes are good*: 'Having . . . the appropriate qualities; adequate, satisfactory, effective . . .'. Another is that of 'Morally excellent or commendable; virtuous'. To distinguish a 'value' from a 'human propensity' is not always easy. But another relevant use is cited in the *OED*, from 1548: *Let him resorte to me and I will be secrete and good to him*. Being good to someone is also what Huddleston and Pullum would call an 'agentive activity', and it is with such a transferred sense that the progressive, as in *I am being good to him*, was to become possible a few centuries later.

Nice too may be basically evaluative, but denotes a human propensity, displayed on a particular occasion, in *They are being nice to me*. So does *true* in, for example, *I am being true to my principles*. Its basic sense is distinguished, in Dixon's typology, as of 'qualification'. This is the use, to be precise, that we may take as basic in Modern English. But its earliest sense, defined in dictionaries as 'loyal' or 'steadfast', has survived with a complement in *to*. *Correct* is another adjective, in origin a participle, whose earliest sense, attested from the end of the Middle Ages, is of qualification. For an adjective of that semantic type the progressive would not be expected: one would not say, for example, *You are being correct*, to someone who has given the right answer to a question. But in later uses *correct* has come to denote a way in which a person behaves. Compare, in the *OED* from 1800: *He is . . . as a clergyman, extremely zealous and correct*. Its use there is characterizing; but in addition one could now say, for example, *As a clergyman he is simply being correct*.

It is important to note, moreover, that where adjectives have transferred senses, their positions will quite often be restricted. Both *true* and *nice*, for example, are in general both predicative and attributive. But the meaning of *a true man* is like that of *a real man*: the adjective has a sense more like that of an intensifier than the sense it has, in predicative position, in *true to my principles*. *He is a nice man* could be a straightforward judgement of value, as is *It was a nice dinner*. But that sense of *nice* is not the one it would have in *The man was just being nice*. The transferred use of *big*, as in *He was being big about it*, is first attested in the early to mid-twentieth century, when it conformed to a pattern of usage, by then well established, which was and is specifically predicative.

9.5 A meaning 'human propensity' can also, of course, be basic. That is true for *stupid*, as for *tactful*, *conscientious*, *wise*, *intelligent*, *sensible*, and many others. All these can be used as *stupid* is in *They are being stupid*, to express what can be classed as we will as either a form of behaviour or a state that is temporary. But there are other adjectives, such as *ashamed* or *angry* or *livid*, which denote states that are not characterizing. It might be wrong to exclude, for example, *I am being ashamed of what I have done* or *They were being livid with rage*: the marked form is there as a model for what would be said. If the progressive, however, is inhibited, it could be because, for adjectives such as these, the unmarked *I am ashamed* or *They were livid* are already explicit.

One group that may belong together is that of participial adjectives in *-ed*. It is not always easy for pigeon-holers to decide which category words of this form belong to. But if one were to say, for example, *They were being satisfied*, the construction is at least more obviously that of a participle. The situation expressed, again in Huddleston and Pullum's typology, would be dynamic, and would be expressed, as usually, with a verb. This may also have a bearing on the use of other adjectives in *-ed*, such as *ashamed* or *flabbergasted*, to which no verb corresponds. Many other adjectives are used normally, in the predicative position, to describe states that are temporary. Wherever this is so, if we are right, the marked form would not normally be needed to make the situation more explicit.

Take, for example, *busy*. In attributive position it is used of a state which will be typical of a person referred to. *She is a busy lawyer* could thus distinguish someone who is habitually busy from other people, including other lawyers, who have less work. If the distinction is from other lawyers, the adjective might be intonationally prominent: *She is a* BUSY *lawyer*. If not, *busy* could be a non-restrictive modifier: *She is a busy* LAW*yer*. In either case, however, the phrase would not refer to someone busy merely at the time of speaking. One could also say, for example, *It was a busy office*. What is described would be an office, or a set of people in it, typically full of work. Compare this, however, with *The office is busy*. This could be said of an office that is in general, over a wider period, very slack; but, at just that time, it did have plenty to do. *She is busy* would say nothing, likewise, about someone's life in general. The person referred to would be simply occupied, or described as occupied, at the moment of speaking.

The predicative use of *busy* may not always have been so restricted. In an example from around 1470, *He in wer was besy, wycht and wyse*, a man is characterized as busy in fighting, just as he was valiant (*wycht*) and wise. This use is cited in the first edition of the *OED*, with another from late Middle English, to illustrate a sense 'Devoted to business, diligent, active, industrious'. Of the two adjectives joined with it, *wise* is one of many still used in the same way. Others now of its type are *stupid* or *tactful*, as we have seen. But the sense of *busy* was marked as obsolete. While *He was wise* can still have a meaning like that of *He was a wise man*, the uses of *busy*, in *He was busy* and *He was a busy man*, are now subject to complementary restrictions.

In an analysis which appeals to situations, we might make the distinction implied in passing, between states, in Huddleston and Pullum's sense, that are temporary and those not temporary. A sentence such as *He was stupid* does not distinguish between them, while the marked *He was being stupid* does. Adjectives which make a distinction between states may be the majority, and may have been so in earlier stages of the language also. It is where there is no distinction, however, that the use of the progressive is inhibited. To be precise, if this analysis is right, it is not needed.

9.6 Take, for a final example, *Your friends were being helpful.* The situation expressed could be the same objectively as one expressed, without the progressive, by *Your friends were helpful.* Once more, therefore, it is easy to slide into vacuity. The difference, as we would be tempted to explain, is that in using the progressive a speaker focuses subjectively on the activity and on the intentions of the people referred to. The situation is accordingly perceived and presented as dynamic. Where there is no progressive, a speaker is focusing on no more than a property the people exhibit, temporary as it may be. The same situation would in that way be perceived as static.

As the analysis stands there is nothing to support this other than the analysis itself. One condition, however, under which *be* takes the progressive is that the subject should refer to an individual or individuals that can be in control of their behaviour. One could say, for example, *The government is being unreasonable*; or for that matter, where the verb is different, *The river is acting strangely.* But one is less likely to say *The river is being unnavigable.* The same holds if adjectives are replaced with noun phrases: compare *The government is being a nuisance* with *The river is being an obstacle.* But this condition is not sufficient; nor is it sufficient that an adjective should be one of human propensity: one is again less likely to say *She is being good at arithmetic.* What is crucial may instead be the principle of markedness: that, where the progressive is used, it makes explicit what might not be explicit otherwise.

In the case of *helpful* a clause without the progressive, such as *Your friends were helpful,* may already express what is temporary. Another nuance, however, can be identified. Where the progressive is not used, one could perhaps be talking of people who just happened to be helpful, through actions whose motives were different. Compare, for example, *The bastards who opposed our plans were actually rather helpful.* If one were to say, however, *Your friends were being helpful,* the implication is that the help was deliberate. This is at least an explanation about which we can argue. We will add nothing by hypostasizing situations in the minds of speakers.

Copular clauses

9.7 The term 'copular' is applied by Huddleston and Pullum, in a passage cited at the very end of the last chapter, to a clause which, as they distinguish it from others with a similar structure, 'has *be* as predicator' (2002: 218; **8.14**). But is it indeed a predicator, and do clauses like this have the same construction as *It sounds good*, *They seem worried*, *Everyone fell sick*, and so on?

Answers were deliberately left pending. In the light, however, of the use of *be* with the progressive, we can now make clear at least one difference. *Become*, for comparison, is used freely with the progressive. We can say, if we like, that the main verb is the head of a verb phrase and as such 'licenses' the progressive. Alternatively, the progressive heads a larger unit and as such licenses the main verb. The crucial point, however, is that a following adjective or other complement can vary independently. As one can say, for example, *They are becoming stupid*, one can also say *She is becoming good at arithmetic* or *The car is becoming expensive*. The progressive is in turn used freely with most verbs of this type, as with most verbs in general. Compare *The grass is getting ever longer*, *The weather is looking bad*, and so on. *Seem* is an exception: one would not normally say, for example, *They are seeming stupid*. But whatever the reason, it lies in the nature and history of the verb itself. The adjective or other complement has no bearing one way or the other.

Be, on the contrary, neither 'licenses' nor is 'licensed' by the progressive. For a verb such as *seem*, the crudest expedient would be to assign to it, in a lexicon, a syntactic feature [–Progressive]. To exclude, however, a sentence like *The weather is being bad*, the comparable expedient would be to assign such a feature to the adjective. *Bad* would thus have one sense, though it might be one of many, in which, on the one hand, it can be used of the weather and, on the other hand, it too is [–Progressive]. In Givón's analysis (**9.2**), this sense would have been classed more generally as 'stative'. If this were an appropriate form of analysis, the progressive in, for example, *They are being stupid* would be 'licensed' by a sense of *stupid* in which it is used with reference to, for example, people.

For Huddleston and Pullum, as for most other linguists, the verb in, for example, *They are getting stupid* heads a unit in which *stupid* depends on it. We may represent this, for the sake of argument, as part of a larger unit in which it combines with the progressive (PROGR):

(1) [PROGR [get stupid]]

In *They are being stupid*, the head would similarly, if we follow their analysis, be *be*:

(2) [PROGR [be stupid]]

But there is no specific relation between *be* and 'PROGR'; nor, in a larger structure of which (2) would be part, between *be* and any unit other than *stupid*. On what grounds, we might ask, is the adjective not a head in (2), as the verb is in (1)?

9.8 It does not follow that adjectives and verbs belong to the same category, though examples like those explored by Givón formed part of the contemporary argument (3.8) that they did. It does seem reasonable, however, to speak not simply of a 'copular clause' in which the role of *be* is like that of verbs generally; but of a 'copular construction' in which the relation of *be* to, for example, an adjective is different from that of *become* and others.

Which then are the clauses we are concerned with? If the term 'copular' could be, as it were, taken out of inverted commas, we could naturally look at all of them together and ask what kind of structure they have in common. The question has not, however, any easy answer. *Be*, in general, is a word with a wide range of uses. Not all, we can agree at once, are relevant. But whether they are or not depends on the criteria by which different uses, at greater or lesser levels of detail, are distinguished.

The word itself is identified by its inflections, and in two uses, one of which is plainly irrelevant, it is traditionally an auxiliary. In *are being stupid* the first *be*, as has been taken for granted already, is part of the realization of the progressive. It combines with the second *be* just as, in *are dancing*, it combines with *dance*; and in this light the two *be*'s are separate. In *are being eaten*, the *be* of the progressive is followed in turn by what is traditionally another auxiliary. This confirms again that the *be*'s are different; and if the second, with the *-en* of *eaten*, is part of the realization of a passive, it is also different from the *be* of *being stupid*. *Is being eaten* has in that view one syntactic structure; *is being stupid* has another; and it is only in the latter that *be* will be called a predicator. An adjective may naturally be participial, and when in the history of the language such an adjective becomes a separate lexical unit, the change carries with it a change in the role of *be* in relation to it.

The 'progressive *be*' and the 'passive *be*' are two of six uses, as Huddleston and Pullum distinguish them (2002: 113–14). Another is the 'copula *be*' but it is further distinguished from three others. One, called 'quasi-modal', is as in *You are not to tell anyone*. This use of *be* is 'modal', as they explain, in that it has some of the properties that define a modal auxiliary; 'quasi', however, in that it does not have all.

A second is a 'motional *be*', as it is described, in *I have been to Paris*. This 'occurs only' in the perfect: one would not say, for example, *I was to Paris*. Suppose then that someone is explaining why they have not been seen in their office for the past week. If they say *I have been in Paris*, the function of *in Paris* would be that of a locative in relation to, if I have understood correctly, the same *be* as in *I have been ill*. But if they say *I have been to Paris*, the *be* would in this account be different, and the structure of the sentence might perhaps be more like that of *I have gone to Paris*. Even if it were not, the function of *be* would be that of a predicator; but one whose complement would be different.

The final use, in their analysis, is of a 'lexical *be*' in, for example, *Why don't you be more tolerant?* This is 'found with *why* + *do*', and is 'virtually restricted to the negative': *Why do you be so intolerant?* is, in Huddleston's words, 'at best very marginal'. The same *be*, which is 'lexical' in that the *-n't* of the negative is supported by *do*, is distinguished in a construction with *if*, as in *If you don't be quick you'll lose.* Both examples are of a *be* whose complement, as it will then be, is an adjective.

Compare then *if you aren't quick*, or *Why be more tolerant?* By the same criterion, the *be* in these examples is not 'lexical' but must be the 'copula *be*' of *You are quick* or *They are tolerant*. So is, by implication, any *be* whose use has not already been distinguished. They include those with adjectives, as in *are stupid*, or with noun phrases, as in *are silly fools*. Alongside this use, which is ascriptive, Huddleston and Pullum include the 'specifying' use of *be*, as they describe it, in *The chief culprit was Kim* (2002: 266). A copula *be*, or at least a *be* not said to be different, would take what they call a locative complement in *I have been in Paris*. The complement is said to be 'syntactically distinct' (2002: 257) from a predicative complement; and it is worth remarking that in combination with *be* it more firmly excludes a progressive. One could say, for example, *I am staying in the garden* as one could say *I am staying sober*; but even if we reinforce the progressive with an adverb, there seems no reason why one should say *I am deliberately being in the garden*. The same is true of *be* plus what is presumably a temporal complement, as in *The wedding is next week*.

Where *be* does combine with the progressive, as in *He is being tactful*, the meaning may be described as of 'agentive activity' (**9.3**; Huddleston and Pullum 2002: 167). The meaning is again agentive, however, and again with an adjective, in both *Why be more tolerant?*, with a 'copula *be*', and *Why don't you be more tolerant*, where the *be* is distinguished as 'lexical'. The distinctions drawn are real, but they are within a range of uses in which partial similarities of one kind overlap with others, and no single criterion, by which clauses are 'copular' or not 'copular', may be decisive.

9.9 Neither, however, may such a criterion be needed. *Be* will at least be the 'copula *be*', or form part of a copular construction, in clauses such as *They are stupid*; and others may to varying degrees be similar to it. It is this kind of sentence whose nature in Indo-European languages, in particular, has provoked discussion over the centuries. They are languages in which verbs are identified easily by their inflections, and *be* in English, like *être* in French or Latin *esse*, is a verb by that criterion. Is it also, syntactically, a verb like any other; or is 'copular' more than simply a traditional label?

Arguments have been both philosophical and empirical, and there is room for disagreement as to which are which. If we look, though, at the evidence in Modern English, it is difficult not to feel that the construction would be quite straightforward, if only philosophers and theoretical linguists could be persuaded to leave it alone. The problems arise from two ulterior assumptions, neither of them always made explicit.

One is that the construction is not a construction of English only. We are talking instead about a cross-linguistic entity, 'the verb "to be"', whose function is the same, if not across all languages, then at least across the languages of Europe and others like them. It is therefore relevant that in, for example, Latin a copula was optional when the tense did not need be specified. It was not needed, that is, to form what is traditionally a predicate. Therefore, to be valid cross-linguistically, the construction cannot be one in which a verb is obligatory. *Be* happens to be so in English, and there is in consequence what would in this view be a merely superficial resemblance, between *be* and the verbs in general whose role is as predicators. It does not follow, however, that *be* is itself a predicator. As a copula, in the traditional sense, it could be expected to be obligatory in some languages, while optional in others.

A student of English grammar might make a robust reply to this. A second assumption, however, is much harder to shake off. It is obvious, if we return to English, that the *be* which combines with an adjective has most of the detailed properties that distinguish auxiliaries. Like the progressive *be* of, for example, *They aren't coming*, it forms a negative in *-n't*; an interrogative is derived by inversion; and so on. At the same time it is not syntactically an auxiliary. It combines directly with an adjective or other unit, as *seem* does in *She seems well* or *She seems my friend*, or *sit* in *I was sitting in the garden*. As a copula it can itself take an auxiliary, as in *I have been stupid*. One assumption, however, which has been common to many conceptions of grammar, is that words are either grammatical or lexical. The same word, or the same word historically, may be both: *have*, for example, is an auxiliary in *I've got it* but a main verb in *I'll have this one*. But *be* is unusual, on the face of it, in that it has properties, in the same use, that point either way. Many linguists have accordingly sought ways to mitigate what would be an anomaly, by representing *be* in ways that will conform, as far as possible, to one model or the other.

One solution is to classify it as, in the broadest sense, a 'marker'. An inflection, for example, can be said to mark a word as having a certain morphosyntactic feature; *be*, when it is an auxiliary, to mark the progressive or the passive. The *-ness* of *happiness* or the *-ity* of *stupidity* can be said to mark these words as nouns, and in Tesnière's analysis, which was referred to briefly in an earlier chapter, the *be* of *They were happy* would similarly mark the 'transfer' of the adjective, to a category in which its syntax is that of a verb (1959; 3.3). Alternatively, *be* marks a predicative relation, of units other than verbs to their subjects. A 'copula *be*' would thus be different from a 'passive *be*', as in *They were eaten*, only in that, in this last example, the passive is marked not by *be* alone, but by *be* in conjunction with the *-en* of *eaten*. It would be different from both the 'motional *be*', of *I have been to Paris*, and the 'lexical *be*', of *Why don't you be more tolerant?*, in that these would not be markers. Both, in their own right, would be predicators.

As a 'copula', in the traditional sense, forms a link by which an adjective is predicated of a subject, so in an another ancient analysis a finite verb reduces to a copula plus a participle. As James Harris, for example, put it, '*Riseth* means, IS *rising*; *Writeth*, IS *writing*' (1751: 90). All this is familiar and very clever. But another solution, obviously, is the one adopted by Quirk and his colleagues (1972, 1985), by Huddleston (1984), and Huddleston and Pullum (2002), and by most other English grammarians, of assimilating *be*, in this use, to the model of verbs such as *become* or *seem*.

It is therefore a lexical unit, which licenses a pattern of complementation, as Huddleston and Pullum put it, as verbs do generally. Nevertheless the 'copula *be*' shares with the 'progressive *be*' all the properties which in their account distinguish auxiliaries (2002: 108, 113). Is there any reason, therefore, why we should say more than is uncontroversial: that an adjective and certain other kinds of unit can combine with *be*; that *be* is inflected for tense and can combine with appropriate auxiliaries; that the whole can combine with a subject, agreeing as necessary; and that *be* has itself, in other respects, the same character as an auxiliary? The construction is simply in part like, and in part unlike, those of other clauses.

9.10 A clause of this kind, by which individuals or things are said to have a certain property, is copular in the most restricted definition. Others, however, resemble it. They include ones which express what in Huddleston and Pullum's system would be 'occurrences', such as *The tulips are early*. Others include any in which their 'lexical *be*', among others, is compatible with a form of *do*. These are uses that have developed in English over the Modern period, and an obvious problem is how far they have established structures that might be separate.

One crucial change is that of *be not*, in a negative imperative, to *don't be*. *Be not affrighted*, in the Authorized version of Mark 16.6, might thus be replaced, in a modern translation, by *Don't be afraid*. The effect has been to separate the imperative from the corresponding declarative, as in *They aren't afraid*, and at the same time to align it with the corresponding structure of *Don't take fright* or *Don't run away*, where *take* and *run* are lexical.

Another change (4.11) has led to the contrast in a positive imperative, between the *be* of, for example, *Be tactful!* and the *do be* of *Do be tactful!* This can be compared to that between, for example, *Come in!* and *Do come in!*, where *come* is lexical. It is possible, moreover, under conditions like those under which *be* normally combines with the progressive, that the subject refers to someone or something capable of controlling their actions, and that the adjective may or may not be used in reference to specific behaviour. To say *Do be tactful!* is likewise to enjoin a course of action. A similar restriction applies to the uses of *be* that Huddleston and Pullum themselves call 'lexical'. One would not say, for example, *Why doesn't the house be larger?* or *If you don't be thin you'll never wear those clothes again*. But a sentence such as *You are being very tolerant* is also normal, and expresses what they would describe as a dynamic situation, of 'agentive activity' (9.3).

It is easy to imagine an 'ideal' system (in the sense of 4.9) in which clauses formed with *be* would be used only of states. It might indeed be more like that of English in the early Modern period, before these and other uses of *do* developed. It is therefore natural to take for granted that, despite them, the construction is unchanged. *Do* is not used with *be* in declarative clauses, or in straightforward interrogatives. A copular clause in the restricted definition, where *do* would be excluded as with an auxiliary, can simply be extended to include its use in marginal circumstances.

9.11 Let us return, however, to the example of *The bus was late*. This too describes what happened, as opposed to the state distinguished by, for example, *The bus was green*. With one adjective, moreover, there is an ambiguity. *She was sick* could be said, on the one hand, of a person who had been ill: the situation, as for most clauses where *be* is not progressive, would be a state. On the other hand, it could be said of someone who has physically thrown up. The situation it expresses would be, in Huddleston and Pullum's typology, an achievement (2002: 118). The progressive too would then be normal: *She is being sick at this very moment*. *Do be* might also be more natural with this meaning than with the other: thus, in the construction with a 'lexical *be*', *Why don't you be sick somewhere else?*

A sense of *sick* as 'having an inclination to vomit' is dated in the *OED* from the early seventeenth century. In none of the citations in the first edition are we forced to see more than an inclination, and its sense as a lexical unit would be stative. From this, however, there has developed what Huddleston and Pullum represent as a separate unit, '$sick_d$', where the subscript is 'mnemonic for "dynamic"' (2002: 560). The context is that in this sense the adjective is 'never attributive'. But it is also exceptional, in their account, in being 'inherently dynamic in meaning'. The 'use' the subscript represents, as they describe it, is that 'of *sick* in *be sick* with the sense "vomit"'. Is it clear, however, that the meaning is of the adjective alone, as opposed to a combination of *be* plus the adjective? If one were to substitute a verb, as in *She threw up*, the unit it would replace, with a similar meaning, would be not '$sick_d$' but the whole of *was sick*.

One argument, perhaps, for assigning the meaning to the adjective alone is that, with this sense, it could head a postmodifier: thus, for example, *the children sick on the carpet*. Compare, however, a passive participle. In *The children were given ice cream*, a passive verb is realized, in most accounts, by *be* plus *given*. But the participle, on its own, can also form a postmodifier, in *the children given ice cream*. Either the adjective or the participle could be preceded in that position by *being*, and with a similar difference in meaning. *The children being given ice cream* would refer to children receiving ice cream at a particular time, including the time of speaking. *The children being sick on the carpet* could similarly refer to children that a speaker observes, at that moment, to be throwing up. Delete *being* and in either case the occurrence might be one repeated regularly or on several occasions. *The children sick on the carpet* could also refer, for example, to children involved in an incident a week previously, which is now over and done with.

If '*be sick*' is a semantic unit, it does not follow that its syntax must be different. We could describe it, for example, as an idiom whose meaning is in part distributed, on the model of analyses by Nunberg, Sag, and Wasow (1994), across its parts. Still less does it follow that *The bus was late*, where there is no ambiguity and the progressive is not needed, has a construction different from *The bus was green*. What does seem clear, however, is that Huddleston and Pullum's '$sick_d$', as an adjective used in describing a physical action, is the extreme case of a general tendency in late Modern English, for adjectives to be used in expressing, in their terms, occurrences.

9.12 Compare the postmodifier in *Anyone being tactful about this needs their head examined* with that of, for example, *people tactful in such cases*. The case seems parallel to that of the finite *is being tactful* and *is tactful*, and in all four uses the adjective itself can be described as lexically 'stative'. In *The children were sick on the carpet* it would already be '$sick_d$'. But compare again the sense of, for example, *big* in *They are being big about it*. This too is recent; it too can be listed as 'never attributive'; and although the situation would not be that of a physical event, it is at least one of 'agentive activity'. It could it be argued that either a 'big_d', or a combination '*be* plus *big*' has a meaning that is also inherently dynamic.

Take then, for a finer distinction, the use of *awkward* with the progressive, in *They are being awkward*. This could be said, for example, of people with whom one is engaged in a negotiation: compare, in similar uses, *They are being difficult* or *They are being sticky*. It too is recent. The first edition of the *OED* records a sense 'of persons', as 'dangerous to meddle with': the example cited was of *an awkward customer*. 'Not easy to deal with' was another: thus, in a citation from 1860, *an awkward face of rock*. But it was explicitly, as in this example, one of 'things'. As the use which we are concerned with may be later, and was perhaps linked from the beginning with that of the progressive, it may also be restricted to predication. One could say, for example, *They were awkward negotiations*, again in a use which is not of persons. But would that be the natural meaning in *They are awkward negotiators*? We have reached a point where judgements cannot always be trusted and where, if examples are attested, their interpretation may be uncertain. But a more likely sense, perhaps, is one that *awkward* has had since the eighteenth century, of 'not at one's ease, embarrassed'. Compare *He's an awkward speaker*, of someone without the gift of the gab; or, with the adjective in predicative position, *They are awkward at dinner parties*. The meaning, however, of *The other side are being very awkward* would not be that the people the speaker is dealing with lack competence or confidence. They might be very experienced and assured.

It does not follow, once more, that a dynamic construction with *be* should be distinguished from an 'ascriptive' construction, as we might call it, of *The chief is tall* or *The children are bright.* It may, however, be worth asking whether, in the light of developments since the late eighteenth century, such a distinction may be beginning to emerge.

10

The positions of modifiers

10.1 *Premodifiers and postmodifiers.*

Rules and exceptions 10.2 *Adjectives compared with participles.* 10.3 *Postmodifiers vs. single adjectives.* 10.4 *Variations in order.* 10.5 *Lexical exceptions.* 10.6 *Exceptions in specific contexts.*

Single adjectives as postmodifiers 10.7 *What calls for comment.* 10.8 *Postmodifiers as restrictive.* 10.9 *Multiple factors.* 10.10 *Is there a postpositive construction?* 10.11 *Historical influences.*

10.1 A final topic is that of premodifiers and postmodifiers. In *some happy children* a noun is modified by an adjective in the position grammars call 'attributive'. In *some children [kinder to animals]* it is modified by an adjective phrase, in brackets, in a position distinguished as 'postpositive'. A question raised at the beginning (**1.8**) was whether the difference is between constructions, or lies simply in the way a single construction is realized. A more immediate problem, though, is how far we can pin down which positions are possible, or which are normal, for which types of modifier.

We can easily be misled, at this point, if we restrict our attention to adjectives and adjective phrases. The position of *kinder to animals* is also that of, among others, a locative expression in *the house [on the corner]*, or the relative clause in *the woman [I met yesterday evening]*. One would not say *the on the corner house*, or *the I met yesterday woman*, any more than one would say *the kinder to animals children.* We cannot dismiss, at least, the possibility that the same rule applies to all three. While *glass*, for example, may not be an adjective in *a glass door* (**2.9–10**), it too is a premodifier. *A door glass*, as a phrase in which *glass* modifies *door*, is instead excluded; by the same rule, possibly, that would also exclude, at least as normal, a phrase such as *some children happy*.

For some units, as we have seen, orders vary: one can say, for example, either *a window downstairs* or *a downstairs window* (**2.11**). *Outside* is a postmodifier in, for example, *the people outside*; but it has senses in which it is a premodifier, as in *the outside door* or *an outside chance* (**2.12**). We have no reason, in such cases, to fight shy of the term 'rule'. Like the adjective phrase in *children kinder to animals*, or the prepositional phrase in *the house on the corner*, neither *downstairs* in *a window* *downstairs* nor *outside* in *the people outside* calls for any qualifying comment. This is the 'basic' position, following what we may call a 'basic rule', for modifiers of this type. It is when their position is contrary to the basic rule, as in *a downstairs window* or *the outside door*, that specific comments are needed: about, for example, the meaning of the modifier or the range of nouns with which this use is normal.

A 'basic rule' for single adjectives is evidently the opposite. From a historian's viewpoint, the positions both of *happy* in *some happy children* and of *downstairs* in *a downstairs window* illustrate the same broad tendency in English since the Middle Ages, for modifiers that at one time could come or come only after a noun to shift to a position before it. It is crucial, however, for any analysis of the language as it is now, that where single adjectives are postmodifiers they are exceptions to a rule applying to one type of unit, just as *downstairs*, where it is a premodifier, is an exception to the rule applying to another.

Rules and exceptions

10.2 'The basic rule' for adjectives, as Huddleston and Pullum formulate it, is one by which 'single adjectives . . . occur in attributive position'; so too do adjective phrases 'without their own post-head dependents'. Other adjective phrases, which by implication have dependents following the adjective, 'occur postpositively'. As a basic rule this is, however, qualified. 'Special rules' apply, contrary therefore to the basic rule, in phrases such as *someone tall*. 'For the rest', too, 'there are specific adjectives that can or must occur postpositively'. An example of one that can, though it can also be attributive, is *suitable* in *the only day suitable*. Among those that must are *afraid*, classed as an adjective which is 'never attributive', and *elect*, classed in addition as 'postpositive only' (Huddleston and Pullum 2002: chapter signed by Payne and Huddleston, 445).

The order of adjectives and nouns is normally the opposite in, for example, Italian: *una casa piccola* (literally 'a house small'), and so on. Such differences have therefore been a central topic for typologists of languages, in a tradition that includes among others the work of Greenberg (1963). Typologies are based, however, on the kind of difference that researchers see as interesting, which in this case has been one specific to this part of speech, between a single adjective before a noun, in some languages, and a single adjective after a noun in others. The modifier in, for example, *a house smaller than the rest* will have no bearing on this, and the second part of Payne and Huddleston's rule is one of the many complications that typologists will be tempted to discount. In English, however, the position of adjective phrases forms part of a much wider pattern, in which modifiers with a similar internal structure, whatever their category or the category of their head, are basically postpositive.

The closest parallel is between adjectives and participles. The modifier in, for example, *the people nice to us* is an adjective phrase formed by *kind* and a following complement:

(1) $_{AP}$[$_{A}$[nice] to us]

In, for example, *the people eating ice cream*, a postmodifier is formed similarly by a participle and its object. For Huddleston and Pullum, they combine to form a verb phrase:

(2) $_{VP}$[$_{V}$[eating] ice cream]

which is the only constituent of a non-finite clause (2002: 446, 1175). It is also a clause in the analysis of Quirk and his colleagues (1985: 1263), and its place as a postmodifier fits with that of clauses, finite or non-finite, generally. In *some very nice people*, the adjective has no 'post-head dependent' and is attributive. Neither does a present participle, in the same position relative to the noun, in *a rapidly changing population*, or a passive participle in *the long expected explanation*.

As most linguists see it, even single adjectives form adjective phrases. 'Strictly speaking', as Huddleston and Pullum put it, the premodifier would be a phrase in nominals such as *nice people* (2002: 529; 'nominal' as in **5.1**):

(3) $_{Nom}$[$_{AP}$[$_{A}$[nice]] people]

In *a changing population*, the participle would similarly head a verb phrase:

(4) $_{NP}$[a $_{Nom}$[$_{VP}$[$_{V}$[changing]] population]]

which in this position, however, would not be a clause. We could therefore say that participial phrases which are also clauses, such as *eating ice cream*, are excluded as premodifiers. But in another perspective the rule is the same as for a phrase whose head is an adjective. Just as one would not normally say *the nice to us people* or *a troublesome in other ways population*, where adjectives have following dependents, neither would one say *the eating ice-cream people* or *a changing in other ways population*.

10.3 'A postpositive adjective', as Quirk and his colleagues put it in a passage cited twice in earlier chapters, 'can usually be regarded as a reduced relative clause' (1985: 418; **1.9**). In McCawley's account (**3.6**) the same holds for postmodifiers generally. But this is an insight that can plainly be turned round the other way. *The people sitting in the garden*, if we may take a fresh example, can be described as a reduction of *the people who are sitting in the garden*. Regardless, therefore, of whether *sitting in the garden* is a clause, its position is postpositive. *People kind to everyone* would be reduced from *people who are kind to everyone*. Regardless therefore of its category, as adjectival and not participial, the position of *kind to everyone* is likewise postpositive.

The same 'basic rule', if so formulated, would apply to a preposition plus a complement: thus *the people* [*in the garden*]. As treated by Quirk and his colleagues, both non-finite clauses, such as *sitting in the garden*, and prepositional phrases are 'major' types of postmodifier (1985: 1263, 1274). The adjective phrase in, for example, *a mistake* [*typical of beginners*] is of a type said in comparison to be 'minor' (1985: 1294–5). But this is perhaps to lay too much weight on its category. If this were the rule, it would apply to any modifier, whether formed by an adjective, or by a participle, or with a preposition, which can be seen as reduced in this way. It would also apply to modifiers formed without a following dependent. These would include the *downstairs* of *the people downstairs*: it is worth recalling that for Huddleston and Pullum this is a preposition that does not take a complement (2.11). They would also include the participle in, for example, *the people leaving*. Finally, the same rule could apply in principle to a postmodifying adjective, in *the only day suitable* or *all the rivers navigable*. It is at this point, and at this point only, that the category of the modifier may be relevant.

Let us compare again the phrases headed by a participle. As *leaving* is a postmodifier in *the people leaving*, so are *smoking* in *the people smoking*, *speaking* in *the woman speaking*, *destroyed* in *the houses destroyed*, and so on. Like *downstairs* in *the people downstairs*, or *outside* in *a car outside*, they follow a rule and call for no specific comment. Single participles can also be attributive, like *changing* in (4). But such uses tend to be restricted. One is less likely to say *the leaving people* or for example, of the houses wrecked by some disaster, *The destroyed houses were all rather flimsy*. While *the population studied* or *the period investigated* are normal, *the studied people* or *the investigated period* would be less so. The boundary between a participle and a participial adjective is as fluid as they come; but *studied* can be described as an adjective in *a studied attitude*, as can *standing*, for example, in *a standing complaint*. Even where there is no case for conversion, the meaning of a verb may limit what is normal. *Smoking*, for example, forms a premodifier in *the still smoking ruins*; but *the still smoking people*, of people who will not give up tobacco, is less usual.

The basic rule would hold, and *changing* in (4) would represent what we might again call an exception. For a modifier, however, such as *suitable* or *navigable* a rule for a specific category intervenes. As *tall*, for example, is a premodifier in *a tall chief*, so by a basic rule for adjectives, established in English centuries ago, these are premodifiers in *the only suitable day* or in *all navigable rivers*. It is the use of such words as postmodifiers that then calls for comment: thus they are members of a class of adjectives which, as Payne and Huddleston put it, 'can ... occur postpositively'. As such they might indeed be seen as an exception. But it may be relevant that while they form an exception to a rule for single adjectives, or for adjectives without a following dependent, their use does conform in another respect to a rule that covers other postmodifiers.

10.4 What follows a rule and what is an 'exception' depends partly on our viewpoint. It is also obvious that while basic rules, in the sense implied by Huddleston and Pullum, can easily be formulated, they are indeed no more than basic.

A further complication is that adjective phrases can be split. They are phrases, again, in which an adjective is followed by a dependent *X*; and in the simplest case, as in the examples given so far, the whole follows a head noun:

(5) $_{\text{N}}$[ ] [$_{\text{A}}$[ ] X]

For most adjective phrases that have such a structure, (5) alone is possible. In some cases, however, units corresponding to the adjective and its dependent are divided by the head noun:

(6) $_{\text{A}}$[ ] $_{\text{N}}$[ ] X

Compare, for example, *a hard man to find*:

(7) $_{\text{A}}$[hard] $_{\text{N}}$[man] [to find]

If we were wedded to a layered analysis of noun phrases, we might be forced to say that *hard* and *to find* form separate nominals:

(8) $_{\text{Nom}}$[$_{\text{Nom}}$[$_{\text{A}}$[hard] $_{\text{N}}$[man]] [to find]]

while if the order were as in (5), there would be a single modifier:

(9) $_{\text{Nom}}$[$_{\text{N}}$[man] $_{\text{AP}}$[$_{\text{A}}$[hard] [to find]]]

following the rule for a postmodifier generally. The infinitive, however, is in either case a complement of *hard*, 'licensed' by adjectives of one class and excluded by others.

In some cases, moreover, the order varies between that of (6) and one in which the adjective and its dependent are both before the noun:

(10) $_{\text{A}}$[ ] X $_{\text{N}}$[ ]

Thus, for example, in *the sweetest imaginable present*, the superlative, in Huddleston and Pullum's analysis, has *imaginable* as its dependent (2002: 1169). Together, therefore, they would form an adjective phrase:

(11) $_{\text{Nom}}$[$_{\text{AP}}$[$_{\text{A}}$[sweetest] imaginable] $_{\text{N}}$[present]]

which would be excluded, however, from the position that the basic rule, as stated, would indicate. Compare too an example in which the superlative of *hard* takes an infinitive:

the very hardest to help people
(journalist on BBC news programme, 22 October 2008)

The speaker could have said *the very hardest people to help*, with the split order of (6). Delete *very*, and *the people hardest to help* is also possible, with the order in (5) that the rule, however formulated, might lead us to expect. Add *the*, and one could also write, though perhaps one is less likely to say, *the people the very hardest to help*.

For another case where all three alternatives seem possible, compare the order that would be normal for a comparative phrase, as in *a larger deficit than usual*, with *a deficit larger than usual*, which might perhaps be commoner in writing; but also *a larger than usual deficit*. Where orders vary, it can be hard, however, to judge what might be said. In an example from Fanny Burney:

secrets of a nature the most delicate
(*Evelina* 2, letter 20)

the postmodifier is a superlative in *the* but with no following dependent. What was normal, however, in the late eighteenth century may now seem foreign: typical, perhaps, of Agatha Christie's Poirot. *A most delicate nature* would be normal, as would be either *the most delicate possible nature* or *the most delicate nature possible*. But can the older usage be excluded? With the example of *hardest to help* we may compare the premodifier in *a hard to find first edition*, cited, though not attested, by McCawley (1998: 392). In transformational accounts of American English, phrases such as *hard to find* were derived by a syntactic process called '*tough*-movement' (McCawley 1998: 107–10), and their use prenominally constitutes an 'important qualification' to the 'generalization', equivalent to Huddleston and Pullum's 'basic rule', as McCawley states it. It seems clear that all three orders are possible: compare, for example, *an easy to swallow theory* with *an easy theory to swallow* or *a theory easy to swallow*. But how far each is likely may not always be clear.

10.5 A general tendency in English, as noted in the introduction to this chapter, has been for modifiers that are usually postpositive, or that were so earlier in its history, to become more usually attributive. A split order, as in *a man hard to find*, can in this light be seen as intermediate; and in a transformational account, of the kind developed fifty years ago by Lees, could have been a stage in a syntactic derivation that, in the case of many adjectives, was complete and obligatory. This transformation was subject, as Lees put it, to 'many as yet unanalyzed restrictions' (1960: 98; 3.4). We are not concerned here with a process deriving all premodifiers from postmodifiers. But if the basic rule is one by which, for example, *hard to find* would be postpositive, we are dealing with what will be in part equivalent qualifications or exceptions to it.

One factor may be the type of word that a modifier has as its head: thus, for example, a superlative or a comparative. Another may be the type of dependent: while *a larger than usual passenger* may be expected, *a larger than me passenger* might not be. Other exceptions may, however, involve phrases as wholes.

Prepositional phrases, for example, are generally restricted to postposition, as in *the people in the garden*. But *on the spot* is a premodifier, as remarked in passing (**2.12**), in *an on the spot decision*, and *out of court* in *an out of court settlement*. To these we may add, for example, *under the counter* in *an under the counter payment*, or *over the top* in *a completely over the top suggestion*. Such phrases are well established, but restricted to specific collocations: one would not say, except conceivably in word play, *an under the door payment* or *a beneath the top proposal*. *Over the top*, in particular, might for some linguists be an idiom, though not listed by, for example, Cowie, Mackin, and McCaig (1993). The phrases also restrict, through their meanings as wholes, the nouns that they are likely to modify.

Compare again the *downstairs* of *a downstairs window*, which in dictionaries is implicitly converted to an adjective (**2.11**). In a *decision on the spot*, as in *a window downstairs*, the postmodifier would call for no specific comment. It would be a straightforward prepositional phrase, following the noun like any other:

(12) $_{\text{NP}}$[a $_{\text{N}}$[decision] $_{\text{PP}}$[on the spot]]

But in *an on the spot decision* the premodifier could, in principle, be an adjective derived by conversion from a phrase:

(13) $_{\text{PP}}$[X] $\rightarrow$ $_{\text{A}}$[X]

As an adjective, it would be 'attributive only' and its position before *decision*:

(14) $_{\text{NP}}$[an $_{\text{A}}$[on the spot] $_{\text{N}}$[decision]]

would follow from the basic rule applying to adjectives in general. Compare, for example, a conversion proposed by Nanni (1980) for phrases derived by '*tough*-movement', discussed by McCawley (1998) in the passage referred to.

Whether (13) is justified is a question we can leave aside. What is crucial, however, is that while such uses form part of a general pattern, in the history of the language, for postmodifiers to become premodifiers, they affect individual units, perhaps through individual analogies. To that extent, accordingly, the problem is lexical rather than syntactic.

10.6 Finally, however, the more sporadic exceptions tend to be, the less we may expect a hard and fast distinction between those established in the language and ones whose explanation lies more in the passing circumstances in which they are attested.

In a story by Henry James, if we may take a literary example, a character is described as:

Carrying... to the stupid opposite houses the dry glitter of his eyes
('Owen Wingrave', ed. Bayley 1999, 2: 67)

This was published in the 1890s, and usage may have shifted. Compare, however, *the stupid houses opposite.* If James had written that, the order of both modifiers would pass, for a reader more than a century later, without comment. Where *stupid* would follow the basic rule for single adjectives, *opposite* would follow another which, however it is formulated, would also apply to *downstairs* or, with a complement, *opposite the station.* But the postmodifier would or could be read as intonationally prominent: *the stupid houses* OPPOSITE. If so, it would be taken to be restrictive; and in James's story no one set of houses is distinguished from others. What is important is simply that the character is staring out of the window, and thus at the houses on the other side of the road, which of their nature are dumb and senseless. It may be relevant that, on its own, the locative has established uses as a premodifier: *the opposite wall* or again (**2.12**) *the opposite argument.* But a more important factor is perhaps that, in the phrase as written, the noun can be read as prominent: *the stupid opposite* HOUSES. It is not where the houses are that matters; simply that they are houses.

For two other examples, both from Huddleston and Pullum, we may return to words in *a-* such as *asleep.* However they are classified (**2.7**), and however the rule may be stated, their position in phrases is basically after the noun. To the extent that there are no exceptions, they are once more 'never attributive'. But the 'never' of grammar is often like the 'never', as Mary Crawford described it, of conversation (*Mansfield Park* 1, ch. 9). The meaning is 'not very often'. Huddleston and Pullum mark with an asterisk, as 'ungrammatical', *their awake children* (2002: 559; their explanation of symbols, xii). But by adding an adverb, as they point out, 'we can greatly improve the acceptability of the attributive use': compare, with no asterisk, *their still awake children.* It is hard to be sure how much this will reflect established usage, beyond the specific context in which it might be said. Suppose, however, that one were to say *their children still* AWAKE. The modifier is prominent and would be restrictive; the reference could thus be, for example, to two of a couple's children who, unlike at least one other, have not fallen asleep. If *still awake* is a premodifier it will be understood as not restrictive. The reference is to some children and it would be relevant in the context that they have their eyes open. No distinction, however, is implied between these children and others who have dozed off.

Huddleston and Pullum also cite an observed instance: *She flashed me an aware, amused glance*, where a premodifier is expanded, as they explain it, by coordination. Remove *amused* and the example would again be marked as ungrammatical. *Aware*, however, can take a complement, as in *aware of what was happening*; and such complements can be understood. A phrase such as *the people aware* might thus refer to people who know something that others do not. One might not normally say *She flashed me an aware glance.* If one did, however, it would be to describe the nature of the glance itself, without implying that either it, or the woman flashing it, betrayed awareness of one thing specifically.

Perhaps one might not say it. But where exceptions are in general possible, and many uses are well established, it would be unrealistic to expect that exact limits can be set on what is possible.

Single adjectives as postmodifiers

10.7 The basic rule for single adjectives, or for adjectives with no following dependent, is as already given. One would not normally say *a child young*, in place of *a young child*. Where uses call for comment, they will be those in which an adjective that falls under this rule can also be postpositive. Take for comparison the variant orders of, for example, *hard to find* (10.4). This is a phrase in which an adjective is followed by a dependent; and, if the basic rule is as it is stated by, for example, Payne and Huddleston, its use will call for comment only when it is not straightforwardly postpositive. The position of, for example, *suitable* is similarly straightforward when, as in *the only suitable day*, it follows a rule by which it is attributive. It may or may not conform to a conflicting rule when it is used as a postmodifier (10.3). It is that use, however, which in one way or another calls for comment.

'Certain specific adjectives', as Payne and Huddleston put it, 'can . . . occur postpositively' (see again Huddleston and Pullum 2002: 445). It would be a mistake, however, to assume that they are no more than a set of individual words, distinguished individually by a feature such as [+Postpositive]. They may form instead a natural class, or one distinguished by series of shared properties, within what remains Huddleston and Pullum's default type (2002: 553; 1.10, Fig. 1.3). The difference seems, moreover, to be simply one of syntax. In Bolinger's famous example, on which Payne and Huddleston's is modelled, the meaning of *navigable*, as a lexical unit, would be the same in both *the only river navigable* and *the only navigable river*.

In one account (1.8), the difference is one of realization only. What calls, accordingly, for comment is precisely that some single adjectives can be realized in the same position as *nice to us*, *eating ice cream*, *in the garden*, and so on.

In another account, the difference is more fundamental. For Ferris, in particular, an adjective in 'prenominal attributive position' is the exponent of a 'property notion' which qualifies an 'entity notion'. In his notation (8.9), *hungry passengers* has the structure:

(15) P ▶ E

or, if words may be supplied as earlier (Ferris 1993: 36):

(16) hungry ▶ passengers

An adjective, however, in 'postnominal attributive position' represents a property notion in the same relation of 'assignment' as in 'ordinary predicative position'. In *the crimes alleged*, the relation is accordingly as follows:

(17) E ← P

or, to conflate this with what Ferris describes as the 'surface sequence':

(18) [the crimes] ← alleged

What calls for comment, in this light, is the restriction of (17) to certain notions only. 'Why is it', in Ferris's words, 'that some adjectives (and some adjective phrases) can occur quite easily in postnominal position while others, apparently comparable, are limited to prenominal position?' In the logic, however, of his treatment this is paired with another 'fundamental question', about a difference in meaning between (17) and (15). 'What is the difference', as he puts it, 'in effect or value obtained by the speaker who uses postnominal position when prenominal position is equally grammatical?' (Ferris 1993: 43).

10.8 One obvious comment, in the light of what has been said already, is that postmodifiers are restrictive. In *the aircraft which are a*VAI*lable*, the adjective is intonationally prominent, and the clause as a whole restricts the reference of a phrase of which it is part. As such it is distinguished from an appositive clause, which is not part of a referring expression, as in *the* AIR*craft, which are still a*VAI*lable.* In *the aircraft a*VAI*lable*, the postmodifier is reduced in one account by a syntactic process: thus McCawley's 'Relative Clause Reduction' (1998; **3.6**), following Lees. For Ferris, the property notion whose exponent is *available* would stand in the same relation of assignment both as a postmodifier and within *which are available*. But adjectives in the prenominal position can in general be restrictive or non-restrictive. If the problem, therefore, is as Ferris has posed it, it is tempting to argue that, where words like *available* are postmodifiers, the 'effect or value obtained' is to make clear that the meaning is restrictive.

The postpositive position would in that light represent the 'marked' term (in the sense of **9.3**) in an opposition. But the effect a speaker would be said to obtain could also be obtained by varying the intonation. *Desperate* could be non-restrictive in, for example, *the desperate people of Ruri*TA*nia*. The reference would be to a population as a whole, of which, as a whole, a state of desperation would implicitly hold. The same adjective would form a restrictive phrase, with the addition of an intensifier, in *the people truly* DES*perate*. But its use would be restrictive too, as a premodifier, in *the truly* DES*perate people*. So would that of *available* in, with a possible fall-rise, *We need all the a*VAI*lable aircraft*. The intonation here would follow a pattern normal for premodifiers generally: compare *the* LARGE *aircraft*, *the really in*TEL*ligent children*, and so on.

There remains, moreover, Ferris's other question, as to why *available*, for example, is used as a postmodifier while *large*, say, is not. That uses are limited is no mystery: the basic rule is that a single adjective is a premodifier, and such cases are exceptions to it. Ferris's wording is to that extent misleading. How far, however, can we make sense of the exceptions that are possible?

How important is it, for a start, that *available* ends in -[ə]*ble*? While we will get nowhere if we simply list words as '[+Postpositive]', it may also be wrong to suppose that there is any comprehensive principle that will explain all cases. Where a single adjective can be postpositive we may expect that there will be others like it which are in some way similar. *Available* is in this respect like *suitable* and *navigable*; or, for example, *eligible* in *the students eligible*. But other similarities, in morphology or otherwise, may be crucial in other cases. We are dealing with uses contrary to a rule, ultimately by individuals on particular occasions; and analogy is a more plausible principle than anything deeper.

Nor have we reason to expect a clear distinction between what is possible and what is not. It is likely too that, in particular instances, more than just one factor may be relevant.

10.9 Take the postmodifier in *the buildings adjacent*. The example is from Ferris, who argues at one point that the modifier need not be 'salient' or be used in this way 'for the sake of emphasis'. We might add that, while postmodifying adjectives can be intonationally prominent, as in *the aircraft* *a*VAI*lable*, so can the nouns they follow: *the* AIR*craft available* (as opposed to the lorries or other means of transport) or *the* HOU*ses adjacent* (as opposed, say, to the office buildings). He also argues that *adjacent* cannot be 'non-characterizing': 'it could hardly be claimed that the buildings were only adjacent on some particular occasion' (Ferris 1993: 44–5, 48). The reference here is to Bolinger's critique of transformational accounts of English (1967), rather than his earlier treatment (1952) of linear modification across languages. Equally, therefore, we may want to qualify McCawley's interpretation (1998: 392; 3.7), that postmodifiers 'can only express "ephemeral" properties'. We must look for wider similarities, with other modifiers that either can or have to be postpositive.

Three comments may be relevant. One is that *adjacent*, like *available* and others, is morphologically complex. It would be silly to suppose that this is a predicting factor: that all simple words, like *large*, must come before the noun, and any that are complex can come after. One would not say, for example, *I like to deal with people reasonable*. Word-formation could, however, be part of the basis for an analogy.

A second comment is that *adjacent* has a locative meaning. It identifies the buildings by the area where they stand, as would the postmodifiers in *the buildings nearby* or *the buildings [by the river]*. It is classed as an adjective rather than an adverb, on the grounds that not all speakers would say, for example, *They live adjacent*. But it is linked by its semantic type both to phrases, such as *by the river*, that are regularly postmodifiers, and to words such as *nearby*, whose position can vary, in appearance similarly.

A third factor is that being adjacent implies a point of reference. The buildings are 'adjacent to' another building, a building site, or something else that can be understood. This could be made explicit: thus, for example, *the buildings adjacent to ours*. If so, the position of the modifier would be in accordance with the basic rule, as stated by Payne and Huddleston among others, where adjectives have a following dependent. Complements of this kind are in general optional, and their function is distinguished even more than in the case of verbs (8.4) by the criterion that they are 'licensed'. But where complements can be omitted they will often remain latent (Matthews 1981: 126). As *the buildings opposite*, where *opposite* is not an adjective, would refer to buildings opposite some point that would be identifiable in the context, *a friend* WORR*ied* could be used of a friend who is concerned about a given individual or a given situation that might develop. *The students eligible* would refer to students 'eligible for', for example, a prize or entry to a competition. If what it was were made explicit, an adjective phrase would again be a postmodifier: thus, for example, *the students eligible for a research fellowship*. An adjective with a latent complement could then be realized similarly.

10.10 The more this last factor, in particular, is important, the less we will be tempted to assume a difference between constructions. *The eligible students* will also, of course, refer to students 'eligible for' something. At the risk, however, of appearing tiresome, we must emphasize once more that where adjectives are premodifiers they are simply conforming to a rule. We have no need to explain why *eligible*, for example, can be attributive, any more than why *kind* is attributive in *some kind students*. Where it is not attributive, the explanation can be that it conforms to another basic rule, that would apply straightforwardly if a complement were explicit.

In Ferris's intensional analysis, a unit whose exponent is premodifying stands in a relation of qualification:

(19) Eligible ▶ students

while in his 'postnominal' position the relation would be of 'assignment':

(20) [the students] ← eligible

If this were right, we would expect a difference of meaning; or, as Ferris puts it in the passage cited earlier, an 'effect or value' that the construction in (20) would obtain (10.7). It might make clear, on occasion, that a property denoted is 'ephemeral'; or that the modifier is restrictive. This might perhaps reflect a cross-linguistic principle, as Bolinger was arguing in 1952, by which a later position tends to be 'non-characterizing'. Compare again, for an exception that might make clearer a specific meaning, the position of *awake* in *their still awake children* (10.6). But here, as there, there is no regular opposition.

What remains is the parallel, as in other accounts, between postmodifiers and predication. As Ferris represents it, the relation of assignment, as in (20), is the one that would also be expounded in, for example, *The students are eligible*, where the adjective is in his 'ordinary predicative' position (1993: 36; **8.14**). It is perhaps worth noting, and perhaps not merely in passing, that if his analysis were applicable to Old English, an adjective in this relation could only be strong, while as a qualifier it could be either strong or weak (examples in **4.3**). In an equivalent treatment, postmodifiers are related to relative clauses in which adjectives will be predicative. One detail, therefore, is that where an adjective has a sense in which it is not attributive, it can be used as a modifier, with that sense, only if it is postpositive. In *the people actually* READ*y*, the sense of *ready* is the one it would have in *They are ready* (**3.11**), and could not have in *the ready people*. If *the lawyers who are already busy* were reduced to *the lawyers already busy*, we might be tempted to argue that the modifier is 'non-characterizing', as opposed to that of *the busy lawyers*. But the proximate cause lies in the uses, more generally, of *busy* itself (**9.5**).

10.11 When some words are postmodifiers, such as *apparent* in *the heirs apparent*, they are historically relics. Is it still relevant that postmodifiers were once more common?

How far, in particular, can we discount poetic licence? The notion of 'licence' springs from a tradition in which, as in an attributive use of *afraid*, a rule can be seen as 'broken'. It is not surprising, therefore, that in the infancy of generative grammar Levin, among others, could distinguish the language of poetry as 'deviant' (1964: 311). In a line, for example, that we may take at random from Tennyson:

Of that great order of the Table Round
('The Marriage of Geraint' 3)

round would break the rule that would exclude, for example, *We sat at a table round*. There is no implication that *the Table Round* might have a meaning any different from that of *the Round Table*, or that there could be any reason, other than metrical convenience, why the adjective should be so used. When Milton wrote, for example, of:

Chaos and th'inroad of Darkness old
(*Paradise Lost* 3.421)

the function of *old* in relation to *darkness* was similarly no different, ordering apart, from that of *old* to *night* in:

Frighted the reign of *Chaos* and old Night
(1.543)

There is no reason, for example, to take the adjective in the first line as restrictive or as denoting a property that is not 'permanent'.

Since Tennyson's day, in particular, such usage has become still more restricted. It nevertheless persists, in doggerel maybe, but in a register appropriate to greeting cards among others, and familiar to most speakers. There are also literary examples where the order remains natural. The first line of Auden's 'Anthem for St. Cecilia's Day':

In a garden shady this holy lady

would have included, for a grammarian in the ancient tradition, an instance of 'hyperbaton', or departure from the normal order of words, which is in Latin a *virtus orationis* or ornament of utterance, rather than a *vitium* or fault. Since there is no rule for when an adjective can be postpositive, for what is grammatical and what is not grammatical, historical influences may remain one factor.

They are also relevant where specific combinations persist. *A battle royal* has its origin in the late Middle Ages, in a construction which was that of words such as *elect*, that have become postpositive only. It might now be listed as an idiom (thus Cowie, Mackin, and McCaig 1993: 45), but one whose form fits still with knowledge of the poetic style. *Peace eternal* is not an idiom, and may simply vary with *eternal peace*. But if it is more likely than, say, *quiet eternal* it may be partly by analogy with the translation, in the *Book of Common Prayer*, of the Latin *requiem aeternam*:

Rest eternal grant unto them, O Lord: and let light perpetual shine upon them.

11

Envoi

11.1 *Adjectives remain one part of speech.* 11.2 *Functions and categories.* 11.3 *Problems of constituency.* 11.4 *The limits to theories.*

11.1 If this study has a general conclusion it is one that has been clear from the beginning: that the attributive and predicative uses of adjectives have diverged. Their divergence reflects changes in English over the Modern period especially, many dating back to the end of the Middle Ages. The drift, in the sense of Sapir (1921), continues. Among the lexical innovations over the past century, we may pick out, for example, a specifically predicative use of *big*, as in *They are being big about it*, or the sense of *nuclear* as a classifier, which is limited to the attributive position, in *nuclear weapons* or *a nuclear physicist*. The first of these reflects and reinforces the expansion of the progressive with *be* plus an adjective, which is itself attested only from the early decades of the nineteenth century.

The divergence is in both syntax and the lexicon. An adjective in one position is nevertheless the same part of speech, or in another term a member of the same syntactic category, as in any other. In principle, of course, they could be classified differently, and related by conversion. *Love*, for comparison, is a verb in *They love dancing*; but a noun related to it in *their love of dancing*. In the same way, a 'big_1', in predicative position, could be described as 'a predicate', and a 'big_2', in attributive position, as 'an attribute'. Their meanings would not correspond entirely. To the extent, however, that a correspondence does hold, members of these parts of speech could be related automatically: as 'big_1' is to 'big_2', so '$happy_1$' is to '$happy_2$', 'red_1' to 'red_2', and so on wherever there is no block or qualification. Where meanings diverge details may be added, as for nouns and verbs and for any other pattern of conversion, in individual entries in a lexicon.

The technique of conversion is well understood, and in the case of '$love_V$' and '$love_N$' its application is not controversial. In application to adjectives, however, it is unlikely to be taken seriously. One reason might be that, unlike a verb and a noun, 'big_1' and 'big_2' do not have different inflections. That cannot, however, be an absolute objection, since English grammars merrily treat adjectives such as *happy* as a part of speech distinct from adverbs such as *happily*. A better reason may lie in the intermediate status, which again has been clear from the beginning, of adjectives as postmodifiers. Would the *kind* of, for example, *people kind to us* be the '*kind*$_2$' of *kind people* or the '*kind*$_1$' of *People are kind*? If the latter, we could say that only 'adjectives$_1$', which we are calling 'predicates', can take such dependents. But instead of, for example, *people kinder than me* one can say *kinder people than me*. If *kinder* is a form of '*kind*$_1$' when it follows the noun, is it to be reclassified as a form of '*kind*$_2$', which we are calling an 'attribute', when it comes before it? A proposal can be dismissed as silly if it compels us to ask questions such as these.

11.2 Specific conclusions, or proposals at least, have concerned the roles of adjectives in one position or another: relations between them, for example, in phrases like *a nice hot bath*, or their function in clauses like *This drives me crazy*. I will not pander to a fashion for rhetorical overkill by attempting an abstract of each chapter *seriatim*. In any analysis, however, which is not constrained by the syntactic theory of one school of linguists, problems arise that are often partly philosophical. They cannot be resolved entirely, at least in the light of what we know now, by empirical argument. Some of these are perhaps worth drawing out a little further.

Most adjectives are bipositional, and can thus be studied from two angles. One form of analysis is monosystemic, and will focus on the properties that distinguish this part of speech from others. No single function, however, is exclusive to it. A polysystemic analysis will instead establish generalizations which link its members to words and phrases of other categories. *Ready*, for example, is uncontroversially an adjective; *away* is in most treatments not an adjective. But in *the people ready for it* and *the people away from home* the postmodifiers have a similar function, which they share with many other kinds of unit. Compare the adverb of time in *the party tomorrow*, or the prepositional phrase, which we can distinguish from those with a locative meaning, in *a woman with no umbrella*. Units are brought together, in this perspective, by their function in the construction of noun phrases; even though, in a monosystemic analysis, they are plainly separate.

Linguists differ in the importance they attach to such connections. In the view of Huddleston and Pullum, functions such as that of a postmodifier are a 'central theoretical idea' (2002: 23), crucial at all points to their analysis of syntax. We can thus describe constructions as relating modifiers to a head, subjects to a predicate, objects to a predicator, and so on. They also, of course, relate adjectives to nouns, or noun phrases to verbs. But categories are differentiated, in their syntax, by the range of functions, across all relevant constructions, that their members have in common. *Big*, for example, shares with *tall* or *red* or *ugly* the functions it has in *a big house*, *houses bigger than ours*, *Her house is big*, *We must make it big*, and in whatever other constructions an analysis may identify. Categories too are an idea that Huddleston and Pullum see as central. But they need to be established if, and only if, there is some general statement to be made, or some rule to be formulated, which applies to their members as a class. For adjectives such as *big* or *red* or *ugly* that is evidently so. We have no reason to assume, however, that assignment to categories must be exhaustive, or that they always form a hierarchy.

Other treatments stand more in the ancient tradition. For the earliest grammarians, the 'parts of a sentence' were the parts, precisely, of which a sentence was directly composed. Divide sentences into phrases, and in the same spirit the construction of *big houses*, in *Big houses are expensive*, involves no more than the combination in a certain order of an adjective, as a word of one 'part', and a noun, as a word of another 'part'. The unit they form will also have a head; but in many current treatments this is simply a part whose syntactic category, or what Bloomfield called its form-class, is also that of the constituent as a whole. It is the functions, which are fundamental for Huddleston and Pullum, that in this account will be defined as secondary.

Is either view to be preferred? As linguists assign words to categories, so too, it is generally assumed, do children learning to speak the language. In one view, therefore, the learning of syntax might begin with the parts of speech as they were first conceived. *Big* and *red*, for example, will be identified as parts of expressions such as *the big chair* or *the red flower*, with a meaning, in such combinations, that will be perceived as similar. They will accordingly be grouped together, at an early stage of learning, to form one of a set of major categories. Words like *chair* and *flower* will form another; and, as many linguists see it, the major categories to which words belong will be given universally. As learning continues, each is divided in due course into subcategories. *Red*, for example, will be grouped at a lower level with *green*, *blue*, and other adjectives of colour, in the light both of their meanings and the way they combine, in sequences, with *big* or *small*, *ugly* or *pretty*, and others. *Chair* and *flower*, which have already been assigned to the category of what grammarians call nouns, will be assigned more precisely, again at a later stage of learning, to the subcategory they call 'countable'. Such divisions and subdivisions will naturally form hierarchies.

This spells out a view that is perhaps assumed more often than it is made explicit. Have we any reason, however, to believe that it is right? The classes that, on the face of it, a learner might find it easiest to identify are those of words whose uses and meanings are most closely similar. These include, for example, those for colours, such as *red* and *green*; for sizes, such as *big* and *tiny*; for tangible objects, such as *mug* and *spoon*; for animate individuals, such as *Dad* or *Granny*. These too are categories that could be seen as given independently of particular languages. They enter once more into combinations, in which, in another view of syntax, they have similar functions. The function of, for example, *red* in *red mug* might be identified with those of *big* in *big spoon*, of *new* in *new spoon*, of *Dad* in *Dad's mug*, and many others. In the learning of syntax functions would undergo progressive differentiation. But larger categories would be established by a process of abstraction, from similarities first recognized to classes whose functions and lexical meanings are more heterogeneous. At the highest level, one such category would again include all adjectives, as we describe them, such as *red, big, beautiful, new, difficult*, and so on. But we have no reason to assume that such a process of abstraction will be exhaustive, or that one category may not overlap others.

These are large issues, which a study like this raises but can scarcely hope to resolve. If constructions, however, are distinguished in terms of functions, the status of what were the ancient *partes orationis* may deserve to be rethought.

11.3 Another general issue, on which it may be possible to come to more of a conclusion, is that of constituency. It would be perverse to deny that many sentences include smaller sequences, such as clauses, or that they in turn can often be divided neatly into phrases. English in particular is a language in which dependents tend to be adjacent, by rule, to the words on which they depend: one must say *It is a big chair*, for example, not *A chair it is big*. Constituents may therefore be established by the relations between them. While this, however, is familiar and uncontroversial, it does not follow that all relations are between one immediate constituent and another; still less that all divisions are binary.

Problems arise whenever in a sequence of three units:

(1) A + B + C

each stands in some relation, on the evidence of mutual restrictions, to each of the others. We could say that *B* and *C*, for example, form a constituent:

(2) A [B C]

and if *B*, say, were to depend on *C*, it would be natural that *C*, as a head in many theories, should stand in some relation to *A*. But that makes a puzzle of the relation between *A* and *B*. One way out is to insist that, while *A* combines with *BC*, the properties of *BC* as a whole, by which the combination is possible, are those of its head and its dependent together. But if *C* were said to combine with *AB*:

(3) [A B] C

we could argue equally that *AB*, as a whole, has properties that derive from those of *A* and *B* together, by which its combination with *C* could be seen as 'licensed' similarly.

These schemas may seem artificial. But the problem becomes real as soon as different linguists describe relations differently. In *That made me happy*, there is in one view a 'small clause' *me happy*:

(4) [made [me happy]]

In another view, *me* is on its own the object of *made*. If all divisions are binary, they would form a unit *made me*, which would be related as a whole to *happy*:

(5) [[made me] happy]

In either case part of the truth is liable to be obscured, to preserve a principle whose origins are more philosophical than empirical, which has become entrenched from the 1950s onwards.

Or should we embrace another way out? For sentences like this the solution was, in the days of deep and surface structure, that of 'raising'. But raising is merely one instance of a more general recourse to the device of movement. In a recent article, Mathieu (2012) addresses a problem which is schematically like that of, for example, *another* with a dependent numeral (**5.10**). His material is from French; but similarly, instead of saying that, in *another three flowers*, either *another three* is a smaller constituent headed by *another*:

(6) [[another three] flowers]

or *three flowers* a smaller constituent headed by *flowers*:

(7) [another [three flowers]]

we say both; but there is a process of movement that relates them. Theories of phrase structure are now rich in self-protecting mechanisms (Matthews 2007b), and attacks based only on facts will never succeed.

11.4 To say that an issue is philosophical is not, of course, disparaging. The structure of a language is at every level an abstraction, and the criteria for abstraction, especially at the level at which constructions are established, are such that it is hard to separate what is directly open to empirical argument and what will not be. Criteria must therefore be applied with circumspection. To say that in *I like fresh lettuce* a word *fresh* forms a larger unit with a word *lettuce* is to make a statement we can legitimately see as true; we will acknowledge, however, that words are already abstractions. To say that *fresh* is subordinate to *lettuce* remains sufficiently uncontroversial. But what holds for some words *A* and *B*, or even for most *A*'s and most *B*'s, may not hold absolutely. If we conjecture that it does, it is for reasons that go beyond the evidence. It may be argued that theories are simpler if they are not qualified; the concept of headship meshes beautifully with theories of categories; and so on. But how far should analyses be constrained aesthetically?

Huddleston and Pullum speak for many and perhaps most linguists in insisting that 'the languages human beings use are too complex to be described except by means of a theory'. Without a theory, they continue, 'there can be no generalisations'. To 'bring together the principles that sentences all conform to', and on which new ones can be constructed, 'means developing a **theory** [their bold face] of the ways in which sentences can be put together by combining words' (2002: preliminary chapter, 18–19). The scope of such a theory is perhaps left open: it could in principle be one of English only. On the basis, however, of the relation assumed between description and theory, Huddleston and Pullum adopt a 'theoretical framework', in which sentences reduce to tree structures, in which 'most of the categories for larger constituents are based on the ones for words' (2002: 22), and in which lexical categories in English form a 'complete list' of nine. Their theory of syntactic functions is thus grafted onto what is, in many other respects, a standard theory of phrase structure. Functions, in a passage cited in an earlier chapter, are of a smaller constituent strictly in relation to a larger unit that includes it (**8.3**).

In this way among others, Huddleston and Pullum seek to incorporate 'as many as possible of the insights achieved in modern linguistics' (2002: preface, xv). In the first of their grammars (1972), Quirk and his colleagues included no such introductory section, and to me at the time, reviewing it for the *Times Literary Supplement*, its relation to theoretical linguistics was a question insufficiently addressed (Matthews, unsigned 1973). The defect, if it was indeed one, might appear to be remedied in their definitive grammar, by a section towards the beginning of the second chapter (1985: 38–47). This has the title 'Parts of the sentence', and explains such general notions as constituency, 'chain and choice relationships', clauses and phrases, and subordination versus coordination, all of which are central to the analyses that follow. References are given for 'the application of various models or theories to English grammar' (1985: 91). But 'theory' and 'theoretical' are not terms that Quirk and his colleagues themselves use, either in this section or, if the index is reliable, elsewhere. Their aim, moreover, may have simply been to make clear how terms of this kind will be used in practice.

If so, I believe they were right. If I have a general comment, in comparison, on the magnificent work of Huddleston and Pullum, it is that the framework they propose tends to limit both the ways in which a linguist will look at problems, and the range of problems that will be noticed.

The principle of markedness, for example, is an insight in another tradition that has been overworked and very loosely defined: see, for example, the entry for 'marked' in my *Dictionary of Linguistics* (2007a); also a broadside by Haspelmath (2006). But it seems relevant, at least, to the use of the progressive (**9.3**), and we have to be prepared to think beyond a theoretical framework in which it has no place.

One problem this framework fails to draw to our attention is that of the rhythm of noun phrases. Huddleston and Pullum's analyses are not restricted to English as written. A 'supplement', or unit standing in a relation of apposition, can be 'set off... in speech', as they describe it, by intonational phrasing, as, 'in writing, by punctuation'. Intonation 'plays an important role' as a 'non-propositional marker' of the illocutionary force of utterances; a subject and vocative are 'distinguished prosodically' when in initial position; the preposing of phrases can 'accord them a significant amount of intonational prominence'; and so on (2002: passages cited 25, 861, 927, 1374). But a supplement, for example, can be identified by other criteria, independently of the way in which it may be realized. Differences in illocutionary force can also be distinguished, independently of intonation, by constructions such as those of interrogatives and imperatives. None of the entries for 'intonation' in the index, some thirty-odd in all, are to differences whose basis is in prosody alone.

Compare Hill's treatment in the 1950s. In his philosophy of linguistics, 'the description and analysis of language' had to start with that of 'sounds and their patterning' (Hill 1958: 3). He began accordingly at the lowest possible level of abstraction, with the sounds produced as utterances by a single speaker; and in an analysis quite literally of speech, he established distinctions of 'stress' and 'pitch', and of what was at the time called 'juncture', in advance of consonants and vowels. It is not surprising that Hill observed differences in the prosodic structure of phrases, which he could not dismiss as variations with no bearing, as most later theories tempt us to assume, on the nature of syntactic units. If the rhythm of noun phrases is ignored in many recent treatments, it is because, in the philosophy that now prevails, syntax is an autonomous component of a grammar, with its own criteria, with which phonology, as a separate component whose criteria are different, 'interfaces' only where there are blatant correspondences between them.

The moral, perhaps, is not that a description should be neutral between 'frameworks'. It is hard to imagine how it could be. But a framework should not be gratuitously exclusive; nor perhaps, gratuitously precise.

Let us return to the notion of 'a construction'. 'Construction' itself, without an article, was defined by Murray in the original *Oxford English Dictionary* (s.v. II.5.b) as 'the syntactical connexion between verbs and their objects and complements, adjectives and their extensions, prepositions and objects, etc.' This can easily be generalized to cover all kinds of 'syntactical connexion'. But the term has also been used for centuries, as in the earliest of Murray's citations, of one construction as distinct from others. This is also how it has been used here, and it is therefore tempting to demand that, in this sense too, it should be clearly defined. The moment, however, we try to formulate a definition we are plunged into issues that are purely philosophical. Must words in different orders have two different constructions? Or can different orders realize a construction that, at a higher level of abstraction, we can call the same? Are constructions established by a sign relation, between a formal pattern on the one hand and a meaning on the other? These are issues with which Bloomfield wrestled in the 1920s and 1930s, and are those that arise, again in theory, in identifying words. In practice, however, words are not in general in doubt, and where they are, alternative solutions can be assessed in individual cases, as they arise. Are constructions in practice any more perplexing?

I am tempted to compare current thinking about grammar with the state of the Church of England in the mid-nineteenth century. The 'High and Dry' church, of Dr

Grantly and other clergymen in Trollope's *Barchester Towers*, had been and was being rocked by the Oxford Movement on the one hand, and evangelical zeal on the other. It had a tradition, however, of openness, and a tolerance of ambiguity in matters of doctrine that, if examined too closely, could lead one into perplexity. This book is perhaps a study in what we might call 'High and Dry' grammar. It stands in a tradition that has long incorporated ideas from philosophers and theorists, from Plato and Aristotle onwards, when they advance its purpose. But ideas have been from varied sources, and they must prove helpful. Huddleston and Pullum are among the latest practitioners to work in this way.

If linguistics has had an equivalent of the Oxford Movement, it is the theory of Universal Grammar developed by Chomsky and his followers. Those who accept it fully, like those who turned to Rome, have often been attracted by the comfort of submitting to authority. Its aim, however, has not been a disinterested study of a particular language; and ideas original to it have been assimilated into the tradition of writing grammars, over the past three decades, with caution.

If my comparison obliges me to associate 'Cognitive Grammar', as a conscious antithesis, with the low-church Christianity of Mrs Proudie, so be it.

References

Aarts, Bas (2007). *Syntactic Gradience: the Nature of Grammatical Indeterminacy.* Oxford: Oxford University Press.

Adamson, Sylvia (2000). 'A lovely little example: word order options and category shift in the premodifying string', in O. Fischer, A. Rosenbach, and D. Stein (eds.), *Pathways of Change: Grammaticalization in English.* Amsterdam: Benjamins, 39–66.

Baker, Mark C. (2003). *Lexical Categories: Verbs, Nouns and Adjectives.* Cambridge: Cambridge University Press.

Barwick, C., ed. (1964). *Flavii Sosipatri Charisii Artis Grammaticae Libri V*, revised F. Kühnert. Leipzig: Teubner.

Bayley, John, ed. (1999). Henry James, *Collected Stories.* 2 vols. New York: Everyman's Library.

Bazell, C. E. (1958). *Linguistic Typology.* Inaugural Lecture, London: School of Oriental and African Languages.

Betjeman, John (1972). *Collected Poems.* London: John Murray.

Bloomfield, Leonard (1933). *Language.* New York: Holt.

Bolinger, Dwight L. (1952). 'Linear modification', *Publications of the Modern Language Association* 67: 1117–44. [Reprinted in *Forms of English: Accent, Morpheme, Order.* Tokyo: Hokouo (1965), 279–307.]

Bolinger, Dwight L. (1961). 'Syntactic blends and other matters', *Language* 37: 366–81.

Bolinger, Dwight L. (1967). 'Adjectives in English: attribution and predication', *Lingua* 18: 1–34.

Bolinger, Dwight L. (1968). *Aspects of Language.* New York: Harcourt, Brace. [2nd edn. 1975.]

Boyd, Jeremy K. and Goldberg, Adele E. (2011). 'Learning what NOT to say: the role of statistical preemption and categorization in *a*-adjective production', *Language* 87: 55–8.

Breban, Tine (2010). 'Reconstructing paths of secondary grammaticalisation of *same* from emphasising to phoricity and single referent-marking postdeterminer uses', *Transactions of the Philological Society* 108: 68–87.

Bresnan, Joan (1978). 'A realistic transformational grammar', in M. Halle, J. Bresnan, and G. A. Miller (eds.), *Linguistic Theory and Psychological Reality.* Cambridge, MA: MIT Press, 1–59.

Bresnan, Joan, ed. (1982). *The Mental Representation of Grammatical Relations.* Cambridge, MA: MIT Press.

Brown, Lesley, ed. (1993). *The New Shorter Oxford English Dictionary.* 2 vols. Oxford: Clarendon Press.

Bursill-Hall, G. L., ed. (1972). Thomas of Erfurt, *Grammatica speculativa.* London: Longman.

Burton-Roberts, Noel (1997). *Analysing Sentences: an Introduction to English Syntax.* 2nd edn. London: Longman. [1st edn. 1986.]

Carroll, John B., ed. (1956). *Language, Thought, and Reality: Selected Writings of Benjamin Lee Whorf.* Cambridge, MA: MIT Press.

Chomsky, Noam (1957). *Syntactic Structures.* The Hague: Mouton.

Chomsky, Noam (1965). *Aspects of the Theory of Syntax.* Cambridge, MA: MIT Press.

Chomsky, Noam (1966a). *Topics in the Theory of Generative Grammar.* The Hague: Mouton.

Chomsky, Noam (1966b). *Cartesian Linguistics.* New York: Harper and Row. [3rd edn., with introduction by J. McGilvray, Cambridge: Cambridge University Press (2009).]

Chomsky, Noam (1975). *The Logical Structure of Linguistic Theory.* Chicago: University of Chicago Press.

Chomsky, Noam (1986). *Knowledge of Language.* New York: Praeger.

Cinque, Guglielmo (2010). *The Syntax of Adjectives: a Comparative Study.* Cambridge, MA: MIT Press.

Cowie, A. P., Mackin, R., and McCaig, I. R. (1993). *Oxford Dictionary of English Idioms.* Oxford: Oxford University Press.

Croft, William (2001). *Radical Construction Grammar.* Oxford: Oxford University Press.

Croft, William (2003). *Typology and Universals.* 2nd edn. Cambridge: Cambridge University Press. [1st edn. 1990.]

Davidse, Kristin (2009). '*Complete* and *sort of*: from identifying to intensifying?', *Transactions of the Philological Society* 107: 262–92.

Denison, David (1998). 'Syntax', in Hogg, ed. 1992–2001, 4: 92–329.

Denison, David (2006). 'Category change and gradience in the determiner system', in A. van Kemenade and B. Los (eds.), *The Handbook of the History of English.* Oxford: Blackwell, 279–304.

Dik, Simon C. (1968). *Coordination: its Implications for the Theory of General Linguistics.* Amsterdam: North-Holland.

Dik, Simon C. (1978). *Functional Grammar.* Amsterdam: North-Holland.

Dixon, R. M. W. (1977). 'Where have all the adjectives gone?', *Studies in Language* 1: 19–80. [Reprinted as lead chapter in Dixon, '*Where have all the adjectives gone?' and other Essays in Semantics and Syntax.* Berlin: Mouton (1982).]

Dixon, R. M. W. (1991). *A New Approach to English Grammar, on Semantic Principles.* Oxford: Clarendon Press.

Dixon, R. M. W. (2010). *Basic Linguistic Theory*, Vol. 2. Oxford: Oxford University Press.

Dixon, R. M. W. and Aikhenvald, Alexandra Y., eds. (2004). *Adjective Classes: a Cross-linguistic Typology.* Oxford: Oxford University Press.

Edel, Leon, ed. (1967). Henry James, *The Awkward Age.* London: Bodley Head.

Feist, Jim (2012). *Premodifiers in English.* Cambridge: Cambridge University Press.

Ferris, Connor (1993). *The Meaning of Syntax: a Study of the Adjectives of English.* Harlow: Longman.

Firth, J. R. (1957). *Papers in Linguistics 1934–1951.* London: Oxford University Press.

Fischer, Olga (1992). 'Syntax', in Hogg, ed. 1992–2001, 2: 207–408.

Fischer, Olga and van der Wurff, Wim (2006). 'Syntax', in R. Hogg and D. Denison, eds., *A History of the English Language.* Cambridge: Cambridge University Press, 109–98.

Fries, Charles Carpenter (1952). *The Structure of English.* New York: Harcourt, Brace.

Fromkin, Victoria A., ed. (2000). *Linguistics: an Introduction to Linguistic Theory.* Oxford: Blackwell.

Givón, T. (1970). 'Notes on the semantic structure of English adjectives', *Language* 46: 816–37.

Givón, T. (1990). *Syntax*, Vol. 2. Amsterdam: Benjamins.

González-Díaz, Victorina (2009). 'Little old problems: adjectives and subjectivity in the English NP', *Transactions of the Philological Society* 107: 376–402.

Gottlieb, Robert, ed. (1994). Rudyard Kipling, *Collected Stories*. New York: Everyman's Library.

Greenberg, Joseph H. (1963). 'Some universals of grammar with particular reference to the order of meaningful units', in Greenberg (ed.), *Universals of Language*. Cambridge, MA: MIT Press, 73–113.

Grice, Paul (1989). *Studies in the Way of Words*. Cambridge, MA: Harvard University Press.

Halliday, M. A. K. (1985). *An Introduction to Functional Grammar*. London: Edward Arnold.

Harris, James (1751). *Hermes*. London. [Reprinted Menston: Scolar Press, 1968.]

Harris, Zellig S. (1946). 'From morpheme to utterance', *Language* 22: 161–83. [Reprinted in Harris 1981: 45–70.]

Harris, Zellig S. (1951). *Methods in Structural Linguistics*. Chicago: University of Chicago Press.

Harris, Zellig S. (1957). 'Co-occurrence and transformation in linguistic analysis', *Language* 33: 283–340. [Reprinted in Harris 1981: 143–210.]

Harris, Zellig S. (1981). *Papers on Syntax*. Dordrecht: Reidel.

Haspelmath, Martin (2006). 'Against markedness (and what to replace it with)', *Journal of Linguistics* 42: 25–70.

Hays, D. G. (1964). 'Dependency grammar: a formalism and some observations', *Language* 40: 511–25.

Hill, Archibald A. (1958). *Introduction to Linguistic Structures: from Sound to Sentence in English*. New York: Harcourt, Brace.

Hockett, Charles F. (1958). *A Course in Modern Linguistics*. New York: Macmillan.

Hogg, Richard M., ed. (1992–2001). *The Cambridge History of the English Language*. 6 vols. Cambridge: Cambridge University Press.

Holtz, Louis (1981). *Donat et la tradition de l'enseignement grammatical*. Paris: CNRS.

Hornstein, Norbert, Nunes, Jairo, and Grohmann, Kleanthes K. (2005). *Understanding Mimimalism*. Cambridge: Cambridge University Press.

Huddleston, Rodney (1984). *Introduction to the Grammar of English*. Cambridge: Cambridge University Press.

Huddleston, Rodney and Pullum, Geoffrey K. (2002). *The Cambridge Grammar of the English Language*. Cambridge: Cambridge University Press.

Jakobson, Roman (1971). *Selected Writings*, Vol. 2. The Hague: Mouton.

Jespersen, Otto (1909–49). *A Modern English Grammar on Historical Principles*. 7 vols. Heidelberg: Winter.

Jespersen, Otto (1924). *The Philosophy of Grammar*. London: Allen and Unwin.

Katz, Jerrold J. and Fodor, Jerry A. (1963). 'The structure of a semantic theory', *Language* 29: 170–210.

Katz, Jerrold J. and Postal, Paul M. (1964). *An Integrated Theory of Linguistic Descriptions*. Cambridge, MA: MIT Press.

Keil, H., ed. (1855). *Grammatici latini*, Vol. 2. Leipzig: Teubner.

Kuryłowicz, Jerzy (1936). 'Dérivation lexicale et dérivation syntaxique'. Reprinted in *Esquisses linguistiques*. Wrocław/Kraków: Polska Akademia Nauk (1960), 41–50.

Lakoff, George (1970). *Irregularity in Syntax*. New York: Holt, Rinehart, and Winston.

Lass, Roger (1992). 'Phonology and morphology', in Hogg, ed. 1992–2001, 2: 23–155.

Lees, R. B. (1960). *The Grammar of English Nominalizations*. Bloomington: Indiana University Research Center in Anthropology, Folklore, and Linguistics.

Levin, Samuel R. (1964). 'Poetry and grammaticalness', in H. G. Lunt (ed.), *Proceedings of the Ninth International Congress of Linguists*. The Hague: Mouton, 308–14.

Long, Ralph B. (1961). *The Sentence and its Parts: a Grammar of Contemporary English*. Chicago: University of Chicago Press.

Lyons, John (1963). *Structural Semantics*. Publications of the Philological Society 20. Oxford: Blackwell.

Lyons, John (1966). 'Towards a "notional" theory of the "parts of speech"', *Journal of Linguistics* 2: 209–36.

Lyons, John (1968). *Introduction to Theoretical Linguistics*. Cambridge: Cambridge University Press.

Lyons, John (1977). *Semantics*. 2 vols. Cambridge: Cambridge University Press.

McCawley, James D. (1998). *The Syntactic Phenomena of English*. 2nd edn. Chicago: University of Chicago Press. [1st edn., 2 vols 1988.]

Malkiel, Yakov (1959). 'Studies in irreversible binomials', *Lingua* 8: 113–60. [Reprinted in *Essays on Linguistic Themes*. Oxford: Blackwell (1968), 311–55.]

Marouzeau, J. (1951). *Lexique de la terminologie linguistique*. 3rd edn. Paris: Paul Geuthner. [1st edn. 1933.]

Martínez-Insua, Ana Elina, and Pérez-Guerra, Javier (2011). 'An open-sesame approach to English noun phrases: defining the NP', *English Language and Linguistics* 15: 201–13.

Mathieu, Éric (2012). 'Licensing by modification: the case of French *de* nominals', *Journal of Linguistics* 48: 389–426.

Matthews, P. H. (1967). Review of Chomsky 1965, *Journal of Linguistics* 3: 119–52.

Matthews, P. H. (1969). Review of Dik 1968, *Lingua* 23: 349–71.

Matthews, P. H. (1973). [Unsigned] review of Quirk et al. 1972, *Times Literary Supplement*, 2 February.

Matthews, P. H. (1980). 'Complex intransitive constructions', in S. Greenbaum, G. Leech, and J. Svartvik (eds.), *Studies in English Linguistics for Randolph Quirk*. London: Longman, 41–9.

Matthews, P. H. (1981). *Syntax*. Cambridge: Cambridge University Press.

Matthews, P. H. (1982). 'Formalization', in D. Crystal (ed.), *Linguistic Controversies*. London: Edward Arnold, 1–15.

Matthews, P. H. (1993). *Grammatical Theory in the United States from Bloomfield to Chomsky*. Cambridge: Cambridge University Press.

Matthews, P. H. (2000). 'What can we conclude?', in R. M. W. Dixon and Alexandra Y. Aikhenvald (ed.), *Word: a Cross-linguistic Typology*. Cambridge: Cambridge University Press, 266–81.

Matthews, P. H. (2001). *A Short History of Structural Linguistics*. Cambridge: Cambridge University Press.

Matthews, P. H. (2007a). *The Concise Oxford Dictionary of Linguistics*. 2nd edn. Oxford: Oxford University Press.

Matthews, P. H. (2007b). *Syntactic Relations: a Critical Survey*. Cambridge: Cambridge University Press.

Matthews, P. H. (2007c). 'How safe are our analyses?', in Matthew Baerman, Greville G. Corbett, Dunstan Brown, and Andrew Hippisley (eds.), *Deponency and Morphological Mismatches* (*Proceedings of the British Academy* 145), 297–315.

Matthews, P. H. (2009). 'On the microsyntax of attributive adjectives', *Transactions of the Philological Society* 97: 358–75.

Nanni, Deborah L. (1980). 'On the surface syntax of constructions with *easy*-type adjectives', *Language* 56: 568–81.

Nunberg, Geoffrey, Sag, Ivan A., and Wasow, Thomas (1994). 'Idioms', *Language* 70: 491–538.

O'Neill, M., ed. (2006). *Chambers Giant Dictionary*. London: Chambers Harrap.

Palmer, F. R. (1973). 'Noun phrase and sentence: a problem in syntax/semantics', *Transactions of the Philological Society 1972*: 20–43.

Parisi, Domenico and Antinucci, Francesco (1973). *Elementi di grammatica*. Turin: Boringhieri.

Payne, John, Huddleston, Rodney, and Pullum, Geoffrey K. (2010). 'The distribution and category status of adjectives and adverbs', *Word Structure* 3: 31–81.

Percival, W. Keith (1976). 'On the historical source of immediate constituent analysis', in J. D. McCawley (ed.), *Notes from the Linguistic Underground*. New York: Academic Press, 229–42.

Postal, Paul M. (1964). *Constituent Structure: a Study of Contemporary Models of Syntactic Description*. Bloomington: Indiana University Research Center in Anthropology, Folklore, and Linguistics.

Postal, Paul M. (1974). *On Raising*. Cambridge, MA: MIT Press.

Pullum, Geoffrey K. (2009). 'Lexical categorization in English dictionaries and traditional grammars', *Zeitschrift für Anglistik und Amerikanistik* 57: 255–73.

Quirk, Randolph, Greenbaum, Sidney, Leech, Geoffrey, and Svartvik, Jan (1972). *A Grammar of Contemporary English*. London: Longman.

Quirk, Randolph, Greenbaum, Sidney, Leech, Geoffrey, and Svartvik, Jan (1985). *A Comprehensive Grammar of the English Language*. London: Longman.

Quirk, Randolph and Wrenn, C. L. (1957). *An Old English Grammar*. 2nd edn. London: Methuen.

Radford, Andrew (1997). *Syntactic Theory and the Structure of English: a Minimalist Approach*. Cambridge: Cambridge University Press.

Radford, Andrew, Atkinson, Martin, Britain, David, Clahsen, Harald, and Spencer, Andrew (1999). *Linguistics*. Cambridge: Cambridge University Press.

Rissanen, Matti (1999). 'Syntax', in Hogg, ed. 1992–2001, 3: 187–331.

Ross, John Robert (1969). 'Adjectives as noun phrases', in D. A. Reibel and S. A. Schane (eds.), *Modern Studies in English*. Englewood Cliffs: Prentice-Hall, 352–60.

Salmon, Vivian (1999). 'Orthography and pronunciation', in Hogg, ed. 1992–2001, 3: 13–55.

Sapir, Edward (1921). *Language*. New York: Harcourt, Brace.

Saussure, F. de (1916). *Cours de linguistique générale*, ed. C. Bally and A. Sechehaye, with the assistance of A. Riedlinger. Paris: Payot.

Strang, Barbara M. H. (1968). *Modern English Structure*. 2nd edn. London: Edward Arnold. [1st edn. 1962.]

Tesnière, Lucien (1959). *Eléments de syntaxe structurale*. Paris: Klincksieck.

Traugott, Elizabeth Closs (1992). 'Syntax', in Hogg, ed. 1992–2001, 1: 168–289.
Wackernagel, Jacob (1926). *Vorlesungen über Syntax*. 2 vols. Basel: Birkhäuser.
Wells, Stanley and Taylor, Gary, eds. (2005). William Shakespeare, *The Complete Works*. Oxford: Clarendon Press.
Winter, Werner (1965). 'Transforms without kernels?', *Language* 41: 484–9.

Index